ONE HUNDRED YEARS OF

Music

IN AMERICA

ONE HUNDRED YEARS OF

Music

IN AMERICA

Edited by PAUL HENRY LANG

A Centennial Publication

G. SCHIRMER, INC.

New York

GROSSET & DUNLAP *Distributor to the Book Trade*

First Printing August, 1961
Second Printing November, 1961

CONTENTS

[5]

Music as a Field of Knowledge

Music, Government, and the Law

Epilogue

Introduction

Portrait of a Publishing House

By PAUL HENRY LANG

It is all but impossible to guess what may have been in the mind of Ernst Ludwig Rudolf Schirmer, a simple, solid German burgher of Thuringia, when in 1840 he pulled up stakes and left the ancestral home for the New World. Why did he leave Europe for a country not yet known to Europeans as the place where everyone eventually ends up a millionaire? Europe in those days was given the role of the Earth in Ptolemy's system of the universe, the center around which everything revolved; why did he choose America, then in the outer regions of the Ptolemaic system?

If a Martian had been watching the Earth through a magic telescope in the fourth decade of the 19th century, he would have noticed that no part of this planet showed such busy-ness, such unrest, such quarreling, as took place on the small peninsula called Europe. The prima donna of the period's political stage was France. Everyone had to take notice of her. Ruling heads and their faithful retainers were afraid of her, the diplomats hated her, only the intellectual youth of Europe worshipped her. She often betrayed even her lovers, but always remained fascinating. It is doubtful, however, that Schirmer's life was unduly affected by post-Napoleonic France.

The period when Ernst Ludwig Rudolf decided on emigration was the period of Revolution and Romanticism. The *ancien régime,* the old aristocratic society, had not yet fallen; in fact, with the Holy Alliance it seemed to acquire a new lease on life, but this life was pale and had a cadaverous odor. The new middle-class capitalistic society had not yet assumed its rigidity, it was on the threshold of its heroic era, the age of the new robber barons, boiling and eager for extension, and soon for conquest. For a young man about to leave the shelter of the family it promised many possibilities. But Schirmer was not a young man, he was fifty-six, which in those days, even with the sturdy, cast-iron Thuringians, was well past middle age.

It was at this time that luxury in the enjoyment of life's goods was beginning to be extended from the restricted number of aristocrats to the much wider circle of the middle classes. Being instrument maker and piano tuner to the small court in Sondershausen, hence presumably an artisan of some standing, Ernst Ludwig Rudolf must have partaken, if modestly, of this new affluence—why risk it for an unknown livelihood? Who would know, in old Thuringia, whether there were any pianos to be tuned in the land of the Indians?

The orderly, God-fearing artisans and small bourgeois of Thuringia were not plagued by *Sturm und Drang,* or burdened by the ominous weight of Romanticism, nor was the almost uniformly Protestant population subjected to the religious strife that created crises in the more romantically inclined regions. But perhaps we should take a closer look at the Germany Schirmer decided to forsake for America.

Every German state, member of the *Bund,* had its own organization, its army, its corps of public servants, and each one was governed by a temporal or spiritual ruler, or by a minor princeling, in a completely autocratic manner. While the ordinary citizen probably could not even fathom the complications this organized political chaos entailed, Ernst Ludwig Rudolf did divine something of it because he knew the court at Sondershausen. Perhaps while he tuned the pianos in the palace he overheard some conversations, perhaps he caught a faint echo of the past deeds of the House of Schwarzburg, one of the oldest and noblest families in Germany. They were an interesting and colorful lot, the dukes and margraves of Thuringia: Louis the Bearded, Louis the Springer, the Hard, the Pious, the Saint; though there was also an Albert the Degenerate. Maybe Schirmer realized that his was a very circumscribed existence, and that given some liberty, a man may improve his life. He had a brood of children and perhaps he felt that they were entitled to something better than what Providence and a feudal regime provided. These were the ideas and feelings that drove Europeans to our shores.

Ernst Ludwig Rudolf also lived in a country that for musicians is hallowed ground, for this is Bach country. It must have been difficult to abandon the land steeped in history, for Schirmer was musical, he must have heard a good deal of music, and his sons, the American Schirmers, all had a love for music with which they must have been imbued in the country of great cantors and great organists. Furthermore, Sondershausen always had excellent court music. But perhaps we are unduly sentimental, and the bliss was not so untroubled as it may seem to us, for by that time a certain prosaic, everyday quality characterized what was once a glorious tradition. The encyclopedia certainly disenchants the seeker for information, and perhaps its sober spirit is an echo of the passing of the glory. Thuringia is noted "for its production of barley, wheat, and rye, but by far the most land is planted with potatoes." Arnstadt, too, is mentioned—for its gloves, glass, and sausage.

We shall never know whether any or all of these circumstances preyed on Ernst Ludwig Rudolf's mind, but at any rate he must have felt like climbing a ladder without leaning it against something, and considered that a possibility to be found only across the seas.

On his arrival in the United States, Father Schirmer, leading his eleven-year-old son, Gustav, the future founder of the firm, found a settlement quite different from anything European emigrants were acquainted with. To India the white man went to trade and then return with his fortune to the mother country. To Australia he was deported as a felon. Only in America did he find a real second home. Nor did he have to forswear his cultural ties, for while the English, Germans, Irish, and Italians all became good citizens, they largely retained their religious and political views, as well as their language. Only in devotion to their freedom to indulge in all this were they united. Nor was it difficult for the disciplined, hard-working German to get used to the almost religious devotion of the American business man to work, money, and success. This was the beginning of the outburst of American growth, the era of Jackson, the building of railroads, of steam navigation across the Atlantic, the telegraph, etc. No other phase of American history is so remarkable for material development as the elder Schirmer's years in this country. Unfortunately, we lose track of him and know nothing about his activity, but at this point Gustav comes within our view.

Four years after his arrival, the youngster entered the business of music importing and merchandising at the menial level, but by attending night school he acquired an education and considerable linguistic prowess, which in those days, when all "classical" music was imported, was an important asset. Rising steadily, he became in 1854 manager of the firm of Kerksieg and Breusing, music dealers, which seven years later he bought out, going into partnership with Bernard Beer. This was indeed a courageous venture: starting a new business in war time — the Civil War — and a business that had no traditions in the United States. There was ample precedent for the lucrative publishing of popular sheet music, hymnals, etc., but Schirmer aimed at nothing less than the establishment of an American Breitkopf and Härtel. When in 1866 he acquired sole control of the firm and opened a shop at 701 Broadway, the pattern of G. Schirmer's future policy was set, and among the first recognized "interests" was the day's most famous and controversial composer: Wagner. For Gustav Schirmer was not only a good business man, but a man of culture and a capable amateur musician (as was his wife, a fine singer), and his family made music assiduously. Later the family gatherings were enlivened by visits of the leading musicians of the period: the Damrosches, Theodore Thomas, Wilhelm Gericke, Anton Seidl, and many others. In Tchaikovsky's journal of his trip to America in 1891 he gives a lengthy report on his visit to the Schirmer home at 72nd Street and Central Park West.

But we must return to the newly founded firm to sketch the situation faced by the ambitious and idealistic young publisher.

It is perhaps myopic to try to look at the City of New York purely from the musical point of view. After all, when G. Schirmer started its operations the nation's very existence was at stake, while the events that took place in the ensuing years west and east of the Mississippi were more significant from the point of view of world history than all the colorful goings-on in Europe. But Gustav Schirmer realized what many in the music business, in politics, and in education still do not realize, that music is not a mere skill that can be called upon to entertain people tired from the pursuit of happiness (which euphemism everyone is free to interpret in his own way), but an integral and important part of the nation's culture. What he found in the New York of 1861 was far more significant than our brilliant musical life a hundred years later would concede: hundreds of years of Old World development had been packed into a few decades. Individual initiative and imagination were not yet swamped by conformity, and Gustav Schirmer was anything but a conformist.

At the opening of Schirmer's, New York, like most of the rest of the country, was dominated musically by Germans who had flocked to the country in the aftermath of the revolutionary years of 1848. New York was little affected by the Puritan traditions of New England, still a bit suspicious about the arts, or by the relatively long musical past of the genteel South, or by the music of the Pietist enclaves in nearby Pennsylvania. The city had its own traditions, and the future importance and excellence of its musical life were not accidental. Practically from its inception, New York's musical life was characterized by venturesomeness, by receptivity towards new ideals and new enterprises. If in the mid-20th century conductors vied for the privilege of giving the first performance of a new Shostakovich symphony, their more humble predecessors were not a whit behind them. The difference was that they risked their meager fortunes on great masterpieces instead of an ephemeral favorite of the day. Handel's *Messiah* was heard in New York in 1770, two years before its first performance in Germany; the *Barber of Seville* and other Rossini operas were produced in 1825 by a troupe organized by Manuel Garcia; Da Ponte's efforts produced *Don Giovanni* in the same year; Mendelssohn's oratorio *Paulus* reached New York in 1838, two years after its première in Düsseldorf, while parts of *Tannhäuser* were heard in 1852.

Ernst Ludwig Rudolf himself could witness the founding of the

New York Philharmonic Society in 1842, and by the time his son started his business New York knew scores of the most celebrated foreign traveling virtuosos. In 1854 the Academy of Music on Irving Place became a "permanent" home of opera, music schools began to be organized, staffed by the first Americans returning from the German conservatories, and in general there were stirrings everywhere. All this activity, we must remember, was predicated on the availability of scores for study and performance. A publishing firm of the kind Schirmer envisaged must be abreast of the times, but what was more important, both for business success and the good of music, it must also have a good estimate of what the future might require as well as willingness to invest in it.

There is a fundamental difference between book and music publishing, just as there is a fundamental difference in the constitution of the reading public and the listening public. Literature has a public that is decentralized, it is the aggregate of the single readers; everyone experiences the trends of literature as an individual; only the theater requires group response. But musical life depends on a listening public, a centralized, even homogeneous public, in which the individual is practically lost. A developed musical culture demands a secure, well-organized social life, which in turn means urban life, and in more recent history, predominantly middle-class life.

In 1861, New York's musical life was not markedly different from that of a good-sized German city — the German element was dominant. Gradually, with the fantastic development of industry and commerce, and with the influx of many immigrants of other than German extraction, the German trunk of American music began to be covered by vines and creepers. The new accents and new tones multiplied, they brought liveliness to the scene, diversifying its former homogeneous attitude. Gustav Schirmer did not have the advantage of the German, French, or Italian publishers in dealing with a settled, uniform, national, tradition-descended musical culture; he had to sense the trends, anticipate fashions and tastes, and in the meantime put up with the vagaries of the present. And when the time came he would have to acknowledge and further the cause of the American composer, at that time still far below the horizon. Artistic life also partly depends on the reciprocity of

[14]

supply and demand, both of which could be controlled to a certain extent by someone willing to analyze the scene and reach conclusions. In the absence of independent national artistic traditions, a tradition had to be created. Schirmer solved the publishing firm's dilemma by the importing and printing of music from the Continent, which he undertook with an eye for variety and quality. Frequent visits to Germany, to keep abreast with developments and ferret out publishing possibilities, brought him into contact with the Weimar Acropolis presided over by Liszt, and with the other leaders of German music, the road eventually leading to Bayreuth. This, Gustav translated into a movement, and just as he was one of the early backers of Bayreuth, he became one of the first propagandists of the new German School in America. Towards the end of his life he achieved his long-cherished ambition: the collection known as the *Schirmer Library of Musical Classics* was started in 1892. Today, the familiar yellow-covered volumes are nearing the 2000 mark, a remarkable achievement in American music publishing. About the same time a collection of opera scores was inaugurated which also proved to be a valuable contribution, constantly growing in numbers. When on one of his periodic trips to Germany in 1893 Gustav Schirmer died in the Bach town of Eisenach, there ended a productive and imaginative career which left its impress on the musical life of his adopted country.

The direction of the firm devolved on Gustav's two sons, Gustave, 2nd, and Rudolph. They inherited not only a thriving business and a fine store, located since 1880 at 35 Union Square, but what was then the most elaborate music printing and engraving plant in the country, on Sixteenth Street. The sons continued the founder's policies, but being born Americans had somewhat different views from Gustav, who was still bound by many ties to his native Germany. The sons, graduates of American schools and colleges, acquired different tastes, which were soon to be reflected by the firm's policies. The long German hegemony began to pale as Fauré and d'Indy joined Wagner and Liszt. While the stylistic reorientation of the country's musical tastes was unmistakable, it took considerable courage to publish in America such works as Fauré's chamber music.

Continuing the printing of the classics, the development of the

Library, and the miscellaneous other ventures — including the beginning of a complete edition of Bach's organ works prepared by Albert Schweitzer and Charles Widor — Schirmer's also entered upon the publication of books on music. Taking notice of the burgeoning of music education, the firm undertook to supply this vast new field with text and reference books. Among the books on music theory Schirmer brought out various tracts by Goetschius and (later) Wedge which established records for longevity. The whole world may turn altogether dodecaphonic, but these worthies will survive and turn a pretty penny. In 1895 Theodore Baker's *Dictionary of Musical Terms* ushered in the reference works, followed in 1900 by the same author's *Biographical Dictionary of Musicians,* the first scholarly compilation of this sort in the United States. Remodelled by Nicolas Slonimsky, the work reached its fifth edition in 1958, still a leader in the field.

Gustave Schirmer, 2nd, died at the early age of forty-three, and in 1907 his brother Rudolph took over sole direction of the firm. The spirit of progressiveness and of active participation in the nation's musical life remained characteristic of the house (and proved beneficial to both). Rudolph Schirmer, a cultivated and enlightened man, was particularly interested in what he construed to be the civic responsibilities of a music publisher. He assisted in the founding of the Institute of Musical Arts (later the Juilliard School), the New York Oratorio Society, and the New York Symphony Society.

Then in 1915 Rudolph took a step that in those days — or in any day — called for more than courage: vision, and faith in the future. *The Musical Quarterly* was founded, with Oscar G. Sonneck, one of our most distinguished pioneer musicologists (and later Schirmer's vice-president), as editor. Although such a publication, eschewing all popular features and devoted to the highest level of scholarship, can never hope to be self-sustaining, the firm has always supported it, through thick and thin, the worst depression and the war years. From its very first issue, which contained an eloquent manifesto in behalf of musical scholarship, *The Musical Quarterly* maintained uncompromising standards, becoming and remaining one of the outstanding learned musical journals in the world. With

5000 copies printed every quarter, it has by far the largest circulation of any publication of its character.

Carl Engel, the whimsical president of Schirmer's in more recent years, and distinguished second editor of *The Musical Quarterly*, told me once that "A publishing firm such as ours exists for two reasons: glory and money. However, glory can only be reaped if we are careful always to make a little more money than glory." Rudolph Schirmer must have come to the same conclusion, because the firm began publication and promotion of operettas, musical comedies, and "light" music in general. This activity was pursued with the same thoroughness and with the same willingness to risk money and effort as the more esoteric endeavors of Schirmer's. Talents were scouted, nurtured, and launched. Rudolf Friml, Sigmund Romberg, and Victor Herbert are some of the illustrious names in this section of the Schirmer catalogue, to which must be added some of the most successful writers of standard secular and sacred songs and ballads in the country, such as Oley Speaks and, later, Clara Edwards, Richard Hageman, Ernest Charles, Albert Hay Malotte, and Celius Dougherty as well as the able composer and folksong collector and performer, John Jacob Niles.

In the meantime the most modern printing plant was built in Long Island in 1916; besides taking care of the firm's own needs, it prints about half of all music published in the United States. Thus when Rudolph died in 1919 he left to the next generation a flourishing enterprise that still continued in the spirit of its founder although on vastly expanded modern lines. While Schirmer's direction was no longer exclusively in the hands of the family, there was no time when some member was not closely connected with it in an executive capacity. Gustave Schirmer, 3rd, nephew of Rudolph, succeeded the former as president for a short time, then Carl Engel took the office in 1929, and upon his death in 1944 Gustave Schirmer returned as president, retiring in 1957. At present Rudolph Edward Schirmer, son of Rudolph, Sr., is vice president and a director.

It was another vice president, Oscar G. Sonneck, who inaugurated Schirmer's "modern" period. What was dimly envisaged by Gustav, clearly seen and prepared for by Rudolph, was now implemented by Sonneck. Schirmer's decisively entered the arena of contemporary

[17]

music, with a special concern for American composers, among them Charles T. Griffes, John Alden Carpenter, Charles Martin Loeffler, and Ernest Bloch. Sonneck's work in this respect was continued by Carl Engel, a kindred spirit. He added to the Schirmer catalogue young and little-known composers who are today among the country's leading masters —Roy Harris and William Schuman, as well as Samuel Barber, all of whose works, from Opus 1 on, are published by Schirmer. When Schoenberg arrived in this country in 1933 he received substantial help from Schirmer's, the company publishing his Violin Concerto, Piano Concerto, Fourth String Quartet, *Ode to Napoleon,* and other works.

Upon Gustave Schirmer's retirement in 1957, the presidency was once more entrusted to an able professional who, while not a member of the family (though at least a Rudolph), had long associations with Schirmer's. It is significant that Rudolph Tauhert is a noted expert in the technical aspects of music printing and publishing, who developed the Long Island plant into the largest such establishment in the world. A publishing firm's nerve system is actuated by its editorial policies and by its technical efficiency; neither could prosper without the other. Rudolph Tauhert is no less devoted to the century-old policies of Schirmer's than were his predecessors in the president's chair; he surrounds himself with capable executives, and the artistic commitments, the pioneering in contemporary American music, and modern business practices are not only continued but intensified in Schirmer's appropriately modern new headquarters, which the firm occupied in its centennial year.

*   *

*

We have seen in the foregoing that the activity of a music publishing firm, if directed by alert and knowledgeable persons, will parallel the periods of cultural history. Each of these periods is different in construction, and presents a complicated spectacle to discerning eyes, because while following the principal line of development, each period has its preparatory stage in which the blood of the declining age still courses, a flowering, and its own decline. The declining stage is characterized by the carrying to extremes of nearly everything that was the essence of the previous flowering.

However, in the arts, notably in music, this is exactly the style period that interests large strata of the public, a fact that cannot be ignored by a publisher who wants to stay in business. Both this terminal era and the subsequent flowering stage, which to the general public represents the *avant garde,* were handsomely served by Schirmer's.

In the post-war decade and a half, Schirmer's continued all the former activities of the house, while constantly modernizing its holdings. Certain old standbys were completely refurbished and reprinted in new, up-to-date editions. The opera library, extended and modernized, was equipped with new English translations. At the same time, Schirmer's not only took cognizance of the new field of "school opera," but assumed the lead in providing the lively movement with old and new works. Most important in the operatic branch of the house was its connection with Gian Carlo Menotti, whose *The Medium, The Telephone, The Consul, The Saint of Bleecker Street,* and *Amahl and the Night Visitors* it published and promoted.

Another important new tack was the recognition of the role of modern musicology in the editing of older masterpieces. Clearly, the old method of entrusting the preparation of such works to any decent musician on hand are no longer acceptable. Accordingly, Schirmer's engaged such eminent authorities as Arthur Mendel (Schütz, Bach) and Ralph Kirkpatrick (Bach, Scarlatti). Hans David not only prepared a new edition of Bach's *Musical Offering,* but wrote a fine essay on the work, also published by the firm. Once more, 20th-century methods are quietly displacing the older procedures of editing and publishing. But of course, the greatest problem is — as it always has been — the new composer of new music.

Cultural history teaches us that the intellectual products of an era are nothing but particular projections of the period's temper and aspirations, and therefore they are closely connected with the period's social, economic, ethical, and artistic life. Our century began in the sign of rebellion against the old order of decadent Romanticism, and in its seventh decade is definitely headed in altogether different directions. From the fermenting soil that was loosened by the masters of the Romantic and post-Romantic age a new art must rise, an art that is the expression of man and his society in the second half of the century. This of course means that the third and first phases of the periodic development described above, decline and renewal, will run concurrently, though in the very particular case of music, where such a procedure can stretch over the better part of a whole century, this still contains a good deal of the flowering stage, too. Thus we are dealing with all phases of a cultural era simultaneously, which makes acceptance and digestion of the new art doubly difficult. What is the role of such an old and distinguished publishing firm in this era of transition and reorientation?

The generation of Bloch, Douglas Moore, Roy Harris, and even of such younger men as Barber, Menotti, or Leonard Bernstein — all of them Schirmer "properties" in whole or in part — is being gradually supplanted. They are still very much alive, productive, and their music fully enjoyable, but they are becoming senior musical citizens; even Schoenberg has become a "classic" as the new generation demands recognition. Beginning their second century, Schirmer's will have to face the challenge of the new men, the total serialists, the electronic composers, and perhaps the total automatons. And since a healthy corporation outlives its constituent members, it will eventually face the musicians of the utopian era when all machines of destruction, atomic or artistic, will be buried and a modicum of serenity returns to a world that lived in turmoil practically since the opening of the 20th century. A hundred years of shrewd and progressive administration guarantees that the problem will be met by Schirmer's and that the centennial continuity will not be interrupted.   *   *

*

In the following pages the reader will find an informal and very readable history of the hundred years of music in America against which he can measure Schirmer's own hundred years of existence. This is not advertising, it is not a doctored or slanted history, nor a paean; for aside from my little story the firm is hardly even mentioned in the body of the book. The necessary and expected publicity celebrating the firm's centennial will be carried out in the usual way and through the usual channels. As editor of *The Musical*

Quarterly I have been for years a member of the Schirmer organization, hence am not an innocent or unbiased bystander. An old hired hand who has enjoyed both his work and the association, perhaps I am permitted to use at least one drumstick to help the celebration — wherefore this introduction. But what Schirmer asked from the contributors to *A Hundred Years of Music in America* was exactly what the title implies: a study of the currents of our musical life during a period that also happens to encompass the life span of G. Schirmer, Inc. It is offered to the public as a most interesting bit of history, related by distinguished specialists in its various aspects. The reader will find in these chapters the story of one hundred years of significant accomplishments, not unmarked however by frustration and cynicism, for these too were characteristic of the century. Some may conclude that this was a peculiar era by recalling that Bach's Chaconne for unaccompanied violin was played by a hundred-piece orchestra, that a guitar player singing mating calls swept the country, that rock 'n' roll meets ended in riots necessitating police intervention, that managers declared chamber music to be "poison," and that the pianists who at the beginning of the era played *on* the piano, were recently to be found *inside* the instrument. But these curiosities are overshadowed by the positive achievements of the age. We take pride in the unparalleled development of our orchestras, now among the best in the world, in the many fine singers and instrumentalists, in the resurgence of the spirit of patronage of the arts. Operas and symphonies are once more commissioned, not by princes or cardinals, but by universities, foundations, and publishers, orchestras, theaters, and broadcasting companies. But above all, we take pride in our composers who, unknown in 1861, are in the front rank in·1961.

Musical Life

The Evolution of
the American Composer

By NATHAN BRODER

There is a curious ambivalence in the American attitude towards
American composers. It existed a century ago and still exists today.
In 1861 the New York Harmonic Society performed a "choral and
instrumental work," *Praise to God*, by its director, George F. Bristow. The local correspondent of *Dwight's Journal of Music* called
it "a complete success." "This Oratorio," he went on, "is the first
American production ever performed with such signal marks of
approbation. As a work of art it is most excellent, an honor to the
composer, a credit to his country; it suffers nothing from comparison
with standard works, and will rank high as a masterpiece — criticisms from all quarters abound in panegyrics." Well, not exactly *all*
quarters. The *Musical Review and World* said of Bristow and this
work of his: "He seems to be willingly guided by the hand of
Mendelssohn, for instance, and others, without even making an attempt to move independently . . . There is nothing original, nothing
striking about his music, nothing to excite us; no stirring discords,
no flashing bits of new ideas — all goes along smoothly, evenly,
correctly, decently, but occasionally in a very tiresome fashion."
There is here, it seems to me, more than a mere difference of opin-

ion between critics. There is a difference of approach, reflecting the familiar dilemma that faces every critic or historian who attempts to evaluate the music of his time. Is he to judge by local standards or is he to take a world view? And if a world view, should it be restricted to his own day or should it be *sub specie aeternitatis?*

The dilemma becomes especially acute for the historian, and sometimes leads to extreme solutions. There is in process of development, as this is being written, a large recording and publication project that will present American music from the days of the earliest settlers to the present. The aim will be to offer as comprehensive a view as possible of the works produced in this country, and it will be left to the listener to make his own judgments. (Even so, of course, editorial evaluation will be involved, since it will be necessary to choose the composers to be included, and to decide which works represent them best.) As against this plan to give the fullest possible representation to American music of all periods may be cited a history of music that was recently published, written by Americans for use in American colleges, in which American music is given less than two lines.

Once the obvious fact is granted that America has not produced a Beethoven yet, and once the equally obvious fact is granted that not every symphony written in this country is necessarily worth perpetuating in print or on records, it becomes clear to any observer looking at the scene with what might be called sympathetic objectivity that more interesting and exciting music of a "serious" nature has been written by Americans than most Americans are aware of, and that even the 19th century was by no means the complete vacuum in this respect that it is sometimes claimed to be.

Bristow, who not only conducted the Harmonic Society but also played the violin in the Philharmonic, turned out a large amount of music, including the opera *Rip Van Winkle,* which ran for four weeks in New York in 1855. This was the second "grand opera" by a native American to be produced. The first was *Leonora,* based on a play by Bulwer, with music by William Henry Fry, produced in Philadelphia in 1845, at the composer's expense. Its style is derived from Bellini and Donizetti; when Otto Kinkeldey presented portions of the work at a concert in 1929, critics were surprised at the high quality of some of it. Fry also wrote several symphonies, which were performed here in the 1850s. All of them share a curious characteristic of early American instrumental music in the large forms: they are based on detailed programs. Fry's Christmas symphony, *Santa Claus,* has a "synopsis" that occupies more than three pages in Upton's monograph on the composer. Even the sober Bristow, who was not given to this sort of thing, thought it desirable to subtitle the Mendelssohnian scherzo of his F-sharp minor Symphony "The Butterfly's Frolic." The tendency towards excessively detailed extramusical props for long instrumental pieces in America cannot be attributed to exaggerated imitation of Beethoven or Berlioz — it reaches back through the fantastically titled eccentricities of Anthony Philip Heinrich (1781-1861) to the patriotic sonatas of James Hewitt (1770-1827). It seems more likely to have been a drastic device to hold the attention of a musically untutored public. And it did not rule out musical quality: there is considerable imagination and charm, within an orthodox idiom, in Fry's *Santa Claus.*

A less ambitious composer than Fry or Bristow but a far more successful one is their contemporary, Louis Moreau Gottschalk, a piano virtuoso who made a brilliant career out of playing his own works. Many of these were sentimental salon pieces (*The Last Hope*) and popular fantasies on operatic and other familiar airs, but some were pieces making serious use of Creole and other folk material — perhaps the first attempts to employ native American melodies and rhythms in art music.

In 1862 two events took place that had important consequences in American music: Theodore Thomas organized his first orchestra in New York and John Knowles Paine became organist at Harvard. Thomas not only took his orchestra on tour, spreading seeds of symphonic music from which local orchestras eventually grew (the Boston Symphony was one of these), but in his home concerts he welcomed new works, including some by American composers. Paine in 1875 became the first professor of music in an American university, after having overcome strong opposition from members of the faculty who felt that music should not be taught in a university. Paine had studied in Germany — he was one of the earliest of a long line of American composers to do so — and his music shows a technical finish, a skill in symphonic development, hitherto lacking in American music. His students at Harvard include some of the most prominent composers of the next generation.

The most outstanding figure among late 19th-century American composers, Edward MacDowell, regarded by many in his own time as "the greatest musical genius America has produced," suffered an eclipse in the decades following his death in 1908. He has not yet emerged from it; but judged in the context of his period, indeed by any generally accepted standards, the best of his music has a freshness and an individuality that go far to justify his contemporaries' high opinion of it.

Together with Dudley Buck and Horatio Parker, whose choral works are discussed elsewhere in this volume, the composers we have named are the representative American composers of serious music in the 19th century. The century did not, to be sure, produce a composer of operas or symphonies who would attain lasting preeminence in his field, as Stephen Foster did in the domain of the ballad and the minstrel song or Sousa in that of the band march. But, given the historical and sociological conditions, the wonder is not that America did not make a more impressive showing. After all, England, which did not have the excuse that it was consolidating a nation only recently hacked out of a wilderness, presents an equally dismal picture through much of the 19th century. The wonder is that there is enough vitality in some of the music of the men we have mentioned to make it still worth an occasional hearing.

From the turn of the century on, American composers increased rapidly in number. The growth in their production of orchestral and chamber music is a strange phenomenon. There was, in the first two decades of this century, no public demand for it, there was little chance that it would be performed, and there was hardly any likelihood at all that it would be published. Back in the 1850s Fry had emitted bitter statements about the difficulty an American composer had in getting performed. It was a complaint that remained valid until the end of the Second World War. Nevertheless, beginning in the early years of this century, the stream of American symphonies, overtures, suites, quartets, and sonatas grew steadily — imposing testimony to the strength of an aroused creative impulse.

Several styles may be discerned in American compositions of about 1900 to about 1930. The German influences evident in Paine, Buck, Parker, and to some extent in MacDowell are still active in the music of George W. Chadwick, Edgar Stillman Kelley, Mrs. H. H. A. Beach, Frederick S. Converse, Rubin Goldmark, Henry Hadley, and others. But German habits of thinking are no longer the principal guide for American composers. By this time Fauré and Debussy have left their mark on American music. The Americans who absorbed Impressionist influences include E. B. Hill and John Alden Carpenter and especially Charles T. Griffes and Charles Martin Loeffler. Some there were who combined French and German influences in their work: Daniel Gregory Mason, Ernest Schelling, David Stanley Smith. This was the period, too, when the first sustained attempts were made to use American folk material in serious music.

Attempts to write "American" music date back to the end of the 18th century. In the first half of the 19th, Anthony Philip Heinrich wrote many large works on native subjects, such as *Pushmataha, a Venerable Chief of a Western Tribe of Indians,* or *The New England Feast of Shells* (i. e., a clambake). A generation later, Silas G. Pratt, another strange and colorful character (he is said to have announced magnanimously to Richard Wagner when he met him, "Herr Wagner, you are the Silas G. Pratt of Europe"), wrote in the preface to his opera *Zenobia, Queen of Palmyra:* "Should it be found, as I hope it may, that my work has borrowed neither its plot nor situation from the European Opera, and that the music owes no allegiance to any special school, I trust this fact will make it none the less acceptable to American audiences." But there is no trace in this music of anything specifically individual or American. Although there were innumerable fantasies on *Dixie* or *Columbia, the Gem of the Ocean,* it was only in a few pieces by Gottschalk that the special character of native folk music was exploited. In the last years of the 19th century and the first of the 20th, sparked by remarks by Dvořák to the effect that American composers ought to make use of their "plantation songs," several men — Arthur Farwell, H. W. Loomis, Henry F. Gilbert, and others — began a serious attempt to shake off foreign domination. They wrote music employing actual Indian or Negro tunes or invented music in the style of those tunes. Of these works, Gilbert's *Comedy Overture on Negro Themes* eventually attained a measure of success. But the work of the Americanists did not produce an American style. Indian dances or Negro spirituals embedded in late Romantic forms and harmonies and orchestration resulted in late Romantic compositions with a slightly American flavor.

While this music was being written, in the first three decades of the century, another composer was tackling the same problem in a far more original and individual way. Charles Ives, imbued with the ideas of Emerson and Thoreau, put to music the sights and sounds of his New England environment. To convey his visions as he saw them he used extreme dissonance, polyrhythms, polytonality, quarter tones, and other novel and unconventional procedures. America was not yet ready for this. The few compositions by Ives that saw the light of day were published by him at his own expense. It was not until the 1930s, after he had ceased composing, that some attention began to be paid to this bold and thoroughly American spirit.

In the 1920s the pace of serious composition in America began to quicken. One of the manifestations of the new ferment was an attempt to find a rapprochement between jazz and "serious" music. Composers like Carpenter and Louis Gruenberg and the young Aaron Copland mixed jazz elements into their works for the concert hall or the ballet theater, while, from the other direction, George Gershwin constructed symphonic pieces out of jazz and blues materials. While most of the established composers continued to write in their own variants of the late Romantic or Impressionist styles, new ideas and new personalities stirred up a profession that had been on the whole mild, well behaved, and grateful for small favors. It was an era when organized attempts were begun to promote modern music. In 1921 Carlos Salzedo and Edgard Varèse founded the International Composers' Guild for that purpose; two years later the League of Composers was established, for the same reasons. Through the vigorous efforts of especially the League some of the most advanced works of the contemporary European and the burgeoning American *avant garde* were produced in New York. In 1928 Roger Sessions and Copland organized a series of concerts devoted to modern music. Composers belonging to no school began to experiment in various directions. At the end of the previous decade New York had been startled by the savage rhythms and wild dissonances of Leo Ornstein. In the course of the twenties it had the opportunity to hear equally unorthodox but better organized attempts to extend musical horizons — by Varèse, Carl Ruggles, Henry Cowell, George Antheil, and others.

All of this activity built up into an explosion of creative energy in the 1930s. Several forces joined to sustain a great upsurge of musical creativity and experimentation. The financial depression created the WPA concerts, which used large quantities of American music, much of it newly composed. Progressive ideas that had percolated in Europe during the twenties began now to boil over into America; Schoenberg himself settled here in 1933. Most of all, while many composers continued to write along traditional lines, others engaged in a search for new sounds, fresh forms — above all, individual expression. This is the period when the Whitmanesque figure of Roy Harris came out of the West — a side trip to Paris had little effect on him — with a barbaric yawp that thrilled open-minded listeners and some of the younger composers. It is the time when Copland hammered out the powerful dissonant idiom of his abstract pieces and etched the spare, lean but not juiceless style of his ballets and film music, a style that has set the tone for the background music of innumerable movies and television plays. In these years Roger Sessions, having outgrown the influence of his teacher, Ernest Bloch, quietly worked out his own complex, tightly knit, thoughtful manner of composing. Walter Piston, during this time, established his mastery of the technique of composition in works that were traditional in form but fresh in content. It was the era in which two American operas in conservative style — Deems Taylor's *Peter Ibbetson* and Howard Hanson's *Merry Mount* — and the more daring *Emperor Jones* by Louis Gruenberg were produced at the Metropolitan Opera House while the imaginative and extremely unconventional *Four Saints in Three Acts* by Virgil Thomson and *The Cradle Will Rock* by Marc Blitzstein, as well as one of the earliest folk operas written for production by modest forces, Douglas Moore's *The Devil and Daniel Webster,* were done on or off Broadway. American music had finally come of age.

The forties and fifties have been a period of further growth and consolidation. The number of able composers turning out substantial and well-made works is bewildering. So, too, is the variety of styles. In the space that remains it will be possible to mention only a few of these men and idioms. It will not be my aim to pigeon-hole. Each of the men to be named conveys personal qualities in his music — some, of course, more than others. But it is possible — and, for a brief survey like this, useful — to divide them into a few general categories because of certain traits in their music, even though some of these men often cross the lines between categories.

As might be expected, one of the largest groups is that comprising writers who find the traditional tools suitable for their needs. They include such otherwise widely differing composers as Randall Thompson, Paul Creston, Norman Dello Joio. Thompson especially in his choral music, Creston in his orchestral works, and Dello Joio in various media are among the composers who have shown that there are still things worth hearing to be said in the tonal system. Samuel Barber is often included in this category — correctly, as far as his early music is concerned, not so fittingly with respect to his later music. Yet throughout his works, no matter how dissonant, there runs a vein of warm *espressivo* writing. The poetic lyricism of his style has influenced a number of younger men.

Another group has in common a fondness for the type of long lines and counterpoint cultivated by Harris. William Schuman has combined such a texture with lively rhythms and an extraordinary sense of orchestral color into a personal language. Complex rhythms and driving energy characterize the work of Peter Mennin, too, while in the large and varied output of Vincent Persichetti, another member of this group, one striking trait is the thoroughly idiomatic writing for the piano — a rarity in modern music for that instrument. Rather more remote from Harris but like him interested in modally inflected lines and featuring contrapuntal development is Robert Palmer, who also stresses sharp and irregular rhythms.

There are twelve-tone writers of all degrees, from those who only occasionally employ this technique to those whose every note is derived from a row. From this numerous group we may mention Wallingford Riegger, who, using dodecaphony with great freedom, wrote moving and powerful music in such works as his Third Symphony and Second String Quartet. What might be called the middle generation of dodecaphonists includes Ross Lee Finney, whose skill-fully written chamber music combines tonal principles with twelve-tone procedures; Ben Weber, who can infuse the style with considerable feeling content and, at times, even humor; Milton Babbitt, who began to apply serial procedures to rhythm and orchestration before such devices became known in Europe; and George Rochberg, whose interest in theoretical aspects of the system does not affect the high musical quality of his compositions. The composers in their twenties and thirties who are absorbing and applying the principles of twelve-tone writing, especially as employed by Webern, are numerous and widespread.

Some composers share an economy of texture and a kind of purity of style that show the influence partly of Stravinsky but especially of Copland. Alexei Haieff, a fastidious craftsman, is one of these. Another is Arthur Berger, whose concise, solidly constructed pieces also employ principles derived from Schoenberg. Some of the works of Lukas Foss belong in this Coplandish category; recently, however, he has become interested in working out ways by which instrumental ensembles may improvise as groups, on the basis of outlines laid down by the composer. Irving Fine, who writes with elegance and wit, and Harold Shapero, who hews closer to tonality and to Classic formal ideas than do the others in this group, may be mentioned here.

There are writers who, working habitually in an atonal, though not necessarily dodecaphonic, idiom, construct large, complex works — often of chamber music — full of tension and, not infrequently, grandeur. Elliott Carter is such a composer, and his two string quartets and Variations for Orchestra are among the most impressive American works of the last decade. Another writer of this general type is Leon Kirchner, whose impassioned style is displayed in orchestral as well as chamber music.

Some composers have cultivated oriental sounds and compositional procedures. The earliest of these was Henry Eichheim (1870-1942), who made several trips to the Far East from 1915 to 1928 and brought some of the native instruments back, for use in his music. Later writers in this vein include Colin McPhee, Henry Cowell, Lou Harrison, and most recently Chou Wen-Chung.

Of experimenters we have many kinds; perhaps it will suffice to name only three here: Henry Brant, who, influenced by Ives, has among other things prescribed multiple orchestras, seated in various parts of a hall and playing in different tempos; Harry Partch, who uses a scale of forty-three irregularly tuned tones to the octave and has had instruments especially constructed to play his music; and John Cage, who is best known for his use of "prepared" pianos, his predilection for odd ensembles and for silences, and his ideas about composing by chance, which have influenced some younger composers here and abroad. There is a small but growing number of composers working with tape and with various electronic means for producing sound. Most prominent among these are Vladimir Ussachevsky, Milton Babbitt, and Otto Luening.

Finally there are eminent composers who do not fit into any of the above categories, loose classifications though they are. Perhaps Quincy Porter should be mentioned here. Of the Harris-Copland-Sessions-Piston generation, he has gone quietly along, avoiding isms of any kind, working out his own style, which features long, curved lines and harmony spiced with dissonance. Definitely in this unclassifiable class is Gian Carlo Menotti, whose success is due to a remarkable concatenation of skills — as composer, librettist, stage director — and has given powerful impetus to the writing and performing of operas in this country. Another maverick is Leonard Bernstein, who has not yet produced a work in the "serious" field to equal *West Side Story* but from whom anything may be expected.

William Henry Fry, who used his position on the New York Tribune to fulminate against our country's indifference to its composers, was a voice crying in the wilderness. Today there are composers spread across the land, writing, teaching, studying. The most celebrated of them are besieged by more commissions for new works than they can handle. It is still necessary for almost all of them to do something else to make a living. This has always been true of most composers. Lassus at Munich or Bach at Leipzig or Haydn at Eszterháza had many duties to perform in addition to writing new music; indeed, it is doubtful that they had as much time to devote to composing as does John Smith, composer-in-residence at a Midwestern university. The amazing thing is that in the United States, which is supposedly anti-cultural, a few composers — because of commissions, performance fees, royalties, income from performing rights societies — *can* live on the proceeds of their music alone.

What of an "American style"? There have been American pieces — that is, pieces entirely built from the characteristic qualities of native folk music — from Gottschalk's *Bamboula* to Copland's *Hoe-Down*. And in the last three decades certain elements appeared in our music that could coalesce into an indigenous style. Traits of rhythm and melody that strike one as peculiarly American turned up in such disparate works as Randall Thompson's Second Symphony, Copland's *Appalachian Spring*, Schuman's Third Symphony, Virgil Thomson's *The Mother of Us All*, Moore's *Ballad of Baby Doe*. But any possibility that such traits would be fused into an American idiom is being swept away in the swift current that bears contemporary music along today. There is no American style now, any more than there is a French or a German or an English or an Italian one. There are only American (and other) dialects of the several international musical languages.

The American Symphony Orchestra

By HELEN M. THOMPSON

The history of American symphony orchestras is, in its simplest terms, a reflection of the history of the economic development of this nation. Revenue from ticket sales has been the traditional base for orchestra income here, but, operating in a democratic society, each orchestra has felt an obligation to hold ticket prices to a level that would make symphonic music available to a broad segment of the general public.

As a result, United States orchestras traditionally have been forced to find a way to meet the gap between ticket-sale income and total cost of operation. It is in the methods used to bridge this gap during the last hundred years that we find the history of the economic development of the United States reflected in capsule form.

Geographically, the establishment of orchestras in the United States has naturally followed the growth of the nation. As each population and orchestral frontier opened and developed, the same cycle has taken place. Successively, in nearly every orchestra, the responsibility for subsidizing the orchestra has moved from the musicians themselves in the formative years, to one or a few wealthy patrons whose gifts or endowments, thought to be adequate when made, later proved utterly inadequate, and thence to annual voluntary contributions from the general public.

In this development we see reflected the changes in the nation's economic format—first the amassing of great personal fortunes, next the growth of tax structures that place restrictions on such fortunes, and as personal incomes become smaller the gradual assumption of voluntary financial responsibility for cultural affairs by the general citizenry, business, and industry. This process was encouraged by changes in federal tax laws. More recently, local tax-supported bodies (municipalities and counties) have begun to share in the support of symphony orchestras. Whether or not this policy should or will move on to the federal government remains to be seen.

These developments, in turn, have influenced every phase of the orchestras' operations — the programming, the legal structure, the form of organization, the make-up of the audiences, and the concept of the basic functions of an orchestra.

The histories of practically all United States orchestras were foreshadowed by that of the nation's oldest "permanent" orchestra, the New York Philharmonic. The story is told in John Erskine's account of the *First Hundred Years of the Philharmonic-Symphony Society of New York* (New York, 1943). The orchestra, formed in 1842 by a group of musicians, was operated by the musicians as a cooperative venture for at least fifty years. During this period the musicians paid modest dues to the Society, received a modest fee for playing, and divided the profits earned by the Society at the end of each season. The dividend was $25.00 per musician the first season. The smallest dividend ($17.50) was paid in 1878, and the largest ($225.00) in 1886.

Popular support, evidenced through ticket sales, declined after 1898 and prompted the orchestra to try to regain its position by engaging conductors with commanding personalities who would have a broad public appeal. There followed a brilliant era of "permanent" and "guest" conductors, but the continued financial problems of the Philharmonic resulted in a complete reorganization in 1909, at which time the control of the orchestra passed from the musicians to a Board of Directors who assumed responsibility for meeting the annual operating deficits and who guaranteed a stated salary to the musicians. Upon the death of Joseph Pulitzer in 1911, the Philharmonic Society received a gift of $900,000 with the request that Mr. Pulitzer's favorite composers (Beethoven, Wagner, and Liszt) receive special attention in the orchestra's programs.

Meanwhile, a competing orchestra — the New York Symphony — was started in 1878 by Leopold Damrosch; at his death in 1885 his son, Walter Damrosch, took over the orchestra which, like the Philharmonic, ran into financial difficulties. Walter Damrosch was successful in gaining the interest and support of Harry Harkness Flagler, who began personally subsidizing the Symphony in 1903 and who assumed full responsibility for the operating deficits for several years beginning in 1914.

The next fifteen years of competition between the two orchestras coupled with mounting financial pressures, occasioned in considerable measure by rising salary scales, resulted in the merger of the Philharmonic and Symphony Societies in 1928, with Mr. Flagler becoming president of the combined Board of Directors.

The economic history of the orchestra (and of our nation) can be further illustrated by a quick glance at the orchestra's financial reports. The total cost of operation in 1842 of $2,200 was met from ticket-sale revenue, the musicians' membership payments, and the fines they levied upon themselves for absences. A hundred years later, the total annual cost of operation—$666,700 — was met from ticket sales, broadcast and recording revenue, program advertising, contributions, and income from endowments. By 1948-49, annual costs had nearly doubled, rising to over one and a quarter million dollars. Earned income (ticket sales, recording, broadcasting and program advertising) had more than doubled in the eight-year period, but contributions had fallen behind nearly a thousand dollars and income from investments had decreased by approximately 16%. Then came a period of reorientation. The orchestra initiated many policies and activities that resulted in new and varied services to a greatly widened public. The orchestra's "corporate image" was changed from that of being primarily a concert-giving organization with emphasis still on "exclusivity" to that of being a cultural community institution devoted to concert-giving *and* a wide variety of educational and entertainment activities which appealed to and met the needs of a broad public, representative of all ages, all social, economic, and educational levels. The general public began to feel it had a stake in the New York Philharmonic—and showed it through increased interest, concert attendance, and financial support. In the ten years from 1948-49 to 1958-59, while costs rose to one and three-quarter million dollars, earned income increased by only 15%, and income from investments again decreased to 10% below the 1948-49 level, contributions increased by 500%, with a total of nearly 14,000 contributors making voluntary gifts to the orchestra in the 1958-59 season.

The development of most United States symphony orchestras followed this same basic pattern with the closest of parallels to be found, of course, among the older orchestras. The second United States "permanent" orchestra to maintain continuous operations from the founding date is believed to be the St. Louis Philharmonic, a non-professional orchestra formed in 1860 which proudly retains its "amateur" status so far as organization and finances are concerned. (The St. Louis Philharmonic is not to be confused with the St. Louis Symphony, which was to make its appearance twenty years later.)

By 1900 at least thirty-seven symphony orchestras were in existence, including the following:

A. PROFESSIONAL ORCHESTRAS

Date of Founding	Orchestra
1842	New York Philharmonic
1878	New York Symphony
1880-81	St. Louis Symphony
1880-81	Boston Symphony
1885	Boston Pops Orchestra
1891-92	Chicago Symphony
1895	Pittsburgh Symphony
	(disbanded in 1910, and later reorganized)
1895-96	Cincinnati Symphony
1897	Los Angeles Symphony
	(became the Los Angeles Philharmonic in 1919)

B. COMMUNITY ORCHESTRAS

1855	Columbus Symphony, Georgia
1860	St. Louis Philharmonic, Missouri
1860	San Jose Civic Symphony, California
1866	Belleville Philharmonic, Illinois

1889	Sheboygan Civic Symphony, Wisconsin
1893	California Women's Symphony, Whittier, Calif.
1894-95	New Haven Symphony, Connecticut
1896-97	Bangor Symphony, Maine
1897	Peoria Symphony, Illinois
1899	Battle Creek Symphony, Michigan

C. COLLEGE ORCHESTRAS

1808	Harvard-Radcliffe Orchestra, Cambridge, Massachusetts
1880	Crane Symphony, Potsdam, New York
1883	Bethany College Orchestra, Lindsborg, Kansas
1887	DePauw University Orchestra, Greencastle, Indiana
1887	Capital University Symphony, Columbus, Ohio
1889	Notre Dame Symphonette, South Bend, Indiana
1890	Oberlin College Orchestra, Oberlin, Ohio
1892	Utah State University Orchestra, Logan, Utah
1894	Grinnell College Orchestra, Grinnell, Iowa
1897	Graceland-Lamoni College Orchestra, Lamoni, Iowa

The following college orchestras also were formed prior to 1900:

Brigham Young University Orchestra, Provo, Utah
Cornell College Orchestra, Mount Vernon, Iowa
Ithaca College Orchestra, Ithaca, New York
San Jose State College Orchestra, San Jose, California
Southwestern College Symphony, Winfield, Kansas
St. John's University Orchestra, Collegeville, Minnesota
University of Michigan Symphony, Ann Arbor
University of Wisconsin Symphony, Madison

Among the professional orchestras, the counterparts of New York's Harry Harkness Flagler were to be found in each city. Henry L. Higginson met the Boston Symphony's annual operating deficit of approximately $50,000 from 1881 until 1918, when responsibility for continuing to meet the orchestra's needs was assumed by nine prominent citizens. In Chicago, Mr. Charles Norman Fay provided the leadership and example that prompted other leading citizens to join him in guaranteeing support for the new Chicago Symphony. In Los Angeles, it was William Andrew Clark, Jr., and in Cincinnati it was Mr. and Mrs. Charles Phelps Taft who undertook to provide financial stability for the symphony orchestras of their home cities.

A changing economic order later forced each of these early orchestras to widen its base of financial support. To do so successfully, they also found it necessary to establish a closer and more informal relationship with their patrons, audiences, and the general public, and adjust their activities to the needs and wishes of a wider public. They, too, became community cultural institutions concerned with music education projects of various kinds, with "pops" concerts in addition, of course, to the formal and traditional subscription series. Again, we find the number of contributors to each orchestra an index to the economic history of our nation.

In 1958-59, responsibility for meeting the operating deficits of these pioneer orchestras was shared by thousands of citizens, organizations, and business firms in their respective cities.

Orchestra	Number of contributors to Orchestra Maintenance Fund in 1958-59 season
Chicago Symphony	1,600
St. Louis Symphony	3,500
Pittsburgh Symphony	3,900
Los Ángeles Philharmonic	4,900
New York Philharmonic	13,800
Cincinnati Symphony	17,300

From 1900 to 1920, approximately one hundred new orchestral groups were formed. The growth of orchestras following 1920 has been rapid and steady, reaching into towns and cities of all sizes. Today, at least 1,100 groups (exclusive of secondary-school orchestras) designating themselves "symphony orchestras" exist in American cities, towns, colleges, and universities. The American Symphony Orchestra League has verified founding dates for nearly 70% of these groups. Assuming that the rate of growth among those for which founding dates have *not* been verified follows the same general pattern as for those that have been verified, the following figures give a fairly accurate picture of the numerical development of symphony orchestras in the United States.

Dates	Approximate number of orchestras founded
Prior to 1900	37
1900 to 1919	100
1920 to 1939	330
1940 to 1959	634
	1,101

ORCHESTRAL CLASSIFICATIONS

Obviously among the 1,101 ensembles there are vast differences. The classifications generally used throughout the orchestra world are arbitrary and objective, and refer only to the financial structure on which each orchestra operates.

Classification	Number of Orchestras, 1960-61
Major Orchestras	26
Metropolitan Orchestras	19
Community Orchestras	806
College Orchestras	250
Total	1,101 [1]

A. Major Orchestras

The managers of the larger city or "major" orchestras formed an informal conference some thirty-five years ago and later found it necessary to define eligibility for admission of orchestra representatives to the conference. Upon examination of the financial operations of those orchestras that engaged professional musicians on a full-time basis for a stated number of weeks during the year, it was found that in the mid-1930s such a program cost a minimum of $100,000 per year. Orchestras operating on budgets of $100,000 or more per year were therefore designated "major orchestras," and their managers were admitted to the conference sessions.

In 1940 sixteen orchestras were included in the "major" group. Their annual financial operations ranged from $100,000 to a little over $700,000. Their gross annual expenditures totalled approximately $6,000,000. These are the orchestras:

Boston Symphony	Minneapolis Symphony
Chicago Symphony	National Symphony (Washington, D.C.)
Cincinnati Symphony	New York Philharmonic
Cleveland Orchestra	Philadelphia Orchestra
Detroit Symphony	Pittsburgh Symphony
Indianapolis Symphony	Rochester Philharmonic
Kansas City Philharmonic	St. Louis Symphony
Los Angeles Philharmonic	San Francisco Symphony

During the next twenty years (1940-60) orchestra costs increased sharply, seasons were expanded, audiences and ticket sales increased, contributions increased, and a "major" operation could no longer be financed on a minimum of $100,000 a year. In June 1958 the Major Symphony Managers' Conference re-defined the term "major

[1] The inventory of orchestras compiled by the Amerian Symphony Orchestra League at the *close* of the 1960-61 season shows a total of 1.212 orchestras, including 35 in Canada.

[42]

orchestra" as designating those orchestras that operate on annual budgets of $250,000 and over, and that contract with the orchestra musicians on a per-season basis. Twenty-six orchestras now qualify for the newly defined "major" status. Their annual financial operations range from $257,000 to $1,700,000, with their aggregate expenditures totalling nearly $17,500,000 a year, representing an increase of approximately 300% for the major group of orchestras within a twenty-year period. The twenty-six major orchestras play a total of 2,500 concerts per year.

Of striking significance is the fact that a total of approximately 125,000 contributors in the twenty-six cities are voluntarily giving funds totalling nearly $5,000,000 towards the support of their orchestras each year; and that the uses of these funds include supplementary financing for approximately 550 concerts for children and young people each year. These figures dramatically illustrate our thesis that orchestra operations and financing today reflect the economic changes that have developed in our nation in the last hundred years.

The following twenty-six orchestras are included in the "major" classification as of the 1960-61 season:

Atlanta Symphony	Los Angeles Philharmonic
Baltimore Symphony	Minneapolis Symphony
Boston Symphony	Montreal Symphony
Buffalo Philharmonic	National Symphony
Chicago Symphony	New Orleans Symphony
Cincinnati Symphony	New York Philharmonic
Cleveland Orchestra	Philadelphia Orchestra
Dallas Symphony	Pittsburgh Symphony
Denver Symphony	Rochester Philharmonic
Detroit Symphony	St. Louis Symphony
Houston Symphony	San Antonio Symphony
Indianapolis Symphony	San Francisco Symphony
Kansas City Philharmonic	Toronto Symphony

The ten orchestras that have been added to the 1940 list offer employment to musicians on a professional basis for seasons ranging from twenty to thirty weeks. In the aggregate, this development has opened up 808 major symphony positions for orchestra players within a twenty-year period. The corollary, of course, is that the citizens of ten more American cities have found it within their economic ability to support professional orchestras.

B. Metropolitan Orchestras

In 1958, when the minimum budget for the major symphony classification was raised from $100,000 to $250,000, a number of orchestras found themselves in a rather unpleasant situation. In previous years they had qualified for major orchestra status. Suddenly, in spite of the fact that their seasons, artistic standing, and financing were constantly expanding, they found themselves thrust out of the major group by decree. To provide a classification that could be used by the press and the general public without the implication of a down-graded status, the American Symphony Orchestra League created the classification of "metropolitan orchestras," to be used in referring to those orchestras operating on annual budgets of $100,000 to $250,000.

The "metropolitan" orchestras are a challenging group established, for the most part, in cities with rapidly expanding populations. The orchestras' audiences are growing; the number of concerts played increases each year and ranges within the group from 17 to 73 concerts per season; expenditures and income of the orchestra likewise are on the increase. Several of these orchestras engage their musicians on a full-time per-season basis and are on the threshold of the $250,000 annual budgetary requirement that will admit them to the major symphony classification. The majority of this group of orchestras, however, engage their musicians on a per-rehearsal and per-concert basis and, although the personnel is largely professional, the musicians depend on other employment — usually teaching — for their main source of income. Under these circumstances, the orchestras do not expand beyond a certain point simply because the musicians could not devote the additional time needed by the orchestras were they to lengthen the seasons.

As a result, these orchestras are faced with the difficult problem of deciding on the best way and the proper time to change over to the professional format of employing the musicians on a full-time basis for so many weeks per year — a format that usually entails a dramatic increase in total expenditure without immediate accompanying increase in income. In order to make the change, the board of directors and the community usually must be prepared to assume responsibility for contributing a higher percentage of the orchestra's income during the transitional years. Several of these orchestras already have doubled or tripled their total expenditures and activities within the last three-to-five-year period in order to keep pace with their rapidly expanding communities.

The metropolitan classification at the beginning of the 1960-61 season includes the following 19 orchestras:

Birmingham Symphony. Alabama
Columbus Symphony, Ohio
Florida Symphony, Orlando, Fla.
Hartford Symphony, Conn.
Honolulu Symphony, Hawaii
Louisville Orchestra, Ky.
Milwaukee Symphony, Wis.
Oklahoma City Symphony. Okla.
Omaha Symphony, Neb.
Phoenix Symphony, Ariz.

Portland Symphony. Ore.
Rhode Island Philharmonic
San Diego Symphony, Calif.
Tulsa Philharmonic, Okla.
University of Miami Symphony, Fla.
Utah Symphony, Salt Lake City, Utah
Vancouver Symphony, B. C., Canada
Wichita Symphony, Kansas
Winnipeg Symphony. Canada

C. Community Orchestras

The term "community orchestra" is used to designate approximately 800 orchestras operating on annual budgets of less than $100,000.

The variance in methods of operation and in artistic stature is greater among the community orchestras than in either of the other two classifications. Community orchestras' concert seasons range from one or two concerts to 35 or 40 concerts per year. Budgets range from a few hundred dollars a year to just under $100,000. Playing personnel ranges from orchestras composed entirely of professional musicians to those in which none of the resident performers has had professional training or experience. Numerically, the playing personnel ranges from over a hundred musicians down to thirty-five or forty. Conductors may be drawn from the playing group with little or no conducting training or experience, or may be men of vast professional training and experience widely known in the United States and abroad for their art, knowledge, and professional stature. Management of the community orchestras may be handled entirely by volunteers or by a professional manager whose salary may be greater in some cases than is that of managers of some of the metropolitan or major orchestras.

The artistic level of the community orchestras ranges from "professional" and excellent on through the artistic spectrum of fine, good, fair, mediocre, poor, impossible. Community orchestras are to be found in cities of all sizes, from communities of only 2,500 population up to New York City's millions. In fact, thirty percent of all the orchestras in the United States are sponsored by citizens of cities having less than 25,000 population and there are less than a half-dozen United States cities in excess of 50,000 population in which there is not a symphonic ensemble of some kind which presents public concerts. The community orchestras fill many roles. They may be the prestige musical organizations of an entire area, presenting challenging concerts which include excellent performances of the standard repertory, enterprising programming of contemporary works, presentation of major and local soloists, established and local composers, and guest conductors of renown. Or, at the other extreme, the community orchestra may serve primarily as a training ground for young players, young conductors, young soloists, young composers, and a new audience. In the metropolitan centers, it is not unusual to find a community orchestra composed entirely of highly trained professional musicians whose regular employment (as in the film studios) does not permit them to play satisfying music. A group of these musicians may form a community orchestra for the sheer pleasure of playing the music they enjoy, meeting the expenses of the operation from their own personal resources.

D. College Orchestras

The "college" orchestra classification is self-explanatory and refers to those orchestras sponsored completely by a college, university, or conservatory and in which the entire playing personnel and the conductor are drawn from the faculty and student body of the institution. There are approximately 250 college orchestras. Combination college-civic orchestras are classified under the community orchestras.   *   *

*

Thus, we have in the United States a vast complex of symphonic organizations. Altogether the 1,100 organizations encompass a total of approximately 70,000 playing members and an estimated 80,000 public-spirited men and women who volunteer their services on orchestra governing boards and committees for the purpose of finding ways and means to meet the orchestras' aggregate expenditures, which are conservatively estimated at $30,000,000 annually and of which at least $10,000,000 is met through contributions.

A total of approximately 7,800 live symphony concerts are played in the United States each year (an average of 21 per day) to a total audience estimated at ten million.

These statistics lead to one positive conclusion — that symphony orchestras are the keystone on which the serious-music development in the United States is based. A generation ago nearly every United States city and small town possessed a town band complete with a bandstand in a city park or the courthouse square. Many of the bandstands have given way to parking lots and freeways; the bands have been superseded by symphony orchestras. Sousa and Goldman have lost out to Bach, Beethoven, Brahms, Barber, Copland, Creston, and on through the alphabet of Classical, Romantic, and contemporary composers of serious music. In those communities in which orchestras have been established for a number of years we usually find that the orchestra regularly plays to a greater percentage of the community's adults and children than does any other musical organization and in so doing wields the greatest single influence on the musical development and artistic standards of that community. In countless communities new audiences for serious music are being developed by the local symphony orchestras. To them is given the opportunity of molding audiences of musical discernment and good taste, or of permitting the new listeners to become accustomed to mediocrity through inept programming and performance.

It is interesting to speculate on the how and why of such an unprecedented orchestral development. During the last hundred years we have seen many things, considered in other eras and other societies to be exclusive possessions and privileges of rulers and their courts, become accessible to the great mass of America's citizenry. These have included material possessions, participation in "kingly" sports and hobbies, education, medical care, libraries. Symphony orchestras and symphonic music belong in this list also.

[47]

Development of music education in the public schools had some influence on the growth of symphony orchestras. In the first quarter of the 20th century orchestral ensembles abounded in the high schools of the country, and many of today's musicians, especially in the community orchestras, are veterans of those early school orchestras. The presence today in nearly every community of adults who played in orchestras during their school years undoubtedly has been one of the significant factors in the development of the hundreds of United States community orchestras.

In the 1920s came radio which, in its early days, offered many good music programs and helped widen the audience for symphonic music. Then came the depression of the thirties, which forced people to develop their own entertainment; apparently, many orchestras were formed during those years because people had little to spend on travel, shows, etc. The WPA (Works Progress Administration) projects of that era initiated and gave federal aid to some of the ensembles that now are listed among the nation's significant metropolitan, community, and major symphony orchestras.

The two World Wars, which brought about shifts in our population and rendered it more mobile, undoubtedly accelerated the development of orchestras. Thousands of our young people serving abroad in the armed forces learned something of the musical heritage of Europe and returned home with a greater awareness of the arts. Residents of rural areas moved to the cities and had their first opportunity to sample the arts, in symphony concerts, the opera, museums, etc. The most recent suburban developments brought to outlying areas people who had been accustomed to having access to fine music, and they promptly set about organizing community orchestras and developing sponsoring groups for occasional tour concerts played by the major orchestras.

Development of fine recording and playing equipment augmented the audience for symphonic music as has the increasing music education available in the colleges and universities. All of these factors, plus the general and gradual maturing of the nation, the increase in leisure time, and America's apparently natural love for stirring instrumental music, have been operative in the growth of United States symphony orchestras and audiences.

The interplay between the community orchestras and the major and metropolitan orchestras must not be overlooked as a factor in the development of symphony orchestras. The community orchestras reach into the very small communities which do not have the facilities or financing needed for sponsorship of concerts played by the touring major orchestras. Through the work of these smaller orchestras, however, symphonic music becomes a vital part of the life of the residents of the small communities and the total national audience for symphonic music is thereby increased in size, awareness, and discernment. This, in turn, broadens the market for the recordings of the major orchestras and undoubtedly increases their sale of concert tickets. Furthermore, the work of the community orchestras is a factor in the recruitment of young musicians to the symphonic field, some of whom inevitably find their way into the professional orchestras as players, conductors, or soloists.

The orchestra organizations themselves initiated experimentation and expansion. In the 1940s many orchestras, beset with paralyzing deficits compounded by the disruption of normal activities due to the war, suspended operations temporarily — or permanently, as they thought in some cases. The great majority of them, however, rose to the challenge and it was during the 1940s that orchestras began to study their communities seriously in order to assess the musical and cultural needs that the orchestras might conceivably fill. It was during this period that orchestra associations began to throw off their yoke of traditional exclusivity and started to view symphony orchestras as flexible organizations which could play music where and when people wanted it. Today's symphony orchestras will consider playing concerts in almost any place or under almost any circumstances or sponsorship that will serve a segment of the community, and that will produce revenue, compatible with costs. In this period, the orchestras began to study modern promotion and publicity methods, fashioning and adapting them to fit their own needs. This period marked also the beginning of the rapid development of women's committees or associations — auxiliary units of the parent organization which undertake special activities in fund raising, and educational and promotional projects. Today, scarcely an orchestra exists (the Boston Symphony is a notable exception) that has not established an auxiliary unit of several hundred women, highly organized into subcommittees responsible for assisting the governing board and association employees in sale of tickets, fund raising, and development of a wide variety of promotional and educational activities. The time, talent, energy, and money contributed annually to symphony orchestras by their women's associations is incalculable and a constant source of inspiration and of vital, practical assistance.

Another significant step taken by the orchestras themselves during the 1940s was their banding together in order that they might learn from each other. That is how the American Symphony Orchestra League came into being in 1942. It gradually developed into a strong, central, coordinating research and service agency of, by, and for major, metropolitan, community, and college orchestras.

The League was able to provide the coordination needed for success when the orchestras decided it was time for the federal government to quit collecting excise taxes on symphony tickets. The repeal of the tax legislation was a financial boon to orchestras operating at all levels.

As a result of the pooling of resources through the League, it became unnecessary for each orchestra individually to go through long and costly trial-and-error experimental periods. Successful plans and ideas were made readily available to any groups wishing them, thus giving rise to more rapid expansion and stabilization of existing orchestras and accelerated development of new orchestras.

Another aspect of the orchestras' initiative in dealing with major problems was their voluntary assumption of responsibility for improving their own work and product. They knew this to be absolutely necessary if they were to compete successfully in the open market for the entertainment dollar against television, the movies, hi-fi, and the many other things that caught the eyes and ears of the buying public. The orchestras raised performance standards, provided variety and new ideas in programming by delving into very old or seldom played music, by introducing more and more contemporary music and young artists, and by occasionally borrowing from the repertories of opera, oratorio, dance, musical comedy, and jazz. During the last few years there even have been notable and controversial efforts to break down the traditional austerity and formality of symphony concerts.

Whether or not *all* of these changes should be applauded is a moot question, but the fact remains that today more symphony orchestras are playing more music for more people than ever before, and more people are participating in the support and activities of symphony orchestras than ever before.

There is no space to do more than merely mention the large subject of the role and influence of the conductor in this hundred-year development of American symphony orchestras. Every orchestra bears the indelible imprint of its conductors. To the conductor goes the glory or the blame for vision or the lack thereof; for the presence or lack of vibrant leadership — on and off the podium; for the presence or absence of the artistry, knowledge, and skill necessary for the re-creation of great music so that it becomes part of the very life blood of a community. The conductor's role throughout the years has been varied and changing. He frequently is at once the cause and the victim of basic changes in the economic life of symphony orchestras. Nevertheless, it often has been the conductor's assessment of the orchestra's true function in the life of the community that has proved valid and correct. The conductors of America's orchestras have trained them, nurtured them, created them, and, on occasion, destroyed them. To many of the conductors is due the nation's expression of thankfulness for their perception of a changing order in which great music must become the possession of all the people, and in which true culture must grow from within.

In orchestra circles today the focus of attention is on the musicians. Of paramount concern to symphony orchestras is the manner in which year-round income and stabilized employment may be made available to their musicians. Employment of musicians on a "piecework" basis — which is what the present contracts for so many orchestra services per week for so many weeks per year amounts to — belongs to a bygone era. It is a remnant of the days when it was considered normal for "labor" to be insecure and "management" secure. Symphony salary scales have been steadily rising the last twenty years. The length of seasons has increased somewhat, but the combined increase in salary scales and length of seasons still falls far short of full-time employment, reasonable income, and security for the majority of musicians in most of the major and metropolitan orchestras.

I have no doubt that an art and a profession possessing the strength and stamina of music in America plus the support of the general public that has been earned and is now enjoyed by the symphony orchestras of this country will be able to find the solution to this pressing problem, meanwhile continuing the extension of symphonic music until it truly is available to our *entire* citizenry. Although the present total symphony orchestra audience is estimated at ten million people, the surface of the potential audience has barely been scratched. It may well be that in the solution of the economic problem of providing adequate income for professional symphony musicians, there exists also the key to making symphonic music available in much greater quantity to all the young people and adults of this nation.

Opera, the Story of an Immigrant

By PHILIP L. MILLER

On January 21, 1861, New York's opera season opened at the Academy of Music on 14th Street, east of Union Square, with Mercadante's *Il Giuramento*. "To this work," wrote the critic of *The Musical Review and World*, "is attached a high reputation abroad; and whenever the modern Italians would point to something classical, pure and elevating in their own music, they exclaim 'Mercadante,' and add immediately *Il Giuramento*. Both these words have a magic spell for every true Italian. Why this is, it is very difficult to say, if it is not because very few know anything about the work, for it is seldom performed . . . The performance offered one fine feature — the acting as well as singing of Miss Phillips, as Bianca. If there ever was a painstaking, earnest, studious member of an opera troupe in this country, it is this lady. Her execution is much more correct than that of many of her Italian colleagues, and her trill, for instance, compared favorably with that of Mad. Colson (Eloisa), in the really fine duet for soprano and contralto in the third act. Let her not relax in her studies . . ." English-born, Adelaide Phillips had been brought to America as a child, and such was the promise of her voice that Jenny Lind encouraged her when she met her here.

Miss Phillips had made her début at the Academy in 1856.

Both the American singer and Italian opera were now accepted features of New York life. Since the coming of the Garcias in 1825 there had been numerous more or less sketchy attempts to produce opera here, climaxed by the visits of a thoroughly professional company from Havana in the late forties. The Academy of Music had been opened in 1854 with Grisi and Mario in *Norma;* other celebrated singers from abroad had appeared with success, notably the contralto Alboni (whom Walt Whitman described as "the best songstress ever in America") and Henrietta Sontag, creator, years before, of the soprano parts in Beethoven's *Ninth Symphony* and *Missa Solemnis.* Jenny Lind, to be sure, had sung here only in concert, though her triumphs could not fail to stimulate interest in opera. But the most significant event leading into the Schirmer century was the début as Lucia of Adelina Patti, aged sixteen, in the Academy of Music, November 24, 1859. Though born in Madrid of Italian parentage, Patti had been brought to New York as a child, and while it may be stretching a point or two to claim her as an American (in her mature life she never made her home here) the fact that her unequaled talents were first disclosed in New York inevitably meant much to the coming American singer.

American opera, too, had already made its start. William Henry Fry, critic of the New York Tribune and a champion of opera in English, was the first native composer to hear his own grand opera professionally performed. *Leonore,* based on Bulwer-Lytton's *Lady of Lyons,* was produced (in English) in Philadelphia in 1845 and revived in New York (in Italian) in 1858. George Frederick Bristow, presumably spurred by a prize offered as part of an ambitious program conceived by the famous Norwegian violinist Ole Bull (who had leased the Academy of Music for a season of opera in 1855), composed the first grand opera by a native American on an American subject, Rip Van Winkle. It was given at Niblo's Garden in 1855. Luigi Arditi, who first came to New York in 1847 as conductor with the Havana troupe and was active for a number of years thereafter in the operatic life of the city, paid us the compliment of producing his opera *La Spia* (based on Cooper's novel) in 1856.

The big event of the 1861 season at the Academy was the début on February 27 of the nineteen-year-old Clara Louise Kellogg, as Gilda in *Rigoletto*. Miss Kellogg was not, though she liked to think herself so, the first American prima donna, but it is true enough that the names of her predecessors, Julia Wheatley, Elsie Hensler, Cora de Wilhorst, and even Adelaide Phillips, are remembered today only by historically minded opera enthusiasts, while that of Miss Kellogg is a part of our heritage. (In the case of Miss Hensler — the first American singer to appear at the Academy of Music, making her début in 1856 — an American girl became something of a legend by marrying the former king-regent of Portugal in 1869. She died at Lisbon in 1929, aged ninety-three.)

Verdi's *Un Ballo in Maschera* had its American première at the Academy on February 16, 1861. "With regard to the music," wrote the critic of *The Musical Review and World*, "we are happy to say, that some portions of it indicate an effort on the part of its author to raise himself above the cheap and vulgar style of patchworking, with which most of his former efforts were produced . . ."

Across the river in Brooklyn, we read in the same journal, another Academy of Music opened its doors, which "in size appears to be a little larger than our Winter Garden. In fact, it looks very much like any ordinary theater on Broadway, with this difference, that we have seldom seen in any building of this kind, such a profusion of red and brown colors . . . The opening consisted of a speech and a concert . . ." The Academy stood on Montague Street until 1903, when it was destroyed by fire. The present building on Lafayette Avenue replaced it in 1908.

Meanwhile in New Orleans on February 6, Adelina Patti sang her first Gilda at the French Opera House. Opera had been a fixture in the Louisiana metropolis long before it took root elsewhere in the country; as early as 1808 there was an opera house there, and we read of a French troupe from New Orleans visiting New York, Boston, and Philadelphia in the 1820s. There was now to be a pause, occasioned by the austerities of the Civil War years, but New Orleans remained the real center of French opera.

In September 1862 New York had its first season of German opera, under the direction of Karl Anschütz. Works of Mozart, Beethoven, Weber, Auber, Lortzing, and Flotow were presented by a company that boasted no stars. "The scenic arrangement was not brilliant," writes Frédéric Louis Ritter in his *Music in America*, "indeed, it was rather modest—but it was complete, and in a certain harmony with the idea of the work: the performances were artistically rounded off. There was an excellent orchestra, a sufficiently strong and intelligently drilled chorus, all in the hands of an experienced, energetic conductor—Anschütz himself; thus the whole force made a satisfactory ensemble." Unfortunately things did not go too well in New York, and the company moved to Philadelphia. The next stop was to have been Washington, where the cautious manager of Ford's Theater had carefully avoided calling attention to the fact that this was not an Italian composer. But in Philadelphia things went from bad to worse, and Anschütz was unable to move his troupe. "Mr. Ford," according to C. D. Hess (*Cosmopolitan,* December 1901), "immediately placed announcements in the papers offering to refund all moneys received. Leonard Grover, then manager of a rival theater, quietly sped to Philadelphia by the first train, and in less than twelve hours from the moment of his arrival in the Quaker City he had contracts signed with Director Anschütz and every artist, chorus-master, musician and other employee of this great company; and the Washington Sunday papers on the following morning, before Ford's apology had reached the eyes of very many, contained half-page displays, advertisements of 'A Season of German Grand Opera' to be given at Carusi's old theater on Eleventh Street near Pennsylvania Avenue under the direction of Leonard Grover . . ." Thus the Anschütz company was saved, but after five successful years it fell a victim of star trouble. Aside from the singers' salary demands, Hess tells us, "Jealousy became common among them. It occurred several times that Karl Formes and Joseph Hermanns, the rival bassos of the company, stepped before the curtain one after the other to address the audience and explain their individual importance."

To Philadelphia fell the honor, on November 18, 1863, of witnessing the first American production (in German) of that most popular of all operas, Gounod's *Faust.* New York heard it at the Academy of Music (in Italian) on November 25, with Clara Louise Kellogg in the part of Marguerite. "Miss Kellogg's voice," wrote Richard Grant White, "is a high soprano, very clear, very pure, very fine, close and firm in quality, and capable of the most exquisitely delicate and tender inflections. Her intonation is remarkably correct.

Her dramatic power is suited to her voice; and all that she does is marked by a fine and pure intelligence which has a certain sweet homeliness in its mode of manifestation. Hence her performance of Marguerite — toward her conception of which she had no help nor even any model — was ideal and purely poetical in its character. It had no marked individuality, and very little local color; but it was feminine, lovely, tender, and above all, pure. There was a simplicity about it, too, that gave it character — such character as the tint and perfume of the lilac among roses and lilies . . ."

A second opera of William Henry Fry, *Notre Dame of Paris*, was staged in Philadelphia, May 9, 1864. W. G. Armstrong has left us the following brief note: "Was produced for the benefit of the Sanitary Fair. It was written in nineteen days, and was placed on the stage in the most liberal manner at Mr. Fry's expense. Ninety in the orchestra and hundreds on the stage. I saw the opera but once, but was struck with the beauty of the orchestration. The vocalists were, generally, very inferior. It was performed seven times."

St. Louis had its first real season in 1865, Jacob Grau's Grand Italian Opera coming from New York to De Bar's Opera House with a repertory including Pacini's *Saffo*, Donizetti's *Il Poliuto*, Meyerbeer's *Robert le Diable* and the new *Faust* of Gounod. Another company from New York had visited St. Louis as early as 1837 with what purported to be *Cenerentola*, though it was actually a mélange of various Rossini operas.

Chicago's Crosby Opera House was to have opened on April 17, 1865, but the event was postponed until the 20th because of the assassination of President Lincoln. It was the Grau company again, presenting *Trovatore*, that delighted "one of the most brilliant audiences ever assembled in Chicago." A previous venture had ended in tragedy in July 1850. A very small traveling company was performing in *Sonnambula* when a fire spreading from a neighboring building reduced the house to ashes. Fortunately there were no human casualties. But Crosby's Opera House, too, magnificently redecorated for a gala season, was a fire victim, in the conflagration of 1871.

Another youthful American prima donna made her début on October 13, 1866. This was the fourteen-year-old Minnie Hauk, and the scene was the Brooklyn Academy of Music, the New York Academy being under repair after a fire. On November 15, 1867, an old question was raised again by the American première of Gounod's *Roméo et Juliette*. As the New York Times critic put it, "Miss Minnie Hauk was a charming representative of Juliet, but lacked dramatic power. It is doubtful if the exigencies of this character could be met by a singer who has not surrendered the charms of youth for the strength and experience of maturity. But this is the fault of the role . . ."

The American debutante of 1870 was Annie Louise Cary, appearing at a concert in Steinway Hall, New York, but destined for a brilliant career in opera. Said Anton Rubinstein: "It is the most beautiful voice I have ever heard in the whole world!" Christine Nilsson, brought to America by the impresario Maurice Strakosch, was billed as a "Second Jenny Lind." But to Richard Grant White she was "a very gifted and highly finished vocalist of the second rank, standing in its forefront . . . Her Margherita had more character than Miss Kellogg's. She was more a creature of flesh and blood, but not so tender, not so ideal, not so expressive of that moral *aura* of the character which Goethe himself suggests but fails to express . . ." It was Nilsson who created for New York the character of Mignon when Thomas's opera had its first American production on November 22, 1871. With her in the cast was the favorite French tenor, Victor Capoul, "the most ardent and fascinating lover known to opera in America." On April 3 Adolf Neuendorf, who had served as chorus-master for the Anschütz Opera Company, presented the first *Lohengrin* in America at the Stadt Theater.

The year 1872 is notable for the début of Pauline Lucca, described as "essentially a lyric actress rather than a singer pure and simple," who "had the power of realizing the highest dramatic conception both of poet and composer; she was able to draw inspiration from the abstract idea, and she has been called 'transcendentally human.'" Italo Campanini came in 1873, appearing as Gennaro in *Lucrezia Borgia* on October 1. Philip Hale, in his often-quoted comment written at the time of Campanini's death in 1896, concluded: "Of all tenors who have visited us since 1873 the greatest, viewed from all points, was Campanini." Another visitor of that year was the phenomenally gifted but eccentric soprano Ilma di

Murska; the sterling Spanish baritone Giuseppe Del Puente also began his American career, and Enrico Tamberlik, a *tenore robusto* famous for his high C's, came for the season. At the Academy of Music the first American *Aida* was given on November 26. Ottavia Torriani, Campanini, and Cary (long acclaimed as the foremost interpreter of Amneris) were in the cast, and a new baritone, Victor Maurel, destined to become much better known ("As an actor M. Maurel is magnificent, as a singer he has never had a marvelous organ, but he has used it with exquisite art").

1874 was the year of our first *Fledermaus* (Thalia Theater, November 21) and of Emma Albani's New York début, at the Academy, October 21. Albani was a French-Canadian who had spent a part of her youth in Albany, N. Y. (she denied deriving her stage name from this fact), eventually settling in England, where in 1925 she was created a Dame of the British Empire. In 1876 the imposing Therese Tietjens paid us a visit, appearing at the Academy as Norma on January 24 ("On the stage she was a tragedienne in the highest sense of the term" — Herman Klein). And on February 15 the future great pianist Teresa Carreño appeared as Zerlina in *Don Giovanni*.

The growth of interest in Wagner is evidenced by our records of the first performances of *Die Walküre* in New York and Boston on April 12 and 16, part of a kind of Wagner festival directed by Neuendorff. But Henry E. Krehbiel, looking back on the event, remarked: "the memories of that production were painful when they were not amusing . . ." In Philadelphia, November 8, 1876, *Der fliegende Holländer* had its American première.

After long experience in London, the redoubtable Colonel James Henry Mapleson came to New York in 1878 to take over the fortunes of the Academy of Music. Among his important debutantes were Etelka Gerster, with "a voice of exquisitely musical quality and bird-like tone, trained to execute the most difficult *fiorituri* and cadenzas with the utmost care, and capable of running up comfortably to the giddy height of an F in *alt*. Moreover, the Hungarian soprano proved to be a good actress and a conscientious artist, so that her success was never for a moment in doubt" (Herman Klein). Her first appearance was in *Sonnambula* on November 18. In his contralto wing the Colonel had Zelia Trebelli, who was to be long known for the brilliance and flexibility of her fine voice.

But other operatic events of the year were overshadowed by the United States première of *Carmen*, in Italian, with Minnie Hauk, on October 23. Miss Hauk had had considerable success in the title role abroad, and had created it for London. In fact it was her claim, not altogether without foundation, that she was responsible for the growing popularity of the opera. Certainly until Emma Calvé appropriated it, *Carmen* was more widely associated with Minnie Hauk than with any other singer. Colonel Mapleson tells us in his memoirs about the difficulties he and his London conductor, Sir Michael Costa, had in inducing the supporting cast to undertake roles they considered unrewarding — Campanini, the José; Del Puente, the Escamillo; and Valleria, the Micaëla.

An American soprano with "a voice of unusually lovely quality and extraordinary purity" — Emma Juch — made her début as Filina in *Mignon* in 1881. Of Sofia Scalchi, who joined Mapleson's forces the following year, Henry C. Lahee says: "Since the days of [Marietta] Alboni there has been no contralto singer to whom the adjective 'great' could be so fitly applied." Also in 1882, but in the concert hall, Theodore Thomas presented a Wagner festival, for which he imported the celebrated Amalia Materna, creator of Brünnhilde and Kundry in the first Bayreuth Festivals.

The story of the building of the Metropolitan has often been told. Behind it were social rather than musical forces. New York had grown too big for the Academy, and Fourteenth Street was no longer the fashionable center it had been in the fifties. Shops and theaters were moving uptown. The first season opened under the management of Henry E. Abbey on October 22, 1883, with the opera that was to remain for so long the prime favorite — Gounod's *Faust* (the Metropolitan was many years living down W. J. Henderson's quip when he dubbed it *Das Faustspielhaus*). The prima donna was Christine Nilsson, the tenor Campanini, along with Scalchi (said to have been incomparable in any contralto-in-breeches role), Del Puente, and Novara. Since the new company, like its rival at the Academy, was dedicated to Italian opera, *Faust* was sung in translation. According to Krehbiel, the performance was no revelation. New Yorkers had been concerned about Campanini, who had recently been falling into bad vocal habits, and the critic reports sadly that such fears were well founded. Miss Nilsson he described as irresistible, though hardly an embodiment of Goethe's Gretchen, and Miss Scalchi "did the most artistic singing of the evening." Perhaps it is revealing that the singer of so important a role as Mephistopheles was barely mentioned, treatment he shared with the much admired Del Puente, the Valentin of the evening.

The second performance, *Lucia,* was more noteworthy, since it introduced to America an artist who became one of its long-reigning favorites. "Mme. Sembrich is a lovely singer," wrote Krehbiel, "lovely of person, of address, of voice and her artistic acquirements, in the limited field in which Donizetti's opera called them into activity, at least, are of the highest rank. Her style is exquisite, and plainly the outgrowth of a thoroughly musical nature . . .." On December 20 New York heard its first *Gioconda,* the cast including Nilsson, Fursch-Madi, Scalchi, Stagno, Del Puente, and Novara. The first Metropolitan *Lohengrin* (in Italian) was performed by Nilsson, Fursch-Madi, Campanini, Kaschmann, and Novara. And, according to Krehbiel, there was a *Don Giovanni* "with the finest distribution of women's roles, I dare say, that New York has ever seen, and one that ranked well with the famous London one of Tietjens, Nilsson and Patti. Mme. Fursch-Madi was Donna Anna, Mme. Nilsson Donna Elvira, and Mme. Sembrich Zerlina." Less impressively sung were the Don Giovanni, Leporello, and Don Ottavio of Kaschmann, Mirabella, and Stagno.

But Mapleson carried on at the Academy. A certain Mrs. Norton-Gower, later celebrated as Lillian Nordica, sang Margherita in another Italian *Faust* "with commendable intelligence and taste." Her voice was admired, her acting praised, but Krehbiel found too much effort in her work. Still, he accounted her after Patti and Gerster the best woman singer in the Mapleson company.

At the end of its first season the Metropolitan went through one of those crises all but habitual with opera companies. Mr. Abbey had lost money; and without a guarantee against losing more in another year, he could hardly go on. So it was that a drastic step was taken. Leopold Damrosch, conductor of the Arion Society and of his newly organized Symphony Society, offered to put on a German season with the best company that could be assembled abroad. And so Wagner came into his own in New York. The season opened with *Tannhäuser*. The tenor, Anton Schott, was disappointing, for he belonged to the declamatory school of Wagnerians. The excellent Auguste Kraus (wife of Anton Seidl, who was to be the leading conductor the following year), and Anna Slach, as Elisabeth and Venus, were outshone by Adolf Robinson's masterly Wolfram.

For seven seasons all operas — even *Faust, Aida, Carmen,* and *Trovatore* — were sung in German, with the major efforts going into discovery and exploration in the new and controversial world of the Master of Bayreuth. There were great singers in those days. The second performance of the season introduced Marianne Brandt as Fidelio. "Her voice is brilliant and powerful," wrote Henderson, "her method eclectic, by which we would imply that she has the vigorous enunciation and accent of the German school of song, and no little of the fluency of the Italian, and as an actress she is intelligent, impassioned and forceful . . ." The singer's versatility was quickly shown as she sang successively Hedwig in *William Tell*, Ortrud, Donna Elvira, Fidès, Maddalena in *Rigoletto,* and Fricka in *Walküre*. On January 5, 1885, Materna appeared as Elisabeth in *Tannhäuser*. According to Lahee, "She was not a vocal technician of the school of Jenny Lind, Nilsson, Patti, or Gerster. Her voice, though unable to give phenomenal runs, trills, or cadenzas, was adequately trained, and was of remarkable richness and breadth. The work of the poet rather than the singing teacher was apparent in her interpretations, and the dramatic intensity and passionate force of her delivery were effective even upon the concert stage. It is doubtful whether any singer will ever combine more of the qualities which are essential to the perfect interpretation of Wagner's operas, and Materna may, therefore, be set down as the greatest singer of her school." In the midst of the season Leopold Damrosch fell ill and died of pneumonia. And so his twenty-two-year-old son Walter made his début, conducting *Tannhäuser* with Materna again appearing as Elisabeth.

At the end of the season Edmund C. Stanton was appointed director, and young Walter Damrosch was sent abroad as a talent scout. "I have always been proud," he tells us in his memoirs, "of the four contracts I had ready for Stanton's signature when he, a month later, arrived in Germany. These were Lilli Lehmann, soprano from the Royal Opera House in Berlin; Emil Fischer, bass from the

Royal Opera House in Dresden; Max Alvary, lyric tenor from Weimar, and Anton Seidl, conductor of the Angelo Neumann Wagner Opera Company. These four artists became subsequently the mainstay of the German Opera and in America developed to greater and greater power and fame."

Lehmann made her début on the second night of the season as Carmen, strangely enough. Says Krehbiel: "Lehmann as the gypsy cigarette maker, with her *Habanera* and her *Seguidilla,* with her errant fancy wandering from a sentimental brigadier to a dashing bull fighter, is a conception which will not come easy to admirers of the later Brünnhilde and Isolde . . ." Of Emil Fischer, who made his first appearance on the opening night as King Heinrich in *Lohengrin,* Damrosch has this to say: "His voice was a beautiful *basso cantante* of great range and vibrancy. His tone production was perfect, and his powers as an interpreter equaled his singing. He will always remain in my memory as the greatest Hans Sachs I have ever heard . . ." Max Alvary, who was the José to Lehmann's Carmen, became one of the great matinée idols in Metropolitan history, though there was some disagreement as to the quality of the handsome young man's singing. Another début of the opening night was that of Anton Seidl, a great conductor and one of the leading authorities on the Wagnerian dramas. Seidl remained a pillar of the company until his death in 1898.

One by one the music dramas were presented, from *Rienzi* to *Parsifal* (though the latter was given only in concert form). The 1887-88 season was opened with *Walküre,* the famous tenor Albert Niemann appearing as Siegmund, a role he had created at Bayreuth in 1876. Later he also sang Tristan. A man in his mid-fifties, it is easy to understand that some thought him rather mature to be convincing in these heroic roles, but he won great praise for his artistry. In March 1889 the complete *Ring* was given for the first time in this country.

The German régime continued through the season of 1890-91; then came the inevitable turning of the tide. By this time the gospel of Wagner had been established, and the repertory tended to take on more and more Italian and French operas translated into German. The magnificent casts of earlier years, headed by artists who had grown artistically in the traditions of Wagner's own Bayreuth,

[63]

were no longer available. Of all the prime favorites only Emil Fischer remained in that final year. Even Lilli Lehmann was gone, though she was to return under the new management the following season.

Writing of the triumph of the Germans, then in full tide, Henry T. Finck observed in *The Cosmopolitan* for March 1888: "The lovers of vocal tight-rope dancing and threadbare orchestral accompaniments who insist that Wagner is merely a fashion, and that ere long there will be a return to the saccharine melodies of Rossini and Bellini, show thereby that they have never studied the history of the opera. The history teaches a curious lesson, viz., that operas which had a great vogue at one time and subsequently lost their popularity can *never* be galvanized into real life again. What has become of the threescore and more operas of Donizetti, and the forty of Rossini — some of which for years monopolized the stage so completely the world over that Weber and Beethoven were ignored even in Vienna and the German capitals? They are dead, and all efforts to revive them have been futile."

Opera in English had one of its periodic flings with the American Opera Company, which gave its first season at the Academy under Theodore Thomas in 1885, and lasted until 1887. Among the excellent native singers engaged were Emma Juch, Hélène Hastreiter, Myron Whitney, William Candidus, and Pauline L'Allemand (who created the role of Lakmé for New York). The effort was carried on subsequently by Miss Juch at the head of her own company. Another traveling prima donna who made a fortune taking opera from the highways to the byways of the country was Emma Abbott (fondly remembered as the American who once scandalized her Milanese audience by interpolating *Nearer, My God, to Thee* into *Sonnambula*). But touring opera companies were flourishing everywhere. Julius Mattfeld's *Variety Music Cavalcade* lists the following as active in 1886: Alice Oates Opera Company, Boston Ideal Opera Company, Clara Louise Kellogg English Opera Company, The Emelie Melville Company, Hess Acme (or English) Opera Company, Norcross Fifth Avenue Opera Company, W. T. Carleton Opera Company, William Lyster's English Opera and Opera Bouffe Troupe, Braham and Scanlan's New Miniature Opera Company, and many others.

New York's Academy was the scene of the first American production of Verdi's *Otello*, then only a year old, on April 16, 1888. A company had been brought from Italy by Campanini, with his brother Cleofonte (later of Manhattan and Chicago) on the podium, and Eva Tetrazzini (Cleofonte's wife and Luisa's sister) as Desdemona. Francesco Marconi sang the title role in a rather disastrous first performance. A fine and much admired singer of the old school, Marconi was clearly miscast. Though himself past his best days, Campanini then took over, but *Otello* had to await the coming of Tamagno to make its full impression.

A red-letter day in the history of Chicago was December 10, 1889, when the curtain went up for the first time in the new Auditorium. Patti, Ravelli, Fabbri, and Del Puente sang *Roméo et Juliette*, an auspicious beginning to a golden era. The Auditorium witnessed three famous American débuts on the evening of November 9, 1891. The opera was *Lohengrin*, the new singers Emma Eames and the brothers de Reszke. The language was Italian, and the Ortrud, also a debutante, was Giulia Ravogli (who was to attain some celebrity singing Gluck's *Orfeo* with her sister Sophia as Euridice). The audience, it seems, at once recognized genius in the two men, but reserved judgment on the beautiful Miss Eames. Her Juliet, sung with the de Reszkes the following week, established her in favor. It was with these singers in Gounod's opera that the Metropolitan season of 1891-92 opened.

The New York company was now Italo-French. The tables were turned; such German operas as there were must now be given in Italian. The first season's manager, Mr. Abbey, returned to share the responsibilities with Maurice Grau and with Edward Schoeffel (who functioned, says Walter Damrosch, simply as a hyphen between the other two names). The following year there was no season, owing to a fire in August that destroyed the entire interior of the building, but in 1893-94 a number of first-rank singers were introduced. On November 29 a double bill of Gounod's *Philémon et Baucis* and *Cavalleria rusticana* brought out the admired Swedish soprano Sigurd Arnoldson and Pol Plançon (perhaps the most accomplished basso ever to tread the boards) in the former; but the sensation of the evening was the Santuzza of Emma Calvé, a greater impersonation, some said, even than her Carmen. And on

December 4 Nellie Melba made her début, in *Lucia*. Krehbiel wrote: "to throw out those scintillant bubbles of sound which used to be looked upon as the highest achievement in singing seemed to be an entirely natural mode of expression with her. With the reasonableness of such a mode of expression I am not concerned now; it is enough that Mme. Melba came nearer to providing it with justification than any of her contemporaries of that day, except Mme. Semrich . . ." On December 3, 1894, New York first heard Tamagno and Maurel together in *Otello*. Eames was the Desdemona, somewhat "severe and unyielding," according to Henderson, who felt that Tamagno had lost some dignity since the critic had heard him in this opera abroad, but Maurel "was a revelation to the public of the resources that go to make the art of a truly great singing actor . . ." Maurel was to reap further honors later in the season when he gave New York its first *Falstaff*. Also in the cast were Eames, de Lussan, Scalchi, and a relative newcomer whom Henderson singled out for praise: "Next to Maurel the greatest success was that of the young baritone Signor Campanari, who may be said to have leaped at a single bound into a position he might have been years in attaining by singing familiar roles. His acting was brisk, well conceived, and well carried out." Many years later, in the same opera, history was to repeat itself with Lawrence Tibbett's leap to fame.

The season of 1895-96 was notable in that Jean and Edouard de Reszke sang the first of their many Wagner performances in German. *Tristan* was the opera, Nordica the Isolde. The following season another leading Wagnerian, David Bispham, made his début as Beckmesser in an Italian *Meistersinger*. And on December 30, 1896, Melba made her disastrous attempt to sing Brünnhilde in *Siegfried*, after which she found it necessary to take a year of rest.

When the new régime came in at the Metropolitan, a need had been felt for a company to carry on the work so well begun by Damrosch and his associates. The result was a season of Wagnerian opera given at the Metropolitan in the spring of 1895. This in turn led to the formation of the Damrosch Opera Company, which for four years appeared in various cities, with emphasis, of course, on Wagner. The singers engaged included some of the first rank, notably the sopranos Katharina Klafsky and Rosa Sucher, both long established in Germany, and the younger Milka Ternina and Johanna Gadski. Damrosch's own opera, *The Scarlet Letter,* was produced with some success in Boston on February 10, 1896, with Gadski, Bispham, and Barron Berthold in the leading roles.

Pagliacci had its first American production at the Grand Opera House in New York on June 15, 1893, and Bizet's *Les Pêcheurs de perles* was given in August of that year by the Philadelphia Grand Opera Company. More important was the American stage première of *Samson et Dalila* at the French Opera House in New Orleans, for it introduced to this country the French baritone Maurice Renaud, later to become one of Oscar Hammerstein's leading stars. New York's Academy of Music, approaching its end as a home of opera, did witness the first production in this country of *Andrea Chenier* in November 1896.

Henry E. Abbey died October 17, 1896. The season went forward as scheduled, but the following year there was no resident company. From 1898-99 through 1902-03 Maurice Grau carried on alone. His was chiefly a period of singing in the grand manner. Of important new operas there were few. The outstanding debutante of the first season arrived in New York after a triumph in Chicago. She was Ernestine Schumann-Heink, one of the greatest and most warmly appreciated singers ever to come before the American public. Her début role, both in Chicago and New York, was Ortrud. Actually, however, it was at a Sunday night concert that Schumann-Heink established herself with the New York public. Responding to an ovation after her masterly rendition of an air from Bruch's *Odysseus,* she added the popular *Brindisi* from *Lucrezia Borgia.* Such was the ease and bravado of her singing that the aria was ever after closely associated with her name. On December 14 Anton Van Rooy, noble of voice and style, appeared for the first time as Wotan in *Walküre,* and on November 30 Marcella Sembrich returned in *Il Barbiere di Siviglia* after an absence of some fifteen years. On December 27, 1899, Antonio Scotti appeared as Don Giovanni, beginning a long career as the company's most polished singing actor.

Puccini made his entry into the repertory on December 26, 1900, when *La Bohème* was offered, and he strengthened his position with *Tosca* on February 4, 1901. *Bohème,* which Mr. Krehbiel thought

[67]

degrading, strenuous, and superficial in expression, owed its production to Mme. Melba, who found in the role of Mimi the answer to her need for lyrical singing, unencumbered with floridity. She worked hard in mastering her part, spending one summer coaching with Puccini himself, and her dramatic art was said to have deepened considerably thereby. In spite of Krehbiel, of course, *Bohème* had come to stay. It is amusing today to read reviews in which critics confess themselves nonplussed by the complexities of the score. In *Tosca* Milka Ternina triumphed, and Scotti sang the first of his long line of masterly Scarpias. Important newcomers of that season included Charles Gilibert, a fine singer and a beloved character actor; the favorite American contralto, Louise Homer; the fine French basso Marcel Journet; the incomparable soubrette Fritzi Scheff; and the splendid French dramatic soprano Lucienne Bréval. With a performance of *Lohengrin* on March 29, Jean de Reszke sang his last at the Metropolitan.

On February 25, 1902, occurred the famous gala in honor of H. R. H. Prince Henry of Prussia, when Mme. Sembrich, offended by the late arrival and early departure of the guest of honor, left the house without singing. And on March 11, 1903, *Der Wald* by Dame Ethel Smyth was given with Gadski, Reuss-Belce, Anthes, and Bispham in the cast. To this day that opera holds the distinction of being the only work of a woman composer ever to be performed at the Metropolitan.

In October 1902 the composer Mascagni embarked on an American tour designed to make it known that he had other operas to his credit than the best-selling *Cavalleria rusticana*. Unhappily, things went wrong with the management, and the tour was cut short.

The Metropolitan season of 1903-04 opened on November 23 under new management. Heinrich Conried, an Austrian actor, had become prominent in theater production. His régime lasted through the 1907-08 season. On his very first night he produced his greatest star, Enrico Caruso, singing the Duke in *Rigoletto* in a cast with Sembrich, Homer, Scotti, and Journet. Mr. Krehbiel found Caruso "the finest Duke that New York has heard in a generation," and Mr. Henderson opined that the new tenor would "probably grow into firm favor with the public." In a word, it was realized that a star had arrived, but hardly that the newcomer would prove *the* star of the next two decades. The strength of the cast was an augury of things to come in the Conried years.

A notable event of the second season was the first full production of *Parsifal* outside Bayreuth, given in the face of threats and lawsuits instituted by Cosima Wagner. The cast was headed by Ternina, Burgstaller, Van Rooy, and Blass. According to Richard Aldrich, "It was without doubt the most perfect production ever made on the American lyric stage . . ." There were, however, two groups of individuals who took violent exception to the performance — those who felt with Frau Wagner that *Parsifal* should remain the exclusive property of Bayreuth, and those who objected to what they considered its impiety. There was no doubt that Conried had scored a popular triumph, and *Parsifal* has been in the repertory most seasons ever since.

On January 22, 1907, Conried exploded another bombshell, this time with less acclaim. Preceded by a miscellaneous concert including such offerings as the quartet from *Fidelio*, arias and duets from *Don Giovanni*, *Mefistofele*, *The Tales of Hoffmann*, *Rigoletto*, and *Africana*, sung by Fleischer-Edel, Alten, Burgstaller, Goritz, Farrar, Scotti, Lina Cavalieri, Homer, Kirkby Lunn, Boninsegna, Stracciari, and Caruso, two Strauss songs by Sembrich, and the *Faust* trio by Bessie Abott, Rousselière, and Journet, the business of the evening was the American première of Strauss's *Salome*, with Olive Fremstad offering a masterly embodiment of the title role (though she did not attempt to dance), with Burrian an unforgettable Herod, and Van Rooy a noble Jokanaan. This time, as everyone remembers, the moralists won out. Such was the storm of protests in the mails, in the pulpits, and in the press that the board of directors ordered Conried to shelve his masterpiece after only one hearing.

Sensational in another way were the annual "director's benefits" of the Conried period. In February 1905 *Die Fledermaus* enjoyed what was probably the most spectacular production in its history, for not only were such headliners as Sembrich, Edyth Walker, Bella Alten, Dippel, Reiss, and Goritz in the cast, but the second-act finale became the setting for a special concert, with Ackté, Eames, Fremstad, Homer, de Macchi, Nordica, Caruso, Giraldoni, Journet, Plançon, Scotti, Van Rooy, and numerous others either contributing a number or at least putting in an appearance. Though Henderson's wry comment — "Last night's presentation was inflated beyond the market value of operetta" — was typical, the next season saw a similar treatment given *Der Zigeunerbaron*.

Meanwhile, history was being made on other stages. In 1904 Luisa Tetrazzini created a furor at the Tivoli Opera House in San Francisco, from which vantage point she proceeded to her triumphs in London and New York. In 1906 Leoncavallo, following Mascagni's example, made an American tour that did not prove successful. And Oscar Hammerstein, a one-time cigar maker who had been playing around with the theater and music for many years, opened his Manhattan Opera House on 34th Street, with a company designed to prove that Conried had not cornered all the world's great stars. The emphasis was on the French repertory, though the Italian was not neglected. Indeed, the first season opened on December 3, 1906, with *Puritani*, introducing the tenor Alessandro Bonci, who made an immediate hit and was straightway set up as a rival to Caruso, though his voice was by nature much lighter, more lyrical, and more limited. Two nights later Renaud bowed as Rigoletto, the first of his many admired impersonations at the Manhattan. With the début of Mary Garden as Thais in November 1907, Hammerstein's company hit full stride, and the operatic war was on.

"Such an ensemble," wrote Joseph Sohn in *The Forum*, "which the writer so strongly urged upon the management of the Metropolitan years ago, has come at last. It is the achievement of Mr. Oscar Hammerstein of the Manhattan Opera House . . . The star system is the bane of operatic performances. Our drama was once dominated by it; but that time is fortunately passing away; the public is becoming more and more interested in the play itself . . ."

The very list of Hammerstein's productions is still exciting. Mary Garden disclosed her celebrated Louise and then her unapproachable Mélisande. Said Carl Van Vechten: "In her faded mediaeval gown, with her long plaits of golden hair — in the first scene she wore it loose — Mary Garden became at once in the spectator's mind the princess of enchanted castles, the cymophanous heroine of a féerie, the dream of a poet's tale. In gesture and musical speech, in tone-color, she was faithful to the first wonderful impression of the eye . . ." Later, among other things, she took over the title role in Massenet's all-male opera, *Le Jongleur de Notre Dame,* and scored with a *Salome* translated into French which had fourteen performances in the last two Manhattan seasons. The sensation of the 1909-10 season was again Strauss in French. Mariette Mazarin, in the title role of *Elektra*, put so much of herself into the interpretation that she fainted when taking her curtain calls. "The plane of hysteria upon which this singer carried her heroine by her pure nervous force," wrote Van Vechten, "indeed reduced many of us in the audience to a similar state." In November 1908 Mr. Hammerstein enlarged his horizons by opening his Philadelphia Opera House with *Carmen*.

But even in this, Conried's last season, the Metropolitan was beginning to take to heart the challenge of Hammerstein's ensemble. In February 1907 Puccini crossed the ocean to witness the first Metropolitan performance of *Madama Butterfly* (the Savage English Grand Opera Company had already had the new opera on the road). Geraldine Farrar had now found her most admired role, and Caruso, Homer, and Scotti made a strong supporting cast. For the New Year of 1908 *Tristan und Isolde* was given, with Olive Fremstad disclosing for the first time an interpretation long accepted as classic, and the new conductor Gustav Mahler making his début.

When Giulio Gatti-Casazza was brought from Italy to succeed Conried, he was to share his task with the company's tenor Andreas Dippel, whose reputation as a standby for any indisposed tenor in virtually any role has since been rivaled only by the soprano Florence Easton and the mezzo Margarete Matzenauer — who, indeed, was ready with almost any feminine role in any school of opera. As co-manager, Dippel had his troubles, for though the sentiment of a large percentage of the company for their long-time colleague weighed heavily against Gatti's authority, still the Italian was the stronger man, the more able executive. Dippel, therefore, lasted two seasons, then moved on to Chicago, where he ruled the roost until 1913.

The Gatti-Casazza reign, lasting through the season of 1934-35, is recent and well-remembered history; to dwell upon it in detail would take us far beyond the bounds of this brief survey. The grand opening on November 16, 1908, introduced the chief Italian conductor, Arturo Toscanini, as well as the new Czech soprano, Emmy Destinn, as Aida. Caruso, Homer, and Scotti rounded out

[71]

the cast. Outstanding productions down the years included Toscanini's *Otello*, which brought Leo Slezak before the American public, with Frances Alda as Desdemona; his *Orfeo ed Euridice*, with Homer, Gadski, and Alma Gluck; the American première of *Boris Godunov*, also under Toscanini, with a stunning performance of the title role by Adamo Didur (years later the opera was given new interest by the coming of Chaliapin) and a promising début by the young American tenor, Paul Althouse; America's first *Rosenkavalier*, with Frieda Hempel, Margarete Ober, Anna Case, and Otto Goritz, conducted by Alfred Hertz; *L'Amore dei tre re*, magnificently presented with Lucrezia Bori, Edouardo Ferrari-Fontana, Pasquale Amato, and Adamo Didur, under Toscanini; *Samson et Dalila* and *Le Prophète* with Matzenauer and Caruso, conducted by Giorgio Polacco and Artur Bodanzky respectively; *Le Coq d'or*, presented in pantomime by the ballet, with the singers (including Maria Barrientos) in stalls at the side of the stage; *La Forza del destino*, never before heard in the house, with Caruso and the surprise début of Rosa Ponselle; the world première of *Gianni Schicchi* with Giuseppe de Luca; *La Juive*, providing Caruso with his last new role and one of his greatest; *Andrea Chenier*, created here by the young Beniamino Gigli, Claudia Muzio, and Giuseppe Danise; *Die tote Stadt*, introducing the radiant Viennese blond, Maria Jeritza; *Falstaff*, revived for Scotti, but affording Lawrence Tibbett his chance to become a star; *Pelléas et Mélisande*, with a superb cast—Bori, Edward Johnson, Kathleen Howard, Clarence Whitehill, Louise Hunter, and Léon Rothier, conducted by Louis Hasselmanns; *La Vestale* with a great role for Ponselle; *Turandot*, in which Jeritza wore a train that filled the stage; *Norma*, another step in Ponselle's career; *La Rondine*, Puccini's flirtation with light opera, charmingly sung by Bori, Fleischer, Gigli, and Tokatyan, Vincenzo Bellezza conducting; Respighi's *La Campana sommersa* with brilliant singing by Elisabeth Rethberg and Giovanni Martinelli, conducted by Tullio Serafin; *Jonny spielt auf*, Krenek's jazz opera, starring Michael Bohnen; *Don Giovanni* under Serafin, with Ponselle, Rethberg, Fleischer, Pinza, and Ludikar, which brought Mozart back permanently into the repertory; and *Simon Boccanegra*, with Tibbett in perhaps his finest role.

American opera was tried from time to time. As early as 1910

Gatti mounted Converse's *The Pipe of Desire* (it had been given in Boston in 1906); a second work was Parker's prize-winning *Mona,* with Louise Homer in the title role, in 1912. Cadman's *Shanewis,* given in 1918 with Sophie Braslau in the leading role and Roberto Moranzoni conducting, lasted into a second season. Deems Taylor was even more successful with *The King's Henchman,* with a libretto by Edna St. Vincent Millay and a cast including Easton, Johnson, and Tibbett in 1927, so much so that he followed it with *Peter Ibbetson* in 1931. Bori, Johnson, and Tibbett headed a strong cast.

There was considerable operatic activity outside the Metropolitan in those years. In 1909 the big news was the opening of the Boston Opera House under the direction of Henry Russell, an Englishman who had brought a traveling troupe to this country a few years previously. The new company was launched in November with *Gioconda,* starring Nordica and a Spanish tenor then reaching the height of a very successful American career, Florencio Constantino. Many of the best artists in the country appeared in turn, some by an exchange arrangement with the Metropolitan and Chicago companies — Destinn, Fremstad, Matzenauer, Gerville-Réache, Alice Nielsen, Slezak, Zenatello, Baklanoff, Muratore, de Cisneros, Garden, Maggie Teyte, Edmond Clément, and Lucille Marcel, American wife of the company's chief conductor, Felix Weingartner. The repertory was mostly standard, though there was at least one American novelty, Converse's *The Sacrifice,* given in 1911 with Nielsen and Constantino in the leading roles. The Boston Opera Company enjoyed a brilliant if brief career, ending with a spring season in Paris in 1914 (the Metropolitan had appeared in Paris in 1910).

The most successful of all traveling companies in this country, the San Carlo Opera, under the direction of Fortune Gallo, began in 1913 its mission of bringing the standard operas to the farthest reaches of the land. Aside from pioneering, the company served as a proving ground for many rising stars. Queena Mario, Mario Basiola, Vincent Ballester, and Dorothy Kirsten are a few who went on to the Metropolitan; well-known guest stars included Marcella Craft, Lydia Lipkowska, Marie Rappold, Anne Roselle, Anna Fitziu, Alice Gentle, Sydney Rayner, Guido Ciccolini, and Henri Scott. The

Japanese sopranos Tamaki Miura and Hizi Koyke became famous for their impersonations of Madame Butterfly with the company. Among the noted conductors were Henry Hadley, Gaetano Merola, and Cesare Sodero.

Hammerstein's brilliant company at the Manhattan continued to threaten the existence of the Metropolitan until 1910, when finally the impresario was forced to sell out with the understanding that he would produce no more opera in New York for ten years. At the same time he surrendered to the Metropolitan his interests in Philadelphia. He had meantime set up his stakes in London, and opened a new house there. Failing to make his mark in the British capital, he returned to New York and in direct violation of his agreement proceeded to build yet another house, on Lexington Avenue, with the intention of starting a new company. This, however, he was prevented from doing.

Just at the time of his surrender it happened that the good people of Chicago and Philadelphia felt the need of a permanent company, and this need was filled largely with Hammerstein artists and repertory. It may have been providential, too, that Andreas Dippel became available at the time, so there was no long search for a manager. The Philadelphia-Chicago Opera Company got off to a flying start with *Aida* on November 3, 1910, the cast including Jeanne Kerolewic, Eleanora de Cisneros, Amadeo Bassi, and Mario Sammarco, Campanini conducting. On February 25, 1911, a great deal of publicity was climaxed by the production in Philadelphia of Victor Herbert's grand opera *Natoma*, in which Mary Garden (who protested in the press that it was impossible to sing opera in English) played an Indian girl and John McCormack a naval lieutenant. A hit was scored in Chicago in 1912 by the production, with the composer present, of Wolf-Ferrari's shocker, *I Giojelli della Madonna*, and in it the reputation of the soprano Carolina White was made. In Philadelphia, on November 12 of that year, Titta Ruffo took the town by storm as Rigoletto. In 1913 Campanini became general manager, and in 1915 the company was reorganized as The Chicago Opera Company. Mary Garden had a season as manager in 1920-21.

Notable singing actors whose opera careers in this country were launched or centered in Chicago included Amelita Galli-Curci, whose début as Gilda on November 18, 1916, was one of the sensational opera events of the century; Edward Johnson, later of the Metropolitan, who stopped the show in Giordano's *Fedora* in 1920; Lucien Muratore and José Mojica, tenors often matched with Mary Garden; Rosa Raisa; Claire Dux; Antonio Cortis; Tito Schipa; Eva Turner, perhaps the greatest of Turandots; Frida Leider, Maria Olczewska, and Lotte Lehmann, who were members of the Chicago company before coming to the Metropolitan. The final performance in the Auditorium was given on January 26, 1929, the famous house ending as it had begun with *Roméo et Juliette,* the cast headed by Edith Mason and Charles Hackett and conducted by Giorgio Polacco, now artistic director of the company. The Chicago Civic Opera then moved into its new building. In 1932, a victim of the bad times, it went out of existence.

The San Francisco Opera Company was founded in 1923 by Gaetano Merola, who guided its destinies until his death in 1953, when he was succeeded by Kurt Herbert Adler. Many of the foremost artists already mentioned have been on its roster, and since the opening of the War Memorial Opera House in 1932 many important débuts have taken place there. Renata Tebaldi, Tito Gobbi, Margarete Klose, Elisabeth Schwarzkopf, Cesare Valletti, Elena Nikolaidi, and Set Svanholm are a few who made their first American operatic appearances there. Among the outstanding American premières, Strauss's *Die Frau ohne Schatten* may be mentioned.

During the First World War all German operas had been dropped from the Metropolitan repertory, and it took a number of seasons to restore Wagner, Strauss, and the rest to their proportionate place in the New York house. Taking advantage of this situation, a German Grand Opera Company toured the country, giving an extended season in New York in 1923-24. Siegfried Wagner and Edouard Mörike were principal conductors, and Meta Seinemeyer, Eva von der Osten, Ottilie Metzger, and Theodor Lattermann were a few of the important singers. Editha Fleischer and Friedrich Schorr remained in this country as leading artists at the Metropolitan. The company in subsequent seasons joined with another group brought over with Johanna Gadski as the special star.

In 1933 a Russian company opened a season at the New Amsterdam Theater in New York presenting many works in the repertory long established in Russia but little known abroad. For some seasons The Art of Musical Russia continued this missionary work.

Popular-priced opera had its big day in New York during the depression years of the thirties. The old Hippodrome, for long the home of the super-spectacular in the New York theater, was idle and available. For a time under the direction of the former Metropolitan baritone Pasquale Amato, but chiefly run by the indefatigable Alfredo Salmaggi, the standard operas of the Italian, French, and German masters were presented, mounted in whatever way proved possible, and never over-rehearsed. Nevertheless, there was no lack of spirit, and sometimes there were real stars — Sigrid Onegin, Bernardo de Muro, and Amato himself on occasion sang with the company. Bruna Castagna made her first appearances in America at the Hippodrome, proceeding thence to the Metropolitan. The principal conductor, Giuseppe Bamboschek, had previously served long years at the Met.

An event far ahead of its time was the first opera broadcast from the Metropolitan stage. On January 13, 1910, equipment was set up in the house to transmit portions of *Pagliacci,* with Caruso, Alten, and Amato. Of course there were no home radios in those days; but that the opera was heard outside the house was a real achievement. Broadcast opera could be taken more seriously when the Chicago Civic Opera inaugurated it in 1927; the Metropolitan entered the field on Christmas Day 1931, with a complete *Hänsel und Gretel* with the then standard cast of Fleischer, Mario, Dorothee Manski, and Gustav Schützendorf.

A few American premières outside the established houses may be mentioned: Schoenberg's *Die glückliche Hand* (Philadelphia, 1930); Berg's *Wozzeck* (Philadelphia, 1931); Virgil Thomson's *Four Saints in Three Acts* (Hartford, 1934); Stravinsky's *Mavra* (Philadelphia, 1934); Gluck's *Iphigénie en Aulide* (Philadelphia, 1934); Shostakovich's *Lady Macbeth of Mtzensk* (Cleveland, 1935).

With the departure of Gatti-Casazza it was announced that Herbert Witherspoon, a former basso of the Metropolitan, would be the next general manager, with Edward Johnson and Edward Ziegler as assistants. Fate willed otherwise, however, for Witherspoon died suddenly. The season of 1935-36 opened under Johnson's direction, and he remained in charge through 1949-50. These were difficult years, beginning in the depth of the great depression and continuing through the Second World War and the post-war years. Johnson, always a good colleague, was well liked by his singers, and he was able to maintain good relations with his public and his board of directors. It was in his time that Mrs. August Belmont, Miss Lucrezia Bori, and others organized the Metropolitan Opera Guild, thus adding new strength to the opera's following. It was a period notable for the number of American singers who came into their own—Helen Traubel, Gladys Swarthout, Risë Stevens, Eleanor Steber, Rose Bampton, Dusolina Giannini, Grace Moore, Richard Crooks, Leonard Warren, Charles Kullmann, John Charles Thomas, Robert Weede, Jan Peerce, Richard Tucker, and Robert Merrill were among Johnson's stars. Mozart flourished, with notable revivals of *Le Nozze di Figaro* and *The Magic Flute* (in English); the roster of conductors gained strength by the presence of Bruno Walter, Sir Thomas Beecham, Fritz Busch, Fritz Stiedry, George Szell, Fritz Reiner, and Erich Leinsdorf. Wagner came into his own by the grace of Kirsten Flagstad, Lauritz Melchior, Friedrich Schorr, Karin Branzell, Kerstin Thorborg, Alexander Kipnis, and others. And for the Lucias, Gildas, and Lakmés, there was Lily Pons.

Rudolf Bing, who took the reins from Johnson after the close of the 1949-50 season, has presented many notable stars, and like Oscar Hammerstein he has been vitally interested in ensemble and quality of production. To this end he engaged the eminent Shakespearean authority, Margaret Webster, to stage his very first opera, *Don Carlo*. His list of novelties has included Stravinsky's *The Rake's Progress* (1953); Strauss's *Arabella* (1953); Barber's *Vanessa* (1958); Verdi's *Macbeth* (1959); and Berg's *Wozzeck* (1959). Glamorous new productions of the light classics, *Die Fledermaus*, *Der Zigeunerbaron*, and Offenbach's *La Périchole*, all sung in English, have been added. Other operas sung in translation included *Boris Godunov*, *Eugene Onegin*, *Alceste*, *Così fan tutte*, *Arabella*, and *Wozzeck*. An interesting experiment in the 1952-53 season was the presentation of *Bohème* in a new translation by Howard Dietz, followed later in the year by the original Italian. The public was asked to make known its preference; the house reverted to regular Italian performances the following season.

In 1943 the City of New York acquired the Mecca Temple on 55th Street, which had served as a concert hall, thus making possible the formation of the New York City Center, devoted to drama, opera, and the dance. Here many promising talents have been developed during the semi-annual seasons, some to move downtown to the larger house, some to go abroad and establish enviable reputations. There have been guest performances by such artists as Maggie Teyte, Rose Bampton, and Dusolina Giannini; the conductors and general managers have included László Halász, Joseph Rosenstock, Erich Leinsdorf, Tullio Serafin, and Julius Rudel. In recent seasons, with the help of a Ford Foundation grant, the company has presented a spring program of American opera, offering such works as Douglas Moore's *Ballad of Baby Doe*, Carlisle Floyd's *Susannah* and *Wuthering Heights*, Vittorio Giannini's *Taming of the Shrew*, Menotti's *Maria Golovin*, Robert Ward's *He Who Gets Slapped*, Blitzstein's *Regina*, Dello Joio's *Triumph of Saint Joan*, and Hugo Weisgall's *Six Characters in Search of an Author*.

With companies blossoming in many cities, notably Chicago (where at the Lyric Theater such notables as Maria Callas, Giulietta Simionato, Gré Brouwenstijn, and Christa Ludwig have made their débuts), Dallas, Washington, and Santa Fé; with opera long established as a part of the program at the Berkshire Festival, the Empire State Music Festival, and New York City's Stadium Concerts; with small "off-Broadway" companies like the Amato Opera running continuously in New York, and with opera workshops in many of our universities and conservatories, unprecedented opportunities are offered today for the native singer, without the necessity of going abroad to gain experience. And the outlook for the ambitious composer is ever brighter.

At the same time there is renewed interest in older and often forgotten operas, despite the prophecies of Mr. Finck three-quarters of a century ago. And with this interest goes a serious endeavor to recapture something of the proper performance styles. This could hardly fail to have a beneficial effect upon the singing of our time. Sometimes operas are mounted without scenery and with a minimum of acting by such organizations as The Little Orchestra Society, led by Thomas Scherman, and The American Opera Society. In this way New York has heard, among others, Bellini's *Puritani* and *Il Pirata*, Donizetti's *Anna Bolena* and *Il Duca d'Alba*, Gluck's *Paride ed Elena* and *Iphigénie en Tauride*, Berlioz's *Les Troyens* and

Béatrice et Bénédict, and Hugo Wolf's *Der Corregidor.* The enthusiasm of the audiences is enough to prove that these operas are not dead yet. As they become increasingly familiar (along with many others of their schools, thanks to the recording companies), a more sophisticated audience is developing. Perhaps the time is ripe for a revival of Mercadante's *Il Giuramento.*

Church Music:
A Century of Contrasts

By ROBERT STEVENSON

The gallery of sacred works bequeathed us by the last hundred years houses in an upper alcove a respectable number of choice canvases from eminent men, on the main floor a sprawling maze of well-intentioned *Gebrauchsmusik,* and in the bargain basement a terrifying jungle of poster art with no other intent than to stimulate quick "decisions." In music, as in other phases of American church life, the keyword has been diversity. With good reason the most influential book on religion by a 19th-century American author boasts a title beginning with the word *Varieties.*[1] When summarizing religious history in the United States from 1800-1914, our best church historian writes: "for richness of variety the Christianity of no other region or age" equals it.[2]

Already by mid-century the denominations had so drawn their social lines that some ministered to the wealthy and the élite in big cities, while others served the common folk on farms and frontiers.

[1] William James's *The Varieties of Religious Experience* (1902) incorporates his Gifford lectures at Edinburgh (1899-1901).

[2] K. S. Latourette, *A History of the Expansion of Christianity,* New York, 1941, IV, 177.

Speaking of one "élite" domination in a course of historical lectures given at Berlin in 1854, Philip Schaff claimed that the Protestant Episcopal Church had addressed itself "heretofore almost exclusively to the higher classes of society, and had rather discouraged the poor man from joining it."[3] With such a constituency, the music published for use in Episcopalian churches in the year that the Confederacy was established sounded quite a different tone from that prevailing in publications for frontier churches, or even for middle-class urban churches.

For instance: Henry Wilson, "organist of Christ Church, Hartford, Connecticut," published in 1861 a second edition of his *Christ Church Collection of Sacred Music.*[4] On the title page, he swathes his choices in purple by claiming that he has cut the cloth for 40 of his 65 psalms, hymns, and canticles from composers so distinguished as "Mendelssohn, Mozart, Rossini, Schumann, and others." His "others" include Handel, Haydn, Weber, Marschner, Thalberg, Herz, and Hérold—but no Americans except himself. Because he withholds the names of the specific originals of his contrafactures, the identification of the sources pleasantly tests our present-day acquaintance with these composers' works. Mendelssohn's *Lieder ohne Worte,* Op. 38, No. 3, Op. 53, No. 2, Op. 19, No. 1, Op. 30, No. 3, and *If with all your hearts* from *Elijah* (to other words) prove to be the easily identified originals for Wilson's Psalm 72, Hymns 177, 51, 167, and 18; Mozart's *O Isis und Osiris* as the source for his Psalm 87; Handel's *I know that my Redeemer liveth* as the music for his Psalm 18; and Weber's *But now there falls a milder light* (Huon's aria) as the original for his Hymn 172. Even when he condescends to so commonplace a text as Toplady's *Rock of Ages* (Hymn 139), he elevates it by wedding it to Schumann's *Widmung.* Apart from a dozen suavely Mendelssohnian items by himself, he makes room for a *Benedic anima mea* of his fellow Hartford organist—Henry Greatorex—whose name is still kept alive in every hymnbook today with a *Gloria Patri,* but who was American only by adoption.

[3] Philip Schaff, *America,* New York, 1855, p. 164.

[4] Published by S. T. Gordon (538 Broadway), this 68-page collection of "sacred quartetts" typifies its time in its format. After the Civil War, such an oblong format was no longer used for choral music.

"Elevated" as were Wilson's musical intentions, a higher level yet was sought in the 203-page *Cathedral Chants including the Gregorian Tones. Adapted to the Canticles, and Occasional Services of the Protestant Episcopal Church ... by S. Parkman Tuckerman, Mus. Doc.*, published at Boston by Oliver Ditson in 1858. Dr. Tuckerman, successively organist in New York City of Trinity Chapel (1855) and St. Paul's Church (1863), must surely be the first editor of an American collection to have added Mus. Doc. after the names of everyone from William Crotch to Edward Hodges[5] who gains admittance to his select book. He proves also to be the morning star of that large group of American church composers whose lights have shone only in prize contests, by including at pages 191-203 his own *Te Deum,* "written in competition for a prize of One Hundred dollars offered by the last General Convention of the Protestant Episcopal Church." Further to forestall the future, when nothing is so important as length, he prefaces his *Te Deum* at page 191 with the coy promise that "the time of performance should not exceed seven minutes."

Wilson and Tuckerman appealed around 1860 to a metropolitan seaboard sector of the American public; and—if Philip Schaff was right[6]—offended the masses by their "exclusiveness and pedantry." The middle group in the more established parts of the country looked instead to publications by such successful entrepreneurs of culture as Lowell Mason and William Bradbury for their new hymns and anthems. When Mason in 1846 published his fifth[7] large miscellany of church music—the 350-page *Carmina Sacra*—he justified his continuing stream of church music publications by the motto *Excelsior.* "Every well organized choir, if kept up with interest, must have a constant succession of new music; without this there will be no advancement," he claimed in his preface. Because no copyright laws prevented him from carrying as much

[5] Edward Hodges (1796-1867), born in Bristol, England, and holder of a Cambridge D. Mus. (1825), arrived in New York from Toronto in 1839.

[6] Schaff, p. 115.

[7] In the preface to his *Carmina Sacra,* Mason lists his earlier miscellanies as 1) Handel and Haydn Society Collection, 1822; 2) Choir, or Unison Collection, 1832; 3) Boston Academy's Collection, 1835; 4) Modern Psalmist, 1839. Only in the last of these did he imitate German practice by printing the four parts on two staves (now the universal custom in all hymnbooks).

European grist as he pleased, he was able to keep his mills active continuously. He not only borrowed and adapted any music for which he saw a chance of success, but also the lengthy pedagogical introductions that were a prime buying attraction of such works as *Carmina Sacra*—teaching how to sing, defining 276 musical terms, and explaining the principles of chant.[8] To disarm the critics who stood ever ready to accuse him of plagiarism, he freely admitted his sources in footnotes. He claimed the Gregorian Tone I formula as the inspiration for his *Hamburg* written in 1824 while he was serving the First Presbyterian Church in Savannah, Georgia—a tune now widely used with Isaac Watts's *When I survey the wondrous cross*. At the opposite extreme from plainsong he found in the popular ballad *Oft in the Stilly Night* the source from which he adapted his tune *Bethany*, published in the Andover *Sabbath Hymn and Tune Book* of 1859 with Sarah Flower Adams's lyrics, *Nearer, my God, to Thee*.[9]

His *Carmina Sacra*, after going through thirteen editions in the 1840s and '50s, sold half a million copies.[10] Such commercial success—unprecedented in America—shaped American hymnody so decisively for a century to come that even today the largest single Protestant denomination in the United States incorporates more hymns "by" Lowell Mason than from any other source.[11] He was so well able to gauge middle-of-the-road American musical taste that many of his hymn tunes were on the lips of the common folk within five years of their first publication. *Nearer, my God, to Thee*, for instance, was considered within two years of publication to be one of the thirty most popular hymn tunes[12] by the American

[8] Although he acknowledges the Pestalozzian G.-F. Kübler as the German authority from whose *Anleitung zum Gesangunterrichte in Schulen* (Stuttgart, 1826) he adapted his *Manual of Instruction of the Boston Academy of Music*, he curiously reverts to atomistic teaching method in his *Carmina Sacra* introduction.

[9] Robert G. McCutchan, *Our Hymnody*, New York, 1937, p. 381.

[10] Leonard Ellinwood, *The Hymnal 1940 Companion*, New York, 1949, p. 499.

[11] *The Methodist Hymnal* (1935) contains 28 tunes by John Bacchus Dykes, but 32 by Lowell Mason. In descending order, the next most popular tune composers in this hymnal are Joseph Barnby, Arthur S. Sullivan, William Bradbury, and the American gospel-song composer, W. H. Doane (1832-1915).

[12] *Bethany* (No. 26 in this collection), *Coronation, Happy Day, Maitland, Missionary Hymn, Toplady*, and *Webb* are still sung in every Protestant church. All were American-composed except *Happy Day* (adapted from E. F. Rimbault).

[83]

Tract Society music committee that sponsored publication of the first Civil War hymnal for soldiers and sailors.[13]

Following long-established American precedent[14] Mason's books were usually published in oblong format, two hymns to a page with the four voice parts on separate staves and the bass part heavily figured throughout. He justified his always hearty emphasis on "new" music by repeating this rhetorical question in every preface: "How many poets would have written since Milton if none had been encouraged but those who were as good as himself?" The two other hymn tune composers who made a triumvirate with Mason during the decade of the Civil War were Thomas Hastings (1784-1872), Lepidus of the three with over a thousand hymn tunes[15] and fifty volumes of music to his credit, and William B. Bradbury (1816-1868), Antony of the three with sixty songbooks.[16]

Hastings—whose name is still kept alive with three tunes, *Ortonville*, *Toplady*, and *Zion* (*Majestic sweetness sits enthroned*, *Rock of ages*, and *Guide me, O Thou great Jehovah*)—never enjoyed the advantages of European travel and study, as did both Mason and Bradbury; but even he liberally sprinkles such books as *The Manhattan Collection of Psalm and Hymn Tunes ... of the New York Academy of Sacred Music* with what he considers to be the best European music: for example, adapting the Larghetto of Beethoven's Second Symphony to *Lord, how secure and blest are they*, *Nun freut euch* (1535) to *He reigns, the Lord, the Saviour reigns*, and *Winchester Old* (1598) to *Long as I live*.[17] In his first hundred pages of this typical collection he prints hymns "with music from" Arne (96, 114), Handel (137), Haydn (52, 115), Thomas Morley, "Bachelor of Music in the reign of Queen Eliza-

[13] *Hymns, Religious and Patriotic, for the Soldier and the Sailor*, Boston, 1861, begins thus: "You are in arms to avenge an insulted flag, to crush a most atrocious rebellion, and to reëstablish the supremacy of the Constitution throughout the length and breadth of the land. A more sacred cause never sounded its call to battle. Those who answer to this call can not be too careful to maintain a tone of moral sentiment in keeping with the dignity of their errand."

[14] See Allen P. Britton, *Theoretical Introductions to American Tune-Books*, Ann Arbor: University Microfilms, 1949, p. 127, on the roots of the oblong tradition.

[15] *The Hymnal 1940 Companion*, p. 455.

[16] McCutchan, p. 168.

[17] *The Manhattan Collection*, pp. 68, 34, 112.

beth" (114), Mozart (130), Purcell (117),[18] and Sacchini (78). Strict Presbyterian though he was, he set a precedent by being one of the first Americans to draw freely on contemporary Roman Catholic collections. Even the Webbe *Tantum ergo* tune now sung in every American Catholic parish is in *The Manhattan Collection* (242), with new words beginning "May the grace of Christ." *Brazil* (140) "arranged from the Portuguese Cathedral Service" is another such borrowing.

Like Mason, both Hastings and Bradbury prefaced most of their oblong books with a "rudiments of music" section.[19] Hastings and Mason surprise us also by insisting so frequently on figuring their basses, until the very eve of the Civil War. In the usual collection of these triumvirs, the leading melody is printed not on the top staff of the four for SATB, but rather on the third staff down. Bradbury—somewhat more sentimental than Mason or Hastings— leaves us *Woodworth* (1849), now known to millions as the tune for *Just as I am, Saviour like a shepherd lead us* (1859), *Sweet hour of prayer* (1860), and *He leadeth me* (1864), as his tokens of immortality. A Baptist, Bradbury is represented by 36 tunes in *The Baptist Praise Book* of 1871, a collection "richer in the precious gems of hymnology than any other volume extant."[20] *The Hymnal, 1940* (Episcopal) still retains his tunes for *Just as I am* and *He leadeth me,* and even *The Lutheran Hymnal* (1941) holds fast to his *Just as I am.* No doubt Bradbury would have preferred to be remembered also by such a cantata as *Esther, the Beautiful Queen*[21] and by his anthem *And it shall come to pass in the last days* ("sung at the closing services of the Broadway Tabernacle Church on April 26, 1857"); but at least his maudlin *The Blind Orphan Girl*—a solo to melodeon accompaniment overlain with many a *rallentando con espressione,* harmonized with barbershop chords, and conclud-

[18] *Burford* is a dubious ascription; see *The Hymnal 1940 Companion,* p. 259.

[19] Britton's dissertation is the classic study of such rudiments of music sections in pre-1800 American tune books. Only with the advent of gospel hymnody, frankly designed for rote learning, did the rudiments sections fall out of favor.

[20] For the best study of "old" Baptist music, see G. P. Jackson, *The Story of the Sacred Harp (1844-1944),* Nashville, 1944, pp. 7-16. *The Baptist Praise Book,* New York, 1871, was much too citified to be pristinely Baptist, according to such scholars as Jackson.

[21] See W. B. Bradbury, *The Jubilee,* New York, 1858, p. 333.

ing with an operatic flourish on "I'm blind, O! . . . I'm blind"—no longer rises to reproach his musical taste.

Apart from their tunes, Hastings, Mason, Bradbury, and their confreres occupy a central niche in American hymnody because they standardized the Protestant hymn in the form now universally accepted by all standard-brand denominations. Because they chose to lodge within the camp first pitched by Hans Gram in *The Massachusetts Compiler* of 1795, they assured Gram's cause eventual victory. A German immigrant, Gram had demanded an end to the homespun type of worship music perpetrated by such uninformed persons as William Billings, David Belknap, Asahel Benham, Daniel Read, and Timothy Swan[22]—if for no other reason than that "good, musical emigrants are daily seeking asylum in this country." As if to symbolize the overthrow of America's homely past, he was the first to propose replacing the name crotchet with quarter-note, and of quaver with eighth-note. Under the influence of Gram and others like him, native music and native practices were already so on the wane by 1807 that Elias Mann could inveigh safely in *The Massachusetts Collection* against "those wild fugues, and rapid and confused movements, which have so long been the disgrace of congregational psalmody." When New England became too refined to sing any longer the native American repertory, other less urbanized sections of the country fell heirs to it, and built upon it. Particularly in those sections that clung to the shape notes originated by William Little and William Smith (*Easy Instructor*, 1802) did the native repertory linger on.[23]

George Pullen Jackson—the Vanderbilt University philologist and folklorist who has most intensively studied the rural hymnody pushed out of New England, eventually to find its last home in the upland South[24]—sees between 1860 and 1870 an especially sig-

[22] Cf. Britton's *Bibliography of Early Religious American Music, 18th Century* (supplement to his Ph. D. dissertation, University of Michigan, 1949), for the publications of these nativists; data on Gram at pp. 238-39 of the dissertation.

[23] *Ibid.*, p. 334.

[24] See *White Spirituals in the Southern Uplands*, Chapel Hill, 1933, pp. 15-24, for the spread of the shape-note tradition. All of Jackson's later books—*Spiritual Folk-Songs of Early America*, New York, 1937; *White and Negro Spirituals* (1943); *Another Sheaf of White Spirituals*, Gainesville, Fla., 1952; and *Down-East Spirituals*, Locust Valley, N. Y., 1953—are devoted to a study of this repertory, and its offshoots.

nificant shrinkage of the area where the fasola folk held their singing conventions, preserved their fuguing tunes, cherished their folkishly modal hymns, and reveled in open and consecutive fifths. After the Civil War, the *Sacred Harp* territory shrank from the mountainous parts of every state along the Eastern seaboard to a smaller area bounded by Kentucky on the north and dipping into lower Alabama at its southernmost.[25] The kind of hymn sung by rural upland folk throughout the South contravened every principle of the tidy "good music" that Mason and his genteel devotees were trying to inculcate. The tunebooks of the fasola folk might well enough be printed in the North—William Walker's *The Southern Harmony* (1835) in New Haven, B. F. White and E. J. King's *The Sacred Harp* (1844) at Philadelphia, William Hauser's *The Hesperian Harp* (1848) and *The Olive Leaf* (with Benjamin Turner, 1878) at Philadelphia, and Joseph Hillman's *The Revivalist* (1868) at Albany. But this was so merely because the South lacked music presses.[26]

The freedom of the Kentucky and Tennessee camp meeting spiritual songs exceeded that of all other rural types. The manner of singing not only the camp songs but also the rest of the rural repertory offended city musicians' ears, always—because of the nasalism, the rhythmic vagaries, the "uncertainty" of the pitch, and the attendant disdain for such civilized helps as the organ.[27] The so-called "gospel song" movement associated in the North with such names as Ira D. Sankey (1840-1908), P. P. Bliss (1838-1876), W. H. Doane (1832-1915), and Philip Phillips (1834-1895) differs from the "sacred harp" tradition on all these crucial issues. Sankey always played the organ to accompany his singing; pitch in even the most banal gospel songs is a fixed ideal. When Beverly

[25] *Another Sheaf of White Spirituals,* pp. xii-xiii.

[26] Charles Seeger in *Contrapuntal Style in Three-Voice Shape-Note Hymns,* in *The Musical Quarterly,* XXVI (1940), illustrates printing at Pumpkintown and Knoxville, Tenn. (1838, 1849) in his plates opposite pp. 485 and 489. But Richard B. Harwell in *Confederate Music,* Chapel Hill, 1950, shows in his bibliography at pp. 159-60 that the South could not print her own music, even when there was most incentive to do so.

[27] Jackson, *Some hearers don't like it. Why?,* in *The Story of the Sacred Harp,* pp. 28-36.

Shea,[28] Ira D. Sankey's present-day successor, sings *How great Thou art,* he affects none of the mannerisms of country singing, but instead adopts the manner of a sentimental light opera star. Furthermore: in "gospel" singing whether in tent or tabernacle, minor mode hymns are never sung, women have the congregational lead, chromatically altered chords often sentimentalize the harmony, the third of a chord is never omitted, and wearisome successions of thirds and sixths are the rule. It is these treacly mannerisms that turn forthright critics such as Charles Seeger against the "thoroughly messed-up and often depraved banality of Protestant Church music."[29]

If the "sacred harp" repertory still waits outside the doors of "respectable" denominations, the Negro counterpart of the rural repertory does begin to find a welcome. So staid a denomination as the Congregational Church now uses a 1958 edition of *The Pilgrim Hymnal,* edited musically by Hugh Porter, late head of the Union Theological Seminary School of Sacred Music in New York, that includes seven Negro spirituals (against nine tunes by Mason, five by Bradbury, and eleven by the indomitable John Bacchus Dykes [1823-1876, Church of England priest]). *Were you there, Lord, I want to be a Christian,* and *Go tell it* are the pentatonic melodies among the seven spirituals in this hymnal. Many Negro spirituals, if such investigators as George Pullen Jackson are right, were variants made by Negroes from songs taught them by the missionaries of Baptist and Methodist persuasion who converted them. In his *White and Negro Spirituals: Their Life Span and Kinship* (1943), Jackson backs up this thesis with 114 melodies culled from "white" sources: pitting these against what he believes to be their

[28] Marvin L. McKissick, *A Study of the Function of Music in the Major Religious Revivals in America since 1875,* Univ. of Southern California Ph. D. dissertation, 1957, studies the repertory and methods of both Billy Graham's soloist, Shea, and his group leader, Cliff Barrows. *I'd rather have Jesus,* with words by Rhea F. Miller and music by Shea, seems to be his most popular composition (p. 139). The music used at the Los Angeles kickoff meetings (1949) is studied at p. 120; and of the Boston campaign at p. 125. *Blessed assurance* is probably the all-time favorite in Graham revivals (p. 133), but *What a friend, Revive us again,* and *Near the Cross* have proved close runners-up (p. 125). The Graham meetings differ from the Moody and Sunday revivals in failing to inspire very much "new" music. Shea's clinching solo, with "He's got the whole, wide world" for a refrain, is adapted to an old tune.

[29] Foreword to Jackson, *Another Sheaf of White Spirituals,* p. viii.

Negro derivatives. He finds "white originals" in rural songbooks for even such widely known spirituals as *Go down, Moses, Go tell it on the mountain, Old-time Religion, Swing low, sweet chariot,* and *Were you there.* (Interestingly enough, just at the moment when Negro spirituals—with texts and harmony "scrubbed up"—begin to enter denominational hymnals, the Negro churches are themselves singing them less and less, and Negro soloists are allowing them to rust as reminders of a past that is better forgotten.)

Whatever their affinities with identifiable originals in rural songsters, Negro spirituals have now gained not only the cachet of hymnbook respectability, but also the salute of art composers so dignified as Daniel Gregory Mason, who based his String Quartet in G minor, Op. 19 (G. Schirmer for S.P.A.M., 1930) on such spirituals as *Deep River,* and Leo Sowerby, who dedicated a prelude on *Were you there* to Vernon de Tar (H. W. Gray, 1956). By contrast, the "sacred harp" kind of hymnody has awaited quotation by less academic composers. Charles Ives rises to a climax in his great solo song, *General Booth Enters Into Heaven* (composed 1914, published 1915, on a text by Vachel Lindsay), with a straightforward quotation of the pentatonic *Cleansing Fountain* cited as a "Western Melody" in Asa Hull's *Pilgrim's Harp.* Ives ends his Violin and Piano Sonata No. 4 (*Children's Day at the Camp Meeting*) with the same *Shall we gather at the river* of Robert Lowry that Virgil Thomson varies for the last of his set, *Variations on Sunday-School Tunes* (composed at Paris 1926-27, published 1954). Ives's whole repertory is indeed so shot through with quotations of old American hymns that a dissertation on his borrowings remains for the writing. Those most likely to discuss his use of *Watchman* (1830) in his First Sonata for Violin and Piano (composed 1903-08), of *Diligence* (1864) in his Fourth Sonata, and of *Nettleton* (John Wyeth's *Repository of Sacred Music,* 1813) in his Second Sonata can praise Ives for having countered the trend of history. Previously, sacred composers had borrowed *Adieu mes amours, Mille regretz, Mein Gmüth ist verwirren,* and *Desilde al caballero* from the secular repertory. Now, Ives permits sacred tunes to interlope in secular environments. So does Thomson, whose masterly *Symphony on a Hymn Tune* (Southern Music Publishing Company, 1954) exploits *Foundation,* an early American tune traced to Jesse Mercer's *The*

Cluster of Spiritual Songs, 1817 (third edition).[30] From the collection of Mercer, a Georgia Baptist preacher, this pentatonic melody passed first to *Sacred Harp* (1844), and thence to the *Hymn and Tune Book of the Methodist Episcopal Church, South,* 1889.

In summary: the history of American hymnody in the last hundred years keeps pace with the denominations themselves. The activist, mission-minded denominations, from Mormons[31] to Methodists, have sponsored official hymnals with a hard core of dignified hymns surrounded by the juicy fruit of *Blessed Assurance* (a long-time favorite in Billy Graham campaigns[32]), *I need Thee every hour* (one of Mrs. Mary Baker Eddy's three favorite hymns, which must never be omitted from Christian Science hymnals[33]), and other like-minded "Songs of Salvation." Side by side with the official denominational hymnal, the same activist denominations have allowed a dense orchard of Sunday School and "auxiliary" hymnbooks to grow up, fruited with hymn tunes by such gospel composers as B. D. Ackley, E. O. Excell, W. G. Fischer, Charles H. Gabriel, Phoebe Palmer Knapp, B. B. McKinney,[34] G. C. Stebbins, John R. Sweney, and Will L. Thompson. The composers of the popular tunes in the Sunday School type of books have usually

[30] McCutchan, p. 342. However, Thomson himself seems to consider this tune Scottish in origin. See his program notes for the San Francisco Symphony concert he conducted on Feb. 12, 1958, p. 365.

[31] William L. Wilkes studies intensively the musical complexions of successive Mormon hymnals (1889, 1908, 1927, 1948, 1950) in his *Borrowed Music in Mormon Hymnals,* USC Ph. D. dissertation, 1957. The famous Mormon hymn, *O ye mountains high,* is adapted to a mid-century Scottish air (*O Minnie, O Minnie, come o'er the lea*), later known as *Lily Dale. The Songs of Zion* (1908), with 260 tunes, shows more "gospel tune" influence than any other Mormon hymnal. The Latter-Day Saints have gladly used such tunes as that of *In the gloaming,* but have so strenuously objected to *In dulci jubilo* that it had to be taken out of the 1948 hymnal when revised (1950); see Wilkes, p. 59. The 1889 Mormon hymnal emphasized music for the choir, and reached a "high-water mark of self-consciousness in Latter-day Saint hymnody" by including many more tunes of Mormon origin than any other edition. The 1948-50 hymnal still retains tunes by John Tullidge (1806-74), George Careless, Ebenezer Beesley, and other early Mormon worthies; Alexander Schreiner, LeRoy Robertson, and Crawford Gates represent the present generation.

[32] Words by Fanny Crosby, music by Mrs. J. J. Knapp. See note 28.

[33] *Christian Science Hymnal* (1910), preface, p. iii.

[34] McKinney's *Send a great revival in my soul* was the theme song of the 1949 Graham campaign in Los Angeles (rocketing him to national fame). Cf. McKissick, p. 120.

been as innocent of any academic training as Dan Emmett. Bricklayer, shoe salesman, or plumber, these composers have found formal musical instruction no more useful than Moody and Sunday found Hebrew and Greek.

Within the last fifty years, their same class of hymn tune has entered numerous Roman Catholic hymnals designed for American use. One of the most successful of these, *Crown Hymnal,* includes 169 English hymns with tunes that range in quality from T. Haweis's *Chesterfield* (123) and an adaptation of Mozart's first-movement theme in the *Turkish March* Sonata (34) to a *Softly and tenderly* tune (11) and an equally insipid *In the garden* melody (113) that vie with the popular Protestant *Old rugged Cross*[35] for sentimental effusiveness. The musical give-and-take in such a hymnal with imprimatur as this[36] is interestingly paralleled by the hymn texts. Charles Wesley, co-founder of Methodism, is in this book at No. 36, for instance—but without credit line.

At the same time that Roman Catholic hymnals in this country were succumbing to the musical idiom of the weaker Protestant Sunday School songs, the vogue of the *Brighten the corner where you are, By and By, There is glory in my soul,* and *O that will be glory for me* type of song[37] was sweeping to distant and alien shores. From Cairo to Honolulu, and from São Paulo to Madras, American evangelical missionaries have so thoroughly imbued converts with this kind of song that "gospel" music now dominates nearly every foreign language hymnal. The proof of how quickly this kind of music has won friends in alien fields can be found in even such a book as *Standard Buddhist Gathas and Services* (published at Kyoto in 1939), the English-language section of which (items 501-557) is filled with "a body of good, worthy hymns and services" that would do credit to a Homer E. Rodeheaver[38] collection.

[35] In a poll taken by Army chaplains in 1945, this hymn with the Rev. George Bennard listed as composer was rated the most popular in the Army-Navy Hymnal (among Protestants).

[36] Published in 1912 by Ginn, this book was typical of the many designed to implement the 1903 *Motu proprio* at the parish level. See *Crown Hymnal,* p. iii. The Rev. L. J. Kavanagh and James M. McLaughlin edited it.

[37] Charles Gabriel composed all these; they gained popularity during the Billy Sunday revivals.

[38] John T. Howard prints Rodeheaver's apologia for his type of music in *Our*

Even in Europe, gospel hymnody has not lacked its advocates. After the mammoth Moody-Sankey campaign of 1875, Lord Shaftesbury claimed that had the American evangelists done "nothing more than teach the people to sing such hymns as 'Hold the Fort, For I Am Coming' [P. P. Bliss] they would have conferred an inestimable blessing on Great Britain."[39] Cliff Barrow and Beverly Shea did not find that American gospel songs had lost any of their mass appeal when Graham conducted his London campaign in 1954. But Eric Routley in *The Music of Christian Hymnody: A Study of the development of the hymn tune* (1957) has qualms as to the "inestimable blessing" bestowed by this class of American tune. "At best this music is honestly flamboyant and redolent of the buoyancy of the civilisation that created New York and Pittsburgh and Chicago; at its worst it is flabby and futile," is his opinion.[40] Horatio W. Parker (1863-1919)[41] and Winfred Douglas (1867-1944) did something to rescue America from "the slough of sentimental music-hall sloppiness and camp-fire heartiness" into which it fell after the Civil War. But "American taste has proved itself hard to rescue," he concludes. Even so adept a master of the popular idiom as Stephen Collins Foster could not write anything with religious words that equalled his *Camptown Races, My Old Kentucky Home,* and *Old Folks at Home.* Foster's twenty Sunday School songs, divided between Horace Waters's *Golden Harp* and *Athenaeum Collection* (1863), never approach anywhere the vitality of *Old Black Joe* (1860) or *Beautiful Dreamer* (1864). For his hymn *The pure, the bright, the beautiful* he chose two stanzas by so eminent an author as Charles Dickens (*The Athenaeum Collection,* pp. 212-13). However, he failed to rise above the Sankey-Bliss level

---

American Music, New York, 1946, pp. 611-12. For further defense, see my *Patterns of Protestant Church Music,* Durham, N.C., 1953, pp. 151-62, and *Evangelistic Song,* in *Religion in Life,* XXVI (1957), 436-43.

[39] *Patterns of Protestant Church Music,* pp. 152-53.

[40] Routley, *The Music of Christian Hymnody,* London, 1957, p. 166. He considers *John Brown's Body* our best 19th-century hymn tune. For his further remarks on gospel music, see his précis *On the Billy Graham Song Book,* in *The Hymn,* VI (1955), 26, 36.

[41] *Mount Zion* by Parker "is probably one of the best hymn tunes of its age" (*The Music of Christian Hymnody,* p. 166).

whether setting Dickens's poetry or his own.

*　　*
*

Since hymn tunes are preeminently the food of the common man, their importance in church history exceeds that of all other musical types in a nation so democratic as America. But during the last half of the 19th century, city churches began nearly everywhere to depend also on ensembles of paid soloists for their more pretentious Sunday fare. The mixed quartet in a side gallery or above the pulpit became the norm in such churches, even in the newly settled West. As early as in 1856, when the *San Francisco Bulletin* published a series of articles on local church music, the reporter thought it odd that "The First Presbyterian Church has a choir of ten instead of the fashionable quartet so much in vogue in other churches."[42] In Episcopalian churches throughout the West — whether at Virginia City in boom days or in Los Angeles at the predecessor of the present cathedral[43]—the taste in the 1870s and 1880s was just as much for the quartet as in the East, where Dudley Buck (1839-1909) reigned as king of church music.[44]

In silk stocking parishes—such as Incarnation in New York, where a paid quartet was installed as early as 1855—the repertory during the two decades after the Civil War reached out to include not only Mendelssohn's *Hymn of Praise* and excerpts from *Creation, Elijah,* and the inevitable *Messiah,* but also Rossini's *Stabat Mater* and the Cherubini Requiem in English. To the orthodoxly Calvinistic, such fare did not qualify as "church" music. A. J. Rowland, a doctor of divinity, spoke for his own denomination in the *Baptist Quarterly Review,* V/20 (Autumn 1883, p. 414) when he decried even "anthems and voluntaries" as "no adequate part of worship." The Puritan conscience spoke through him when he continued: "God is not to be praised by proxy ... The only office that a choir can serve is to lead the congregation in the singing."

Viewed from this dogmatic position, much of the religious music

---

[42] Cornel Lengyel, *Music of the Gold Rush Era,* San Francisco, 1939, p. 59.

[43] Howard Swan, *Music in the Southwest,* San Marino, Calif., 1952, pp. 65-66, 117.

[44] Ellinwood, *The History of American Church Music,* New York, 1953, pp. 114-15.

[93]

to be discussed in the rest of the present essay cannot be called church music at all. It is merely concert music set to religious texts. However, in defense of discussing the cantatas, oratorios, and Masses of Horatio Parker, Randall Thompson, and Roger Sessions is the patent fact that even works so ambitious as Haydn's *Lord Nelson Mass,* Beethoven's Mass in C, Mozart's, Verdi's, and Fauré's Requiems are now sung in whole or in part as acts of worship in churches so protestant as the First Presbyterian of Princeton, Highland Park Methodist of Dallas, and First Congregational of Los Angeles. Just how worshipful are these acts of worship is, of course, a question to be endlessly discussed. The Wycliffes have the best reason on their side when the music is meretricious, poorly performed, and adapted.

Describing the music in the leading Episcopalian church, a writer for the Los Angeles Express wrote in the issue of March 22, 1875, that the "air of the prayer in the opera of *Zampa*" provided a "delicious conclusion to very interesting services." The two female soloists were Miss Florida Nichols with a soprano voice "which would attract attention in any choir" and Miss Belle Mallard whose "notes are fresh as a bird's." For such singers as these, Dudley Buck composed scores of highly successful anthems, many of which still "deservedly remain upon our choir programs," according to Peter Lutkin, who praises him above every composer of his generation. Even though "most of his music was intended for the quartette choir, it was a marked advance on anything which had preceded it."[45] Lutkin attributes Buck's weaker moments to his "too frequent cadences giving something of a patchwork effect," and his "oversentimental" approach to the historic texts of the Bible and the liturgy. Buck—born in the same year as his fellow New Englander John Knowles Paine, educated in Germany as was Paine, honored by Theodore Thomas with exposition commissions at Philadelphia in 1876 and again at Chicago in 1893 (as was Paine, also)—"stood more nearly for a distinctive style of American Church music than any other composer." In Lutkin's opinion, Buck's approach to an American style sufficiently condones his faults.

Buck turned his hand to any text, Latin or English, with the

[45] Peter C. Lutkin, *Music in the Church,* Milwaukee, 1910, p. 253.

same easy facility and tuneful zest. His *Ave Maria* and *Requiem
aeternam*—quartet choruses in *The Legend of Don Munio* (a
cantata published by Oliver Ditson in 1874 as Buck's Op. 62) —
bow just as low to *Vierhebigkeit* and round off the musical cliché
just as smoothly as does the choral finale from the same cantata in
praise of the Protestant Jehovah, *In thankful hymns ascending*.

Besides Buck, several other New England composers wrote
cantatas and oratorios that were printed by Oliver Ditson in the
1870s. Eugene Thayer, born at Mendon, Massachusetts, in 1838, and
one of the first native-born Americans to gain a Mus. Doc. degree
at Oxford University, returned to Boston to take up an organist's
career;[46] in 1872 Ditson brought out Thayer's *Festival Cantata*. Two
years later, the same firm followed with John Knowles Paine's
oratorio, *St. Peter* (given its première at Portland, Maine, on June
3, 1873). This was Paine's first large work performed in this
country. A smaller choral work, his sacred ode for four men's
voices and orchestra, *Domine salvum fac,* had been sung at the
inauguration of Thomas Hill as president of Harvard University
on March 4, 1863; it was repeated for the inauguration of Charles
Eliot, October 19, 1869. Abroad, he had garnered praise in the
German press with a Mass in D, which he directed at Berlin in 1867.

Oliver Ditson's other large sacred publications continued with
Dudley Buck's *46th Psalm* in 1877, and the *Redemption Hymn* and
The Blind King by James Cutler Dunn Parker (1828-1916; no
relation to Horatio W.), issued in 1877 and 1883. J. C. D. Parker,
for twenty-seven years organist of Trinity Church, Boston, wrote
also a *St. John* oratorio. *The Life of Man,* his last oratorio (first
performed in Boston by the Handel and Haydn Society in 1895),
had a powerful Resurrection scene, in the opinion of Louis Elson,
and showed "masterly canonic writing in the portrayal of the seven
churches of Asia." So evanescent are such triumphs, however, that
few students of American music would today recognize a *Doppel-
meister* problem.

A Parker so much more eminent rose in the 1890s as to over-
shadow not only his Harvard-trained namesake but all American
sacred composers of his century. *Hora Novissima,* Horatio Parker's

[46] Louis C. Elson, *The History of American Music,* New York, 1915, p. 265. He
was Chadwick's teacher.

first large choral work (Op. 30), breathed the spirit of the times when he chose Latin for his language. Even Mrs. H. H. A. Beach was in February of 1892 making her Boston début as a composer with a Mass in E-flat, Op. 5, performed by the Handel and Haydn Society under Carl Zerrahn. Two months later Parker finished scoring *Hora Novissima,* which he had started to compose in the spring of the previous year.[47] His daughter alludes to his many personal griefs in the year that he wrote this stirring oratorio to thirty-five six-line stanzas from *De contemptu mundi.*[48] The poem had been a favorite of his father, Charles Edward Parker, who died in the year Horatio was working at *Hora Novissima.* So also did Mary, Horatio's younger sister, and his only son. From these griefs he turned to the oratorio that more than any other work has kept his name alive.[49] First performed by the Church Choral Society of New York under Richard Henry Warren on May 2, 1893, it made an ever more profound impression at the Handel and Haydn Society première in 1894 and the Cincinnati Festival performance under Theodore Thomas in the same year. Before its première at the Three Choirs Festival in Worcester (1899) it had already been acclaimed in the English press as a work worthy of comparison with the best that Europe was producing.[50]

In a clearer sense than any of his later oratorios—*The Legend of St. Christopher,* Op. 43 (New York Oratorio Society, April 15, 1898), *A Wanderer's Psalm,* Op. 50 (Hereford, Three Choirs Festival, September 13, 1900), or *Morven and the Grail,* Op. 79 (Boston, Handel and Haydn Society, April 13, 1915) — *Hora Novissima* qualifies as church music: because it was heard first in a church (Church of the Holy Trinity, New York City). On this account it indeed differs from the familiar oratorios of all such European composers as Handel, Haydn, Mendelssohn, and Elgar. To have had it performed first in a church redounds all the more to

[47] Isabel P. Semler, *Horatio Parker,* New York, 1942, p. 77.

[48] *Ibid.,* p. 79. Bernard of Cluny's poem was popularized by John Mason Neale.

[49] This is his only large work recorded to date (ARS 335). The criticisms from Philip Hale and W. J. Henderson (see Gilbert Chase, *America's Music,* p. 377) claim that parts of *Hora Novissima* could have been written by "Hobrecht, Brumel, or even Josquin des Près." Such uninformed criticism, completely wide of the mark for the Flemings or Parker, inhibits any serious study of Parker's masterpiece.

[50] *Musical Times,* Oct. 1893, 586-87.

Parker's credit when we compare its harmonic wealth, the intensity of expression throughout, the dynamic extremes, the bold modulations, and the over-all unifying devices with the usages of such contemporaneous oratorio composers as Parry, Mackenzie, Rubinstein, Saint-Saëns, Gounod, and even Franck. For an example of his unifying devices: the head-motif of the instrumental introduction undergoes inversion to become the vocal fugue subject of *Pars mea* (No. 4). It again appears, in its original form, as the instrumental counterpoint to a new choral melody in the finale of Part 1, *Tu sine littore* (No. 6). Or for another example: the head-motif of the bass aria, *Spe modo vivitur*, suffers a sea-change into major, and emerges as the soprano melody in *O bona patria*. The instrumental theme first heard at mm. 201-203 of the opening chorus, Part 1, returns in the finale of Part 2 at letters "I" and "N," there to serve as a countermelody to the principal theme. Another idea carried over from first to last numbers of the oratorio is the agitated instrumental interlude from mm. 42-49 of the plangent introduction to the opening chorus. This particular chromatic interlude—quoted in No. 6 as well as Nos. 1 and 11—serves so obviously as keystone in two arches that a reviewer in 1893 almost wished to call it a *Leitmotiv*.[51]

Parker never lets down the high emotional pitch established in the first chorus. Each of the two principal parts ends splendidly. Nothing lasts too long. The more voice parts (*Stant Syon* is a double chorus; *Urbs Syon inclyta* pits a quartet against the chorus *a 4*), the more ingenious the conduct of the individual parts. The relief of an *a cappella* chorus for the antepenultimate number of the oratorio proved so fine a contrast that Parker reverted to the same scheme when he wrote his next oratorio (the *a cappella Jam sol recedit*[52] precedes the last scene in *The Legend of St. Christopher*).

His later oratorios do not vie with *Hora Novissima* for popular favor, nor do they leave so homogeneous an impression. Yet parts of each equal the best in *Hora Novissima*. Like Dudley Buck, whose *The Legend of Don Munio* is founded on a Washington Irving tale, Parker describes *The Legend of St. Christopher* on the title page as

51 *Ibid.*, p. 586.

52 Semler, p. 100, quotes D. S. Smith's estimate of this chorus as "Parker's finest and most beautiful composition."

a "dramatic" oratorio. Against his judgment when he was composing it, he even decided at the time of publication to call the principal divisions "Acts." For the poetry of *St. Christopher* he was indebted to his mother (née Isabella Jennings, "Class Poet" at Lasell Seminary when she graduated in 1857[53]); and for the libretto of *Morven and the Grail* to Brian Hooker, the same Yale English professor who provided him with the librettos of his two operas, *Mona* (G. Schirmer, 1911) and *Fairyland* (1915). The "plots" of both *St. Christopher* and *Morven*—despite the different librettists—show some striking similarities. In both, a young low-voiced hero pursues the Ideal, first in the wind, then in the earthquake, then in the fire. Finding the Ideal in none of these, he finally discovers it in the still small voice (or an equivalent). In a general way this is indeed the scheme underlying so secular an oratorio as Schumann's *Paradise and the Peri.*

Parker's gift for composing exciting music did not desert him in either *St. Christopher* or *Morven*. The clamor up to the drawing of the bow in Act I, the raucous meeting with Lucifer in Act II, and the exultant Gloria in Act III, indeed outdo *Hora Novissima.* The repetition of Offerus's vow-motif (score-numbers 17, 34, 55, 91) and of the *Asperges me* music in II, ii and III, ii (=*Tarnhelm* motif) bears witness to Parker's overmastering concern for unity. Throughout *Morven,* he constantly reverts to themes first enunciated at measures 5 and 53 of the Introduction (m. 5 = "Compact" motif in *The Ring,* 53 = "Atonement" in *Parsifal*); and to the "Follow the Grail" motif in the opening quartet (= "Gleaming Gold" in *The Ring*).[54] If he adopts Wagnerian unifying principles, and if he works with a harmonic palette as richly hued as Elgar's, Parker still shows such mastery of his craft that he is no more to be deprecated than Berg for having followed in Schoenberg's wake.

During the years that *St. Christopher* was in gestation (he finished the scoring of the first part in August 1897), his pupils at Yale included Charles Ives. Ives's testimony to Parker's gifts is therefore germane: "I have and had *great* respect and admiration for

[53] *Ibid.,* p. 29.

[54] These correspondences are cited only to give a quick idea of the character of Parker's ideas, and not because he consciously quoted (any more than Brahms quoted Grieg in his Opp. 4 and 79, No. 1).

Parker."[55] Ives continues by praising him for seldom being trivial — even if Parker could toss off a *Valse gracile* that was the first encored number on the only all-American program that Josef Hofmann ever gave.[56] "His choral works have a dignity and depth" that cannot be ignored, even if Parker was too much swayed by the "German rule."[57] One of Ives's classroom experiments was a fugue in which the entries went around the clock of keys from C to G to D to A. Despite his Germanisms, his training under Rheinberger at Munich, his German wife whom he taught to speak English, and his academic honors, Parker's mind was not so closed as to prevent him from experimenting with just such a scheme of clock-entries in *St. Christopher*, II, ii. The voices enter with a subject successively in B, E, and A; and later in a journey through the relative minors. True, the effect is never close to Ives's. But Parker was destined to make his living out of music, to win more large cash prizes than any American composer in history,[58] and to obtain the honorary D. Mus. from Cambridge University—an unprecedented honor for an American. Ives, by contrast, lived so much above the professional world that recognition might never have reached him had not he earned enough from insurance to publish and distribute his music gratuitously.

Parker's other distinguished Yale pupils included David Stanley Smith, Douglas Moore, and Roger Sessions. As early as 1902, Smith (1877-1949) was writing "large and elegant pieces" in Munich,[59] whither he had followed Parker on sabbatical. When praising Smith

[55] Henry and Sidney Cowell, *Charles Ives and his Music*, New York, 1955, p. 33. (Cowell says that "great" is crossed out).

[56] Richard Aldrich, *Concert Life in New York, 1902-1923*, New York, 1941, p. 589.

[57] Cowell, p. 33.

[58] For his Op. 31 he received a $300 prize (National Conservatory of Music); for his Op. 45, $250 (Musical Art Society of New York); for his Op. 54, $500 (Paderewski Prize); for his Op. 71, $10,000 (Metropolitan Opera Company); for his Op. 77, another $10,000 (National Federation of Music Clubs). G. Schirmer was the original publisher of his Opp. 3, 6, 14, 15, 17, 20, 22-28, 33-37, 39, 42, 45, 53, 59-62, 64-65, 67-68, 71, 73-75, 77, and of numerous anthems and solo songs without opus-number. Already before 1900, G. Schirmer had published 12 important church works without opus-number (*Magnificat, Nunc dimittis, Deus misereatur, Te Deum, Salve Regina*, and seven anthems).

[59] Semler, p. 141.

to that other paladin of New England musical culture, George W. Chadwick (1854-1931),[60] Parker wrote from Munich: "He is a good boy and will turn out well, unless I am dreadfully mistaken." Smith did turn out well, if succeeding to the deanship of Yale Music School for two decades (1920-1941) measures success. But Smith, prolific composer of hymn tunes, anthems, cantatas, and oratorio, lived into an epoch when to be "good" was less a cachet of musical esteem than to be "outrageous." He felt his isolation keenly in later years, and tried self-consciously to paste modernisms on his essentially pre-war pieces. His early church music, such as *The Logos,* Op. 21, a Christmas cantata in four parts (H. W. Gray, 1908), is simple, affecting, and rises to full-throated climaxes at the close of Parts 1 and 4 with quotations of *Veni Immanuel.*[61] Smith reached his high-watermark as a churchly composer with his *Rhapsody of St. Bernard,* Op. 38, the "cantata" of oratorio proportions (G. Schirmer, 1918) that brought his name into the national iimelight when it was first given at the Chicago North Shore Festival in the year of publication. The text—translated by Smith himself from Bernard of Clairvaux — begins with *Jesu dulcis memoria:* a stanza that he sets with all the liquid sweetness of the "Victoria" motet. Although he exploits for what they are worth the few dramatic touches in the centonized text, the stanzas stay too close to the pure and the ethereal for much conflict. According to Ives, Parker could become "hard-boiled" on a moment's notice. Smith is never hard-boiled, even in the fugal *Jesu Rex.* Nor does he strive for Parker's over-all unity. In only two numbers does he repeat himself — 1 and 12 (the opening melody returns at "F" in the epilogue). Brahms of *How lovely are Thy dwelling places* (letter "A") looked over Smith's shoulder when he wrote *Jesu decus angelicum.* Brahms's influence also accounts for such rhythmic involvements as Smith devises in *Desidero te millies,* for the intercepted phraseology in *Jesu, flos matris,* for the spare orchestration, and even perhaps for the use of the word Rhapsody in the title.

[60] Neither Chadwick nor the two other hierarchs of Boston music, Arthur W. Foote (1853-1937) and Arthur B. Whiting (1861-1936), did anything consequential for church music. Chadwick and Foote were long-time church organists.

[61] When Smith, or any of his generation, quoted from the past, they always seem to have preferred pseudo-plainsongs such as *Veni Immanuel* to anything of authentic antiquity.

Sessions, who in his *Reflections on the Music Life in the United States* (1956) justly calls Parker "the most significant figure in the American music of his time" after MacDowell,[62] and who praises his religious works for "not only a mature technique, but also a musical nature and profile which were well defined," had the advantage of being twenty years younger than Smith. Such religious music as Sessions's *Mass for Unison Choir and Organ* (1955) speaks to this generation as uncompromisingly as does Stravinsky in his *Canticum Sacrum ad honorem Sancti Marci nominis* of the same year. Both works are so much of their time as to bear all the mid-century stigmata—without which signs no advanced listener will believe that he is hearing music from on High. Denis Stevens, reviewing Sessions's Mass at its première (Cathedral of St. John the Divine, New York, March 11, 1956), saw deeply into its meaning. "His contribution to English liturgical music is an important one, and it is more than likely that new music of this calibre . . . will do much to revive the adventurous spirit that one so often finds lacking in the purveyors of *ars sacra*."[63] Irving Lowens found it "austere music," but of high "specific gravity."

Randall Thompson's *Mass of the Holy Spirit* of the year following acknowledges the past with many more "devices" than does Sessions's Mass. For instance: Thompson resorts to canons (*Christe*, three-in-one canon at the fourth and seventh below; Benedictus, four-in-one at the fifth, ninth, and thirteenth below; Agnus at the octave), incorporates a fugue (*Pleni sunt coeli*), and readily repeats or sequences long strains (*Gloria in excelsis = Tu solus Dominus; Credo in unum Deum = Et incarnatus est; Pleni sunt coeli = Hosanna*). Sessions's Mass, even though he uses key signatures, yields to no conventional harmonic analysis; Thompson's, without such signatures, speaks in an easily assimilable major-minor chordal vocabulary. Throughout, Thompson's Mass is masterfully scored for an *a cappella*[64] group usually of the conventional SATB kind, but sometimes of as many as eight parts (Sanctus). Sessions wisely confines himself—as does also Lou Harrison in his *Mass for Mixed*

[62] *Reflections*, New York, 1956, p. 142.

[63] *Notes from Abroad*, in *Musical Times*, May 1956, p. 269.

[64] A *prima prattica* composer, he writes all his major sacred works for unaccompanied chorus.

Chorus, Trumpet, Harp, and Strings (introduced in New York, February 1954) — to unison or octave singing.[65]

The resurgence of the Mass in settings by Roy Harris (men's voices with organ, New York, May 13, 1948), Harrison, Sessions, Thompson, and even by so "American" a composer as Stravinsky (naturalized September 28, 1945, he published his 17-minute Mass for men's and boy's voices with double wind quintet in 1948, the year of its première) is interestingly paralleled in modern America by the use to which such lights as Samuel Barber, Aaron Copland, Ross Lee Finney, Lukas Foss, Howard Hanson, Alan Hovhaness, Norman Dello Joio, Normand Lockwood, Peter Mennin, Vincent Persichetti, Leo Sowerby, and Randall Thompson have put numerous other classic religious texts. These range from the creation poem in Genesis, psalms in both scriptural prose and the rough-hewn meter known to the 1620 pilgrims, selections from such other books of the Bible as Isaiah, Ecclesiastes, and Luke's gospel, to John Chrysostom's Greek liturgy and selected prayers from Kirkegaard. At mid-century, our established American composers have almost to a man made some sort of "religious" gesture. In doing so, they differ from MacDowell and Charles T. Griffes. Curiously, the gestures of even the most *avant-garde* have been bows to the traditionally accepted masterpieces of religious prose and poetry.[66]

When, for instance, Copland composes his *a cappella* masterpiece, *In the Beginning,* [67] he hews as closely to Scripture as did Handel in *Messiah.* Thompson in his sequence of sacred choruses for unaccompanied mixed voices, *The Peaceable Kingdom,* invokes the Quaker painter-preacher Edward Hicks (1780-1849) as his patron,[68]

[65] Sessions wrote his Mass for the fiftieth anniversary of Kent School. Thompson's Mass was a commissioned work also. The first version of Harrison's Mass was inspired by a report of WPA research in Indian mission music; he "Europeanized the composition" after moving to New York.

[66] Virgil Thomson suggests a reason when in *Harper's,* November 1960, p. 61, he writes: "The music of today, written by no matter whom, is surprisingly noncommittal." It is easier to remain aloof with an antiquated text. Thomson, in his *Stabat Mater* for soprano and string quartet (1932), showed courage with a text that is not liturgical (words by Max Jacob).

[67] For purple prose describing the excellencies of this Copland work, see Hans Redlich, *New Music: A Critical Interim Report,* in *The Music Review,* XVI (1955), 264.

[68] The anomaly of Hicks's patronage is the more keenly felt when the Quaker

but confines himself to passages from Isaiah, so far as text is concerned. Leo Sowerby,[69] the most professionally church-oriented of composers, chooses texts from Revelation for *The Throne of God* (1956-1957) or from St. Francis for the Alice Ditson commission, *The Canticle of the Sun* (Carnegie Hall, April 16, 1945). Even *Christ Reborn* and *Forsaken of Man* with texts "arranged" by Edward Borgers each culminate in Scripture. Sowerby's *The Vision of Sir Launfal* (1928) comes nearer to our time, but no nearer than James Russell Lowell.

In 1958, Sowerby — after surveying the American scene from the organ bench of the Episcopalian cathedral in Chicago—awarded merit ribbons to these native-born composers of church music: Seth Bingham, Everett Titcomb, Philip James, Joseph W. Clokey, Randall Thompson, Normand Lockwood, Richard Purvis, Robert Elmore, and Searle Wright.[70] Mark Siebert, who published a lengthy White List of anthems by contemporary composers in December 1957, largely endorses Sowerby's choices (he adds a half-dozen names not in Sowerby's list).

But such "good music" lists as Sowerby's and Siebert's are perplexingly incomplete in one respect. They almost invariably lack Masses and motets by native-born Americans of Roman Catholic persuasion. From the time of Buck and Beach, American non-Roman Catholics — eminent as composers —have freely set Latin liturgical texts. Where have the eminent Roman Catholics been during the last hundred years? Roman Catholicism during the past century has flourished in big cities with notable orchestras, and has rallied strength from the same floodtide of European immigrants that has given opera stars and touring virtuosos to musical America in abundance. In sacred music, no equivalent contribution has yet been made. Father Robert J. Stahl, Notre Dame seminary instructor in

---

antipathy to all art-music is remembered. Hicks, a fanatic, deplored even his multiple-copy paintings, such as the peaceable kingdoms, as pomps of Satan.

[69] Ronald M. Huntington gives a painstaking account of Sowerby's church works in *A Study of the Musical Contributions of Leo Sowerby*, USC Master's thesis, August 1957. See the sections on organ works, pp. 219-27, choral pieces, pp. 227-37, services and settings, pp. 237-39. His style-criticism at pp. 169-70 is informed.

[70] *Organ and Choral Aspects and Prospects*, London, 1958, pp. 42-43.

New Orleans, summed up the Catholic situation in an article first published in the November 1940 *Notre Damean,* and republished in *Caecilia,* LXVIII/2 (February 1941, pp. 60-61), when he wrote thus: "With rare exception, the music in Catholic churches today is poor, very poor. Gregorian Chant is seldom heard and rarely done well. Harmonized masses of the cheaper variety are in vogue. Many churches are burdened with piano-playing organists whose principal asset, rather than musicianship, is 'loud but not good.'" To comprehend the present impasse, Roman Catholic historians look to the past, and explain that a sea of mediocrity engulfed American Catholic music in the 19th century.

Only a few exceptional leaders arose here and there from the deeps — and these leaders were almost to a man German or Swiss-German immigrants profoundly affected by German Caecilianism. John B. Singenberger (1848-1934) ranks as the patriarch of this select group. Born in German-speaking Switzerland, trained in an Austrian Jesuit college, and a graduate of Innsbruck University in 1870, he crowned his education with a course under Dr. Franz Witt in Munich. Heir to the *Musica divina* traditions of Karl Proske, Witt imbued his pupil Singenberger with both the strengths and weaknesses of Caecilianism. In 1873 Singenberger emigrated to America, settling in Wisconsin. A year later he founded the American Cecilian Society, with headquarters at St. Francis, Wisconsin. In 1875, at a Dayton, Ohio, meeting of the society, he established himself as the leading Catholic conductor in the nation, with a festival performance of the *Missa Papae Marcelli.* In 1882 Pope Leo XIII knighted him, and in 1885 he presided at the first in a series of giant Cecilian festivals that reached its climax in one at Chicago in the year of the World's Fair. His compositions already in 1889 numbered 14 Masses, 16 Vespers, 16 motets, 20 Latin hymns — not to enumerate his pieces included in his popular instruction manuals. Through his pupils, his role at festivals, and his long dominance in the American Cecilian Society, his music came into wide vogue. What is more, it continued to be reprinted even after his death at the age of eighty-six. As late as 1937, for instance, a complete set of Benediction pieces written forty years earlier was republished in *Caecilia* magazine.

According to one pupil, the widely known Indianapolis choirmaster F. J. Boerger, Singenberger taught, thought, and acted in German throughout his long career in America. Such other prominent American Catholic church composers before 1900 as Monsignor Henry Tappert (1855-1929), long-time pastor in Covington, Kentucky, the two Jesuits, Ludwig Bonvin (1850-1939) and Hubert Gruender (1870-1940), and Father J. B. Jung, for many years vice-president of the American Cecilian Society, were also German or Swiss-German by birth and training. Naturally, Singenberger's best pupils were of German descent. At the top of the roster was Sister Mary Cherubim, born Cecilia Schaefer with a Wisconsin organ-builder for her father. Her personal monument was the Alverno College of Music in Milwaukee, which she headed until retirement in 1938. With 16 motets and 2 published Masses to her credit, she became in her active years the most widely performed American-born Catholic woman composer of sacred music.

For composers outside German-descended ranks, the student of American Catholic music in the last fifty years can look on the eastern seaboard to Pietro Yon (1886-1943), J. Vincent Higginson (pen name: Cyr de Brant), Joseph J. McGrath, and Father Russell Woollen. On the west coast, Richard Keys Biggs (b. 1886) has proved the most prolific Catholic composer, with Masses in honor of St. Joseph (1920), the Holy Spirit (1933), and Junipero Serra (1934) typifying a published list that extends to 16 Masses and 30 motets. Biggs, organist and choirmaster of Blessed Sacrament in Hollywood since 1928, was like Mother Georgia Stevens of the Pius X School of Liturgical Music a convert whose musical training was of professional caliber before conversion.

J. Vincent Higginson (b. 1896) has separated his hymnological and editorial self (*The Catholic Choirmaster*) from his creative self by recourse to a pseudonym. Joseph J. McGrath (b. 1889), born at Oswego, educated at Syracuse and later instructor of music in Syracuse University, became music director at Immaculate Conception Cathedral (Syracuse) in 1926. His long list of successful church compositions includes three of the most popular Masses of our day. His *Missa Pontificalis* was the first Mass by a native-born American to win H. B. Collins's praise in *Music and Liturgy*, and has been sung at more than a dozen consecrations of bishops in the past twenty-five years. In such easier compositions as his *Missa Lyrica*,

[105]

Op. 23, and his *Missa Parochialis,* he pleasantly blends an unstudied counterpoint with free-flowing melodies of immediate appeal. Whereas R. K. Biggs in such a Mass as that in honor of St. Francis of Assisi unifies every major movement with a reference to a plainsong (the seventh-mode introit, *Puer natus est nobis*), McGrath unifies by repeating and sequencing his own graceful tunes.

With Pietro Yon, we leave composers whose fame is restricted to Catholic circles. Now remembered principally for his Christmas *succès fou, Gesù Bambino,* Yon was in his lifetime one of the best-known organ virtuosos in America. Born in northern Italy, trained at Turin and Milan, he emigrated to New York at the age of twenty to become organist of the 16th Street Church of St. Francis Xavier. When he was only twenty-four, G. Schirmer published his ambitious Mass in G, in honor of Blessed (now Saint) Jeanne d'Arc. In 1926 he became organist of St. Patrick's Cathedral, and in 1934 his career as a composer was crowned with an oratorio of three parts, *The Triumph of St. Patrick (The Mission, The Return, The Sacred Fire).* Produced with a roster of eleven eminent soloists, chorus, organ, and orchestra in Carnegie Hall on April 29, 1934, this ambitious work was repeated in Chicago in the presence of Cardinal Mundelein on March 9, 1936. Though on an "Irish" subject and though endorsed by Patrick Cardinal Hayes, this oratorio bespoke Yon's truest leanings when he chose for his librettist a fellow Italian, Armando Romano; and when he chose for his publisher G. Ricordi.

Whether the cumulative impression gained from a survey of American church music in the 1950s and 1960s heartens or discourages us depends entirely on our vantage point. For university and college chapels, for heavily endowed metropolitan churches, and for public, ceremonial, and patriotic assemblages where the name of God is invoked, a rich literature by famous contemporary Americans awaits the conductor. Almost invariably the texts have been chosen from elevated historic documents. If the semanticist will permit any religious music written by a composer after naturalization to swell the American repertory, such noble experiments in extending the liturgical repertory as Stravinsky's *Canticum Sacrum* and *Threni,* or Schoenberg's *Kol Nidre,* Op. 39 (1938), and *De profundis,* Op. 50B (1950), permit us to cite America as the footstool of Heaven.[71] Even a nativist such as Lockwood has struck out boldly in such a late work as the "dramatic portrait of Rocky Mountain Methodism," *Land of Promise*, composed for the 1960 General Conference (Denver, April 30 and May 6, 1960).[72] Judaism can boast not only of achievements by Copland and Foss, but also of such definitely liturgic music as Ernest Bloch's *Avodath Hakodesh* dedicated to Gerald Warburg (1934) and Frederick Jacobi's *Ahavas Olom* (1946), one of many such compositions written for and dedicated to David Putterman and the Park Avenue Synagogue Choir.

Against these achievements, the pessimist can pit the saccharine quality of the popular revival melodies, the anodyne banality of numerous anthems sung regularly in "respectable" churches, and the taste of ministers who pride themselves on their sacred settings of Irving Berlin and George Gershwin tunes.[73] The critic can unite with Paul Hume in execrating the music at even so exalted a ceremony as the dedication of the Shrine of the Immaculate Conception, America's largest Roman Catholic Church (he labeled it a "shabby, feeble effort" compounded of titbits from Sibelius, Brahms, Refice, and Selner[74]). The cynic can deplore the vogue of the overly handsome "minister of music" whose high salary depends more on his dynamic quality as a youth leader, his ability to deliver a captive audience to the preacher at the evening hour, and the pliability of his repertory, than on any specific musical qualifications.[75]

So long as America continues diverse enough to be a land in

[71] See Peter Gradenwitz, *The Religious Works of Arnold Schoenberg*, in *The Music Review*, XXI (1960), 24-25, 27-29.

[72] For a bibliography and critique of Lockwood's works, see the brochure, *Normand Lockwood*, issued by Broadcast Music, Inc., 1959. Lockwood, one of America's most sensitive and prolific church composers, considers that quality in church music almost always reflects the morale and vigor of the church itself.

[73] Foundry Church in Washington had a minister who was nationally famous for his use of Irving Berlin in church services. He was Senate chaplain.

[74] *Caecilia: A Review of Catholic Church Music*, Summer 1960, p. 70.

[75] Among several renowned schools specializing in the training of church musicians or ministers of music can be mentioned the Union Theological Seminary School of Sacred Music in New York, the Westminster Choir College in Princeton, the Louisville Baptist Seminary sacred music school, and the Pius X School of Liturgical Music at Purchase, New York.

which 256 different denominations can flourish, we must continue to expect diversity in church music. The tares will probably continue to grow up taller than the wheat; but at least some wheat does grow. The musically sensitive churchgoer who disregards the tares will justify himself in some such words as Charles Ives's father used. Someone asked Ives's father (who was a professional musician) how he could "stand to hear old John Bell (who was the best stone mason in town) bellow off-key the way he does at camp-meetings?" Ives's father replied: "Old John is a supreme musician. Look into his face and hear the music of the ages. Don't pay too much attention to the sounds. If you do, you may miss the music."[76]

[76] Cowell, p. 24.

The Plush Era in
American Concert Life

By NICOLAS SLONIMSKY

On February 20, 1861, President-elect Abraham Lincoln attended a performance of Verdi's opera *Un Ballo in Maschera* at the New York Academy of Music. It was, of course, the censored version, in which the original libretto dealing with the historical assassination of Gustavus III, King of Sweden, was revised to eliminate the perilous suggestion of regicide and replace it by the murder of a mythical "Governor of Boston" named Riccardo.

On the eve of the Civil War, the New York newspapers were filled with stories of "hideous plots" against the life of Abraham Lincoln, and denunciations of the adherents to the Southern American Confederacy, who "urged the plunder and destruction of the opulent classes, and of the man marked as the fount of the popular wrongs." A warning was made to "scan carefully every proposed movement of the President-elect," since "poisoned honey and suspicious boxes have been sent to him, and threats of assassination have been definitely ascertained." But, wherever Abraham Lincoln appeared, "the harmony of incessant cheers was unbroken by indecent language or act of violence," said the New-York Times (New York was invariably hyphenated at that time). The police protection of the President-elect in New York City was under the special care of Superintendent Kennedy, and it was "beautifully demonstrated."

Opera in the United States a hundred years ago was entirely in Italian hands, while orchestral and chamber music was monopolized by the Germans. The New-York Times had some bitter words to say regarding the inability of the Italian opera singers to join in the singing of the *Star-Spangled Banner* in Lincoln's honor.

After the first act [the newspaper reported], when the President-elect's presence had been discovered by a few persons familiar with his appearance, a round of applause brought him to his feet. The curtain then arose, and the artists sang the *Star-Spangled Banner*—at least Mesdames Philipps and Hinckley did, for the Italians, although they have been here for many years, have not yet mastered the difficulties of the language, and could not, of course, condescend to sing it. Intrusted to two American girls, the anthem received the best of treatment, and was vehemently applauded. The President-elect bowed his acknowledgments from the box.

The New-York Herald gave a vivid description of this scene of recognition:

The plain black cravat, the neat shirt collar turned over the neckcloth, the incipient whiskers and good-humored face that sat so demurely in the box, left no doubt in the public mind that Abraham Lincoln of Illinois was among them. All this time the opera singers were doing their best; the chorus chaps were expending their unwearied lungs to the extent of their second-class abilities; and the trumpeters and drummers were blowing and thumping their instruments in the most approved style.

Lincoln's attendance at an opera that treated the subject of political assassination may have inspired some darksome premonitions, but Lincoln left at the end of the second act, and so did not witness the actual scene of murder. Not even the most feverish journalistic imagination could conjure up the vision of another visit to a theater four years thence, when the "hideous plot" became a reality.

*   *

*

Opera, a century ago, was by far the most important social event in the United States. It was the entertainment of the wealthy and the well-born. The New-York Herald of February 21, 1861, describing Lincoln's reception, reported that "gentlemen waved their hats and caps over their heads, and the ladies did the same with their hand-kerchiefs," and then added significantly,

Coming as it did from a class of citizens whom the President-elect could not have had so excellent an opportunity of seeing assembled together under any other circumstances — and in consideration of the wealth, intelligence and respectability of those who were so met together — the demonstration becomes doubly valuable, and will not, as it should not, be readily forgotten by Mr. Lincoln.

Abraham Lincoln, it appears, was regarded as socially inferior to the assembled splendor of American society.

The German Quartette Club of Hoboken, numbering twenty-two members (the designation "Quartette" apparently referred not to the number of singers but to the number of parts in which they sang), serenaded Lincoln at the Astor House, performing various vocal compositions. Then the forty-piece National Guard Band arrived, escorted by 150 "Wide Awakes" with badges. The band played arrangements from Verdi's operas, quicksteps, and other dance tunes.

The Italian-German dominance of American concert life in the 19th century, and well into the 20th, was complete and undisputed. Musical societies were named in honor of German and Austrian composers — the Handel and Haydn Society, the Mendelssohn Quintette Club, a Mozart Verein, a Beethoven Verein, a Wagner Verein. There was a Germania Orchestra; choral societies in New York, Cincinnati, St. Louis, Philadelphia, Washington, were called Liederkranz, Liedertafel, or Sängerbund, and sang German songs. Orchestral conductors up to World War I were Germans, and so were most of the orchestra men. The German language was spoken almost exclusively during symphonic rehearsals in New York, Philadelphia, Boston, Cincinnati, St. Louis, Baltimore.

Time and again, some rebellious American musician would shout a mighty but hoarse shout about music for Americans by Americans. But he would be shouted down immediately: "You want music? Then go to Germany!"

Truth to tell, these early pioneers of American music, whether in composition, performance, or education, were strong on slogans and weak on competence. One of the most picturesque of these was Jerome Hopkins, who shouted his way into American music in the

[111]

1870s and 1880s. The life of Hopkins would make an interesting subject, but unfortunately his entire archives, musical manuscripts and correspondence, which he willed to Amy Fay at his death in 1898, have been apparently lost.

Hopkins imagined himself to be a martyr to the cause, and in one of his statements he mourned the martyrdom of American musicians who had gone to a "drunkard's grave" (Harry Sanderson, T. Hagen, E. Remack, William King, A. H. Pease) or had committed suicide (Candido Berti, Ureli Corelli Hill, H. N. Sawyer). Three musicians, said Hopkins, suffered "early decline and consumption from disappointment" — William Saer, Von Oeckelen, and August Goeckel. U. C. Hill is well known, and his life and death (of poison) are well documented, but who are these other victims of America's indifference to her own sons? Were they worth saving from disappointment and a drunkard's grave?

Brooding over all this, Hopkins wrote an emotional letter to Berlioz expressing his desire to go to Paris to live. Apparently he touched upon a sympathetic string, for Berlioz wrote him a remarkable letter in reply: "Monsieur et cher confrère, I read your letter with considerable emotion. You say you are suffering for art's sake; unfortunately, I am not the person to offer any consolation to you. You have a greatly mistaken idea of the kind of life that an artist (worthy of the name) leads in Paris. If New York is for you the Purgatory of musicians, then Paris is to me (and I know Paris) their Hell. So you should not be discouraged too deeply." Berlioz then extended his welcome to Hopkins to "this Hell" (using the English words) but warned him not to delay his voyage: "Every morning I rise from my bed hoping that this will be my last day. My physical and moral distress leaves me no respite, and I have long said farewell to my musical illusions." Berlioz concluded, half in English, half in French: "But I beg your pardon, Sir, if I give you this counsel. Laissez-moi vous serrer la main et vous adresser les dernières paroles du Ghost d'Hamlet: Farewell, farewell, remember me."

*　　*

*

Idealistic and eccentric Americans have risen time and again to champion the cause of national music. One of the most ambitious among them was Mrs. Jeannette M. Thurber, a wealthy society lady in New York, who organized in the 1880s an American opera company, presenting operas in English, with as many American singers as could qualify for the task. She published a grandiloquent prospectus, in which the superlatives were freely lavished in a manner worthy of P. T. Barnum himself:

GRAND OPERA sung in English by the most competent artists — The musical guidance of Theodore Thomas — THE UNRIVALED Thomas Orchestra — The LARGEST CHORUS ever employed in grand opera in America, and composed entirely of FRESH YOUNG VOICES — The LARGEST BALLET corps ever employed by grand opera in America — Four thousand new costumes, for which NO EXPENSE HAS BEEN SPARED — The armor, properties, and paraphernalia made from models by THE BEST DESIGNERS — The scenery designed by the Associated Artists of New York, and painted by the MOST EMINENT SCENIC ARTISTS of America.

Natives of twenty American cities, said the prospectus, were counted among the members of the American Opera Company, and the chorus represented 26 different states of the Union. The management "distinctly discouraged the pernicious star system" since it felt confident that "there is no lack of American singers who require only encouragement and opportunity to do honor to the musical reputation of their native land."

It is interesting to note that a statement of aims very similar to that of Mrs. Thurber was made in 1923 by the American Opera Company organized by Vladimir Rosing at the Eastman School of Music, Rochester. The names of the two companies were the same; the operas were to be sung in English, and the star system was to be abolished. Mrs. Thurber's plan included the formation of an American school of opera, and a similar opera school was established at the Eastman School of Music in connection with Rosing's American Opera Company. Mrs. Thurber's enterprise lasted two seasons and foundered with a mighty crash of bankruptcy, lawsuits, and countersuits. Rosing's undertaking, backed by George Eastman's money, came to its end peacefully in 1929.

Mrs. Thurber had a splendid list of "Incorporators" for her American Opera Company, with Andrew Carnegie as president. The repertory included *Faust, Lakmé, The Huguenots, Aida, Lohengrin,* and *The Flying Dutchman.* The first season passed auspiciously from the artistic standpoint, but financially it was a failure. To ward off creditors, Mrs. Thurber renamed her enterprise the National Opera Company for the second season, hoping to make a fresh start. It undertook a grand tour to the Pacific Coast, but on the way back to New York it broke down completely, and Mrs. Thurber stopped payment to her troupe. Chorus singers and ballet girls were stranded; some leading singers retained lawyers to collect their fees, and Theodore Thomas himself put in a claim for the six months' salary due him.

"The National Opera scheme, from its boastful and vainglorious start to its miserable and contemptible end," wrote the New York theatrical journal *Truth* in its issue of July 7, 1887, "has been marked by ignorance, vanity, bungling and failure. It was started to satisfy the desire for notoriety of a half-educated woman, possessed of a bank account but very little brains."

With her National Conservatory of Music, possessing "an AD-MIRABLE FACULTY," Mrs. Thurber was more successful. The performing arts were emphasized. There was a Trio Club, which presented concerts of chamber music. Victor Herbert played the 'cello. Ever a go-getter, Mrs. Thurber addressed a petition to Congress, asking for $200,000 for the National Conservatory. In this petition she stated that, should the grant be given, every Senator and every member of the House of Representatives would be given the right to send any deserving young musician of his State to the National Conservatory free of charge.

The reaction to the petition was immediate and devastating. The Boston Gazette of February 25, 1888, declared: "Music is a luxury for the wealthy, and it would seem that Mrs. Thurber should take from her own well-filled pocket all she can afford in the shape of assistance to her pet conservatory." The Indianapolis Journal of the same date wrote: "Imagine a member of Congress facing his constituents after voting to appropriate $200,000 to teach young people how to execute vocal gymnastics, or play on the fiddle. We are not so esthetic as that." Mrs. Thurber's petition never got through, but in 1891 she made a coup that elevated her conservatory to a truly national, and even international, status. She managed to entice Dvořák to head the National Conservatory. Dvořák spent three fruitful seasons in New York, taught a number of talented Americans, and composed the *New World Symphony*. To some Americans, however, Dvořák was just another scheming foreigner bent on collecting money. "The arrival of Herr Anton Dworzak [*sic*]," wrote the New York *Truth*, "increases the already large circle of musical notabilities who are quitting the old fatherland and taking their abode in this 'free country' which is fast becoming the musical Eldorado of the world. Nikisch, Seidl, Xaver and Philip Scharwenka, Dworzak, they are all attracted by the wonderful chromatic sound of the American dollar."

Mrs. Thurber lived a very long life. She died in 1946, at the age of ninety-four.

*   *

*

Grandiosity was not an exclusively American trait in the promotion of the arts. Berlioz, Wagner, and Liszt were glorified and maligned by the journalists of both hemispheres as the prophets of the ultimate noise. A cartoon published by G. Schirmer in 1869 under the caption "The Music of the Future" showed an orchestra of maniacs savagely attacking their instruments from every conceivable angle, supplemented with a scaleful of yowling cats whose tails are pulled by a distracted attendant. The conductor leaps in midair, his arms and legs spread wide apart. On the stand before him is a symphonic poem by Liszt, and propped against the podium, another score inscribed "WAGNER. Not to be played much till 1995."

The year of the Schirmer cartoon was also the year of the Great National Peace Jubilee, held in Boston "to commemorate the restoration of peace throughout the land." Peace was commemorated with a series of "monster" concerts which produced an amount of noise that no music of the future could equal. The word "monster," incidentally, conveyed no pejorative sense, but was used as a synonym for prodigious and phenomenal. The Great National Peace Jubilee was organized and directed by the Irish-American bandmaster Patrick Gilmore, who assumed the proud title of "Projector." The tumult and the commotion of the occasion soon passed with contemptuous cries of "humbug" resounding from the press, but one feature of the affair entered the annals of American music for all time, the *Anvil Chorus* from *Il Trovatore* performed by a huge

[115]

vocal and instrumental ensemble, helped out by one hundred selected members of the Boston Fire Department, attired in red shirts, and hammering the main beat on one hundred anvils.

The mania of grandiosity that possessed Gilmore was not satiated with the Great National Peace Jubilee. Three years later he staged in Boston a super-monster festival, the World Peace Jubilee. A mammoth Coliseum was erected on the wastelands of the Back Bay with an advertised seating capacity of one hundred thousand. (Checking on this figure, a skeptical reporter found that the Coliseum held only twenty-one thousand seats.) There was "the greatest chorus ever organized of twenty thousand trained voices" (eighteen thousand was estimated by the press as a more likely figure). There was a "grand orchestra of one thousand musicians in classical and popular overtures" and "a military band of one thousand members in the most dashing marches and selections" (the newspapers said there were only eight hundred in each). Still and all, the World Peace Jubilee was, as advertised, the "grandest musical festival ever known in the history of the world." It ran from June 17, 1872, to July 4. The *Anvil Chorus* was made a daily feature. The *Star-Spangled Banner* opened the festivities, with all the massed thousands of performers, plus "all the bells of Boston in chime and artillery accompaniment." The bells were rung and the cannon fired "by electricity." (In the mid-20th century, a more sophisticated signal was used to open a festival, when President Eisenhower pressed a button to let a beam of light from Arcturus pass through a photo-electric cell and ring a bell.)

The Sextet from *Lucia* was then sung by a "bouquet of artists" numbering one hundred fifty, accompanied by full orchestra, and conducted by the "Projector." *Farewell to the Forest,* a four-part chorus by Mendelssohn, was performed by twenty thousand voices *a cappella.* The spirit of grandiosity here reached its apogee. Even newspapermen were impressed by such magnification. The Boston Daily Globe ran an editorial solemnly proclaiming that "the moral effect of this grand International Jubilee might be to perpetuate, as well as to celebrate, a state of peace throughout Christendom."

Ironically, far from being deafened by the great noise, some auditors found the effect disappointingly small. Even the hundred anvils, specially imported from Birmingham, England, and weighing from 100 lbs. to 300 lbs. each, failed to produce an impression of overwhelming sonority. Apparently the directors of the World's Peace Jubilee overlooked the Weber-Fechner law, according to which the intensity of a sensory perception is proportional to the logarithm of the stimulus, so that the auditory impression of twenty thousand voices is not twenty thousand times, but perhaps only twenty times stronger than that of a single voice, the exact proportion depending on an acoustical constant.

Military bands were brought over from Europe to take part in the Peace Jubilee. The participation of the Grenadier Guards Band of London created some international tension; there were protests in the British Parliament against exporting the Grenadiers to serve the sensationalism of American tastes.

The great star of the show was Johann Strauss, the Waltz King, expressly invited for the occasion. He led the huge orchestra in the performance of the *Beautiful Blue Danube* and his other waltzes, conducting in the Viennese fashion, violin in hand, and giving cues with the bow. The Boston Post reported that Strauss "veered around vane-like, from one side to the other, and seemed the very impersonation of Terpsichore, while all the musicians under his control resolved themselves into a spontaneous band of Dryads and Bacchantes."

Johann Strauss was apparently the originator of the famous "shaggy dog story," usually ascribed in musical anecdotage to Paderewski. It was reported in the New York World as follows:

It is related of Johann Strauss, the Waltz King, that when he was in St. Petersburg, the fair Russian belles made a frightful series of demands upon him for locks of his hair. Strauss viewed the prospect with alarm. All these souvenirs would leave him bald. Then he had a brilliant idea. His dog was a huge black Newfoundland. Its shaggy coat was of precisely the texture of his hair, and today many a Russian album is enriched by the possession of a cherished lock of hair from Strauss's dog. When he was coming to America, he could with difficulty be restrained, it is said, from bringing along the dog as a precautionary measure for a similar emergency.

*   *

*

Great patriotic anniversaries invariably included musical festivals. In 1876, the centennial of the Declaration of Independence was celebrated by a series of concerts under the direction of Theodore Thomas, held in Philadelphia, the Cradle of Liberty. For this occasion Thomas induced Wagner to compose a special work, the worst he ever wrote, a *Grand Centennial Inaugural March,* dedicated to the Women's Centennial Committee. In a letter to Thomas, Wagner pointed out that the "soft and tender passages" in the march were intended to portray "the beautiful and talented women of North America, as they take part in the cortège." Considering the musical quality of these tender passages, Wagner's opinion of American feminine beauty must have been very low.

Theodore Thomas was also in charge of the musical program of the World's Fair Columbian Exposition in Chicago during the summer of 1893. He invited Brahms to take part, but Brahms declined. He did secure the services of Paderewski and Saint-Saëns.

Among American musical patriots, the figure of Silas Gamaliel Pratt imposes itself. The spirit of grandiosity found in Pratt a faithful believer. But he was also a shrewd organizer, who knew how to raise money for his projects. In October 1891 he conducted in New York, Chicago, and Philadelphia a series of spectacles entitled "The War in Song, a Military and Musical Allegory of the Late Civil War." The music was a medley of popular tunes of the period. Lantern slides provided visual illustrations. Detachments of soldiers marched through the audience to impart a sense of immediacy to the recent conflict. A "Battle Fantasia" was depicted in Pratt's program notes: "The opposing forces rapidly approach! A combat! Crash of Arms! The Retreat! a dying soldier's vision of home! The battle resumed with onrushing cavalry! Heroic resistance! The final charge and Victory!" Here *The Battle Cry of Freedom* overwhelmed *Dixie,* and the Union was saved.

Pratt's "Allegory of the Late Civil War" was produced under the auspices of the Grant Monument Association. A voluminous program book, containing the texts and music of the songs, was published, with lucrative advertisements, the most arresting of which proclaimed the curative powers of Bovinine, "prescribed by more than twenty-five thousand physicians," guaranteed to "create new and vitalized blood," and to "permanently cure nervous prostration, dyspepsia, cholera infantum, and excessive irritability of the stomach from any cause." An engraving of a bull illustrated the advertisement, and a testimonial from General Grant's son assured the public that during the last four months of Grant's life he was fed on Bovinine, and that "it was the use of this incomparable food alone that enabled him to finish the second volume of his memoirs." Other advertisements in the program book extolled Garfield tea for "constipation and sick headache," and "Genuine Pansy Corsets" to constrict the waist and project the bosoms forward.

Monster concerts and musical extravaganzas were to the public of a hundred years ago what television spectaculars in living color and cinematic epics on a wide screen are today. Guest artists on popular television shows are warned to reduce their solo numbers to a skeletal minimum, leaving out a modulation here, a variation there. At one such show, a child pianist was told to cut out an A major portion in Mozart's *Rondo alla Turca* and proceed from F-sharp minor directly to the initial A minor! Opportunistic artists ordered to commit similar atrocities salve their conscience by arguing that it is better to carry to the untutored millions in the mass audience even a monstrously mutilated classical piece than to surrender them completely to a diet of popular songs in symmetrical sequences harmonized to the point of maximum saturation with chromatic progressions of ninth-chords, and crooned by illiterate and voiceless entertainers.

*　　*
*

"One generation passeth away, and another generation cometh . . . and the wind returneth again according to his circuits." American impresarios booking a celebrated European artist "according to his circuits" were as cautious as masters of ceremonies at television shows today not to overload the paying customers with culture, and to insure variety of entertainment. The word "recital," in the sense of a musical performance given by one person, was making its way into American usage, but grudgingly. Reporting Anton Rubinstein's concerts in New York in September 1872, the New York Times used such locutions as "recital of Schumann's *Carnaval,*" and "the pianist recited a suite." Rubinstein played not more than one-third of each program. Besides the violin solos of his joint artist Henri Wieniawski, there were overtures by a makeshift orchestra and popular ballads sung by a soprano and a contralto to

[119]

piano accompaniment. Despite these added attractions, Rubinstein's concerts were poorly attended. The Boston Globe of October 16, 1872, deplored this lack of interest: "We make great pretenses to a refined musical cultivation, but we manifest it by crowding the theater where opera *bouffe* is played by women whose coarseness is their principal claim to popularity. An opera singer, if she be a pretty woman, will fill the house nightly with the élite of our dilettanti, even though her claims to musical genius be not of the highest order."

Opera singers were the darlings of the plush era. Sturdy of frame, ample-bosomed, stern of visage, accoutéred in rich costume, wearing plumed hats and opaque veils, the operatic sopranos and contraltos excited the imagination of the less privileged humanity. Their marriages, their divorces, their unsanctified amours were as eagerly reported in the daily press as similar activities of movie stars are today, and their photographs taken in demurely alluring poses were the pin-up pictures of young America. Sometimes, after the opera, college students would "unhorse" a diva's carriage, and conduct her to her hotel with themselves in harness.

Robert Graves has written a book-length paean in praise of Ava Gardner, the movie star. In the 1870s, moved by no lesser ardor, Longfellow addressed adulatory verse to the singer Marie Rôze:

> Oh Marie! Veil the radiant eyes
> That melt with inner light
> Conceal the brow that o'er them lies
> The bosom warm and bright.
> The dainty chin, whose dimples play
> At merry hide-and-seek
> The mouth with careless laughter gay
> And either perfect cheek!

*   *

*

Some paraphernalia of old concert life disappeared with the advent of a more sober age. Lavish floral tributes, laurel wreaths, gifts of jewelry placed at the feet of an artist, all these tokens of admiration and esteem are gone. Sartorial effulgence among male artists gave way to a sober full-dress suit for the evening, a cutaway for the afternoon. Gone also is the abundant chevelure, bushy hair à la Paderewski (who was once dubbed a "human chrysanthe-mum"), natural curly hair of lesser virtuosos, and the long, falling locks of musical *Wunderkinder*. A great deal of eccentric behavior on the stage, which was an attribute of the plush era, also fell out of favor. The greatest eccentric among pianists was Vladimir de Pach-mann, the "Chopinzee," as Huneker called him. A stenographic report of his mumblings taken at one of his New York recitals read as follows: "I have a nervous in my thumb . . . But I am not tired . . . I work twenty hours a day . . . But I have a nervous in my thumb . . . Ah! Bravo, Pachmann! C'est joli! Schön, schön . . . Bellissimo!"

Philip Hale made an attempt to explain away Pachmann's eccen-tricities.

Why should one be disturbed [he wrote] when the pianist, intoxicated by the beauty of a certain phrase, invites the audience to share joy with him, or points out with an uplifted hand some exquisite bit of tone gradations? There is no one like Mr. de Pachmann; he himself hears his music as though he were one of the audience, and if he calls attention to the heat of the room or exclaims "Schön!" it is as though a neighbor whispered his discomfort or his delight. He smiles to you that you may realize how beautiful the notes are, when they trickle out of his fingers like singing water; he adores them and his own playing as if he had nothing to do with them.

But even Hale became exasperated when Vladimir de Pachmann put on a particularly obnoxious exhibition:

The only thing that was lacking was a stereopticon with views of Chopin's portraits, pianos that he played, women whom he loved, and a series of pic-tures of Mr. de Pachmann from childhood to the year of his first American concert tour. Miss Duncan dances on the stage with bare legs and arms, clad in a garment of thin gauze, illustrating various pieces of Chopin. It is a pity that Mr. de Pachmann cannot do this and play the piano at the same time.

*   *

*

It is difficult to believe that a century ago most instrumentalists performed in public with the music before them, and that playing from memory was exceptional. Anton Rubinstein's ability to dis-pense with the notes amazed American audiences during his tour of 1872. "To play a Beethoven concerto, Schumann's *Carnaval*, and three other pieces," wrote a music critic, "all compositions of the most complicated nature, without a note to assist him, is a feat of itself of no common magnitude." Such effusive praise for something that every conservatory student nowadays takes for granted is astounding. It would seem that memorizing would be a natural result of study, at any time of music history. Conducting an orchestra from memory is another matter, for here the conductor learns the music by inner reconstruction of actual orchestral combinations, and it is therefore at least comprehensible that Toscanini's ability to control an orchestra without consulting the score aroused admiration. But Toscanini's repertory was, with a few exceptions, limited to Classical and Romantic literature, more or less symmetrically constructed, logically developed, and mellifluously orchestrated, so that the music needed only guidance and interpretative genius to make it roll. Then Mitropoulos produced a sensation by conducting from memory works of the ultra-modern school. Yet such feats are no longer rare. Young conductors, some of them scarcely out of school, lead rehearsals and concerts from memory as a matter of routine. Only chamber music groups still continue to use the notes, but some modern ensembles are beginning to break out of bondage and perform from memory.

Commercialism was much more blatant in the musical affairs of the plush era than it is now, and pretensions to artistic aims were more transparently false. Advertising was frankly sensational, with exclamation points strewn all over. The announcements of the "Absolute Farewell American Tournée" of Adelina Patti during the season of 1903-1904 were typical of this sensational commercialism. The management carefully explained that "Madame Patti never before in all her career announced officially, as in this instance, her farewell to the Public," and pointed out that "in order to secure Madame Patti for another tour at all, the management had to outbid all others with whom he was in direct competition, and to evolve a contract that demands the largest honorarium ever accorded to any artist in the history of the world." This was by way of introduction to the greatly raised prices of admission. Adelina Patti herself sang only a few numbers with the orchestra, and gave encores with the piano; the bulk of the program was taken up by a number of assisting artists — a solo pianist, a solo violinist, a solo 'cellist, a contralto, a tenor, and a baritone.

Traffic in child prodigies was very active and apparently profitable. Among the few *Wunderkinder* who rose to great and merited fame was Josef Hofmann, advertised on his first appearance in America in 1887 as "The Greatest Genius of the Pianoforte since the days of Mozart." Like Leopold Mozart, who made Wolfgang a couple of years younger than in biological reality, Josef's father, Casimir Hofmann, who organized his American tour, let the management advertise him as "The Wonderful Child Pianist and Composer Aged Ten," when he was pushing twelve. The program was also typical: Hofmann played Beethoven's First Piano Concerto, accompanied by a small orchestra under the direction of his father, who also conducted an overture, some Chopin pieces, and a few compositions of his own. In addition, there were a violin soloist, a harpist, and three singers. Included in the program was also an "improvisation on a theme given by any lady or gentleman in the audience." At the Boston concert, Chadwick suggested a theme from Frederick Cowen's *Welsh Symphony*, and Hofmann dutifully improvised a variation on it.

Hofmann's appearances ran into unexpected trouble when, on January 28, 1888, the New York Society for Prevention of Cruelty to Children appealed to the Mayor of the City of New York to suspend the permit for Hofmann's further concerts on the ground that the child was being exploited to the detriment of his physical and mental health. Hofmann's father opposed the motion, and arranged for an examination by four New York physicians. They found unanimously that "the boy's physical functions are all in good order, and there are no indications that he has sustained any injury from his public appearances." At that juncture, a *deus ex machina* appeared in the person of a wealthy New Yorker who offered the sum of fifty thousand dollars to Hofmann's father for the purpose of the boy's education, on condition that he would not appear in public until he reached the age of eighteen. The offer was cheerfully accepted, and satisfaction was expressed by all parties concerned.

* *

*

Wars, revolutions, and sometimes partisan politics have affected the programs and the selection of performers of musical works, in

America as well as in Europe. A wave of anti-German feeling during the First World War engulfed even German classical music. German musicians, who enjoyed a virtual monopoly of the American concert stage, suddenly found themselves classified as enemy aliens. Karl Muck, the supernal drillmaster of the Boston Symphony Orchestra, was arrested like a common criminal and interned for the duration of the war. So was Ernst Kunwald, the Austrian conductor of the Cincinnati Symphony Orchestra. Even the German classical composers were cast under suspicion as culture-bearers of militant Prussianism. Walter Damrosch, himself of German birth but an American citizen, pleaded that at least Bach, Beethoven, and Brahms be spared. But Wagner was practically banned from the American opera stage. Nothing as silly happened during World War II despite the fact that Wagner was claimed by Hitler as the spiritual father of Nazism.

The cold war with Russia brought some scattered cancellations of performances of works by Russian composers, and a Hearst columnist actually protested against the playing of Tchaikovsky's symphonies.

The brief interlude of McCarthyism brought discrimination against composers of known radical or liberal views. Aaron Copland's *Lincoln Portrait* was taken off the symphony program at Eisenhower's inauguration in January 1953, at the instigation of Representative Fred E. Busbey, Republican of Illinois, who made this immortal pronouncement: "There are many patriotic composers available without the long record of questionable affiliations of Copland. The Republican Party would have been ridiculed from one end of the United States to the other if Copland's music had been played at the inaugural of a president elected to fight communism, among other things."

Although the American public and even financial backers of musical organizations take a latitudinarian view towards libertine conduct among artists, the ugly specter of moral turpitude was invoked against some foreign musicians ostentatiously living in sin. A French conductor was discharged in the 1940s because of notorious cohabitation. When Scriabin came to America in 1905 with his common-law wife, there were rumors that deportation proceedings were begun against him, but he sailed for Europe before these rumors could be substantiated.

The greatest moralistic ruckus on the American musical scene in the last hundred years was raised by the production of Richard Strauss's *Salome* in New York and Boston. Not only religious and social groups, but even professional journalists and music critics voiced violent objections to the immorality of Oscar Wilde's play and the sensationalism of the music. H. E. Krehbiel, of the New York Tribune, wrote of the "moral stench with which *Salome* fills the nostrils of humanity," and W. J. Henderson, of the New York Sun, opined that to judge by *Salome,* the music of the future would find its mission "in sewer, pesthouse, and brothel." A professional physician declared in a letter to the New York Times that *Salome* was "a detailed and explicit exposition of the most horrible, disgusting, revolting, and unmentionable features of degeneracy."

The shocked stockholders of the Metropolitan Opera and Real Estate Company, among them J. P. Morgan, A. D. Juilliard, and William K. Vanderbilt, served notice on the management to discontinue further showings of *Salome* and to refund money to ticket holders for the three scheduled performances.

In Boston, the notorious New England Watch and Ward Society petitioned Mayor John F. Fitzgerald (grandfather of President Kennedy) to prevent the local presentation of *Salome,* and other politically powerful organizations bombarded him with similar demands. But Fitzgerald stood off the assault with judicious calm.

The Mayor's office [he declared] does not interfere as a rule with the productions in the Boston theaters. Licenses are issued under such conditions as the office makes, and we insist at all times that the productions be up to the proper standard. If any theater violates public decency by the presentation of anything offensive, we can revoke the license. If the people of Boston do not want the opera *Salome* presented and give expression to that view, I do not think that the opera will be given. No theater manager will fly in the face of public opinion.

It was left for Fitzgerald's successor, Mayor Hibbard, to ban the presentation of *Salome* in Boston by the visiting Manhattan Opera Company. He did so on the bland pretext that a Boston lady of his acquaintance had seen the opera in New York and formed a categorical opinion that it was utterly unfit for the Boston public.

Apart from quantitative expansion of audience through the

marvels of electronics, has there been any inherent change in American concert life since 1861? Certain it is that musical mechanization and automation have not killed the individual artist, despite the agitation against "canned music" in the 1930s. On the contrary, careers are now made in America by European artists through their recordings alone, and American music-lovers flock eagerly to concerts by phonograph celebrities. There seems to be no diminution of concert activities by living artists.

Grand Opera is still very much with us, and the nature of its repertory has remained almost unaltered in a century. Operas that have become popular since 1861 are still grand, still make their appeal to distilled sentiment, still follow the twin formulas of Wagnerian and Verdian constructions.

American symphony orchestras have largely preserved the old type of program making — an overture, a classical symphony, an intermission, a solo concerto, and a raucous finale. With the shining exception of Leonard Bernstein, conductors of prime orchestras are still largely recruited from Europe, but the orchestra men are now mostly American-born. There is no doubt that the quality of orchestral playing has advanced enormously. If the famous Theodore Thomas Orchestra were to arise from the dead, its best performance would be completely outshone by even a secondary American ensemble of today. Besides, a 19th-century American orchestra would have been unable to cope with even a relatively mild piece of modern music. The levitated conductor of the Music of the Future in the Schirmer cartoon of 1869 would have been grounded after a few measures had he replaced Liszt's symphonic poem by a 20th-century work.

There remains the intriguing and unanswerable question regarding the true greatness of the virtuosos of the plush era. Were they really insuperable technicians? They could hardly be expected to match the technical dexterity demanded by the modern repertory of contemporary pianists and violinists, and would flounder when confronted with a composition in the new idiom. Their greatness then must have resided in the fidelity of interpretation. Yet there are indications that visiting virtuosos adopted an over-romanticized and sentimentalized interpretation of the classical masters. Some young musicians today, possibly under the influence of the movie portrayals of great virtuosos, are reviving this type of musical histrionics, but it manifests itself mainly by expressive movements of the head and the body rather than by deformations in the music itself. Perhaps it is the sum total of technique, interpretative insight, absorption in the music, and an imponderable personal impressiveness that made for greatness. Perhaps it is true that there were giants in those days whose equals our century could not produce.

Band Music in America

By RICHARD FRANKO GOLDMAN

In 1859, Patrick Sarsfield Gilmore, a twenty-nine-year-old Irish cornet virtuoso, formed his first band, in Boston. This date conveniently marks the birth of what we know as band music in America. To be sure, there had been bands before Gilmore's, but they had been of purely local importance and were musically of negligible character. For the most part, they were civilian brass bands, although there were a few bands attached to the volunteer militia and some with the regular military. Most famous among them were the Boston Brigade Band; the American Band of Providence, Rhode Island; the Allentown (Pennsylvania) Band, said to be the first regularly established civilian band in the United States; the Ringgold Band of Reading, Pennsylvania; and Dodworth's Band in New York City. Of the regimental bands, that of the Seventh Regiment of New York, under C. S. Grafulla, was well known and proficient; but of the national Service bands, the only ones extant before the Civil War were the Marine Band in Washington and the band of the United States Military Academy at West Point. These, however, were small, poorly organized, and unimportant groups. The Marine Band did not begin to enjoy its present reputation until the era of John Philip Sousa, in the 1880s.

Most of the bands mentioned above were organized in the 1830s, but the names of Gilmore's predecessors and contemporaries are known today only to band buffs or students of musical Americana. Gilmore himself arrived in Massachusetts (via Canada) in 1848, and immediately acquired a reputation as a cornet player and band leader. He conducted bands in Salem and other Massachusetts towns, and eventually succeeded Eben Flagg as conductor of the Boston Brass Band, which had been organized in 1835 by Edward Kendall, a famous virtuoso on the keyed bugle. The American Band was directed by Joseph Green, while band music in New York was practically a monopoly of the Dodworth brothers, Allen and Harvey. From all accounts, many of these men were capable band-masters. But it needed the impact of Gilmore and his vigorous personality to produce a forward movement in American band music.

It must also be said that the Civil War stimulated the development of military music in the United States, much as the Revolution and era of Napoleon I had done in France. Gilmore and his newly organized band enlisted in 1861 as a unit with the Twenty-Fourth Massachusetts Volunteer Regiment. Grafulla and the Seventh Regiment of New York also saw service, as did many others. During the war, Gilmore and Harvey Dodworth helped recruit and train new bands, and their work resulted in the establishment of many units which continued after the end of the war. These new bands were in many cases better organized and more active than the pre-war bands.

Gilmore and his band were mustered out after a short term of service. In 1864, Gilmore found himself in New Orleans, following the capture of the city by the Union forces. For the inauguration of Governor Michael Hahn, Gilmore, at the request of General Banks, organized the first of the gigantic festivals with which his name has ever since been associated. The event took place in Lafayette Square on March 4, 1864. Gilmore assembled a "Grand National Band," consisting of some 500 Army bandsmen, plus a number of additional drum and bugle players, and obtained permission to organize a chorus of 5000 school children. The program consisted largely of patriotic tunes, ending up with *Hail, Columbia*. For this finale, Gilmore added thirty-six cannon, which he fired by electric buttons from the podium. The affair was an enormous success, and brought Gilmore's name before the entire American public.

From New Orleans Gilmore returned to Boston, where he gave regular concerts with his band for several seasons. But the taste for the spectacular remained with him, and he devoted his efforts to his dream of a National Peace Jubilee, to be on a scale twice as large as the affair in New Orleans. His Jubilee of 1869 was a triumph. In 1872, again doubling his forces, he successfully promoted and produced a World Peace Jubilee, with a band of 2000, a chorus of 20,000, the whole augmented by cannon, anvils, a huge organ, and other trimmings. This festival, "colossal" even by today's standards, continued for ten days. Gilmore not only imported many of Europe's leading bands for the occasion, but also engaged the services of Johann Strauss and his orchestra, as well as those of a distinguished "bouquet of artists" from here and there. The Jubilee was attended by President Grant and other notables, and was again a triumph for Gilmore. As an organizer and promoter, Gilmore was fabulously gifted; and it should be remembered that despite the vaudevillean character of some of his most famous productions, he did a good deal of valuable work in the popularization of good music. Even Lowell Mason gave his blessing to Gilmore, consenting to appear as a guest of honor at the 1869 Jubilee.

The European bands, including the English Grenadier Guards under Daniel Godfrey and France's Garde Républicaine under Sellenick, had impressed American bands by their obvious superiority and given American musicians an idea of the performance quality of good bands. It is true that some improvement had already taken place in the American bands. The Marine Band under Fries took part in the 1872 Jubilee, and was beginning to grow in size and proficiency. Much of this improvement could be directly traced to the influence of Gilmore and the improved standards he had demonstrated with his own band. For Gilmore, despite his taste for noise and fun, was a sound leader and musician. The instrumentation he adopted for his band, especially in the matter of proportion of reed instruments to brasses, is still the basic instrumentation of the modern concert band in America, and his choice of repertory opened new vistas. Many post-Civil War bands showed this influence; among the leading organizations, aside from Gilmore's own, were the Ninth Regiment Band of New York, under D. L. Downing; the band of Easton, Pennsylvania, under Thomas Coates; and the American Band of Providence, which enjoyed its finest days under the leadership of D. W. Reeves, beginning in 1866.

Gilmore's greatest work was done after 1873, when he accepted the leadership of the Twenty-Second Regiment Band of New York on the condition that he could build it into a concert unit and accept engagements on a business basis. Under Gilmore, this band was the greatest of its time, and probably one of the greatest of any time. His musicians were the best to be found (at one point he had both Jules Levy and Matthew Arbuckle, the two greatest cornet virtuosos of the day, in his band at the same time), and Gilmore trained them meticulously. He made many tours of the United States and Canada, and in 1878 took his band to Europe, where its excellence was quickly recognized. His programs were considerably in advance of anything that had been attempted in this country up to the time. Along with the triple-tongued cornet solos, the quadrilles, polkas, marches, and patriotic medleys, Gilmore offered good transcriptions of standard orchestral overtures and excerpts of works by composers up to and including Wagner and Verdi, his contemporaries. In the way of repertory, it cannot be said that even Sousa advanced beyond the point attained by Gilmore. Typical of his programs is this one:

Saturday evening, December 9, 1877
GRAND CONCERT
by
Gilmore's Full Military Band
with Soloists

Part First

1. Overture, "Stabat Mater"		Rossini
Gilmore's Band		
2. Piccolo Solo, "Canary Polka"		De Carlo
Signor De Carlo		
3. Andante, Fifth Symphony		Beethoven
Gilmore's Band		
4. Cornet Solo, "Fantasie Original"		Hartmann
Mr. M. Arbuckle		

[131]

5. Piano Solo, "Paraphrase on Themes from Rigoletto"   Liszt
    Master Hermann Rietzel
6. Song, "Good-Bye, Sweetheart"   Hatton
    Mr. W. H. Stanley

Part Second

---

7. Grand Opera Fantasie   Meyerbeer
    Including the gems of Le Prophète, L'Africaine,
    L'Etoile du Nord, Les Huguenots and other Operas.
    Gilmore's Band
8. Scene from Il Trovatore   Verdi
    Miss Lillian B. Norton[1]
9. Saxophone Solo — Variations on "Casta Diva"   Bellini
    Mr. E. A. Lefebre
10. Overture, "Jubel"   Weber
    Gilmore's Band

Which brings us, of course, to Sousa himself. Two days after Gilmore's death on September 24, 1892, Sousa gave his first concert in Plainfield, New Jersey, with his newly formed civilian band. This event marks the beginning of the next era of American band music. Sousa had for twelve years previously been leader of the United States Marine Band, which he had made into an organization rivaling Gilmore's famous group. But the Marine Band, despite Presidential permission to enlarge its scope and activities, was not enough for Sousa. Gilmore had demonstrated that a band could tour with great financial success, and indeed from about 1880 to about 1910, the band was perhaps the greatest popular musical attraction in the United States.

There were several reasons for the band's popularity. First of all, there was little competition from orchestral music, and none at all from motion pictures, radio, television, or recordings. Secondly, the repertory of the concert band was calculated to please unsophisticated tastes. This repertory, with Gilmore and Sousa, consisted of dance music and characteristic pieces, potpourris from popular operas and operettas, cornet and trombone solos, and a scattering of standard overtures or other orchestral pieces in transcription. Neither Gilmore nor Sousa worried very much about "educating" the public, although their efforts certainly had the incidental effect

[1] Nordica.

of introducing many thousands of people to music, and to the names of Verdi, Wagner, Meyerbeer, Rossini, and occasionally even Beethoven and Mozart. In a history of music in America, one should not entirely overlook the "educational" accomplishments of the really great bands.

A third reason for the great popularity of bands, especially Sousa's, was that the march enjoyed a vogue as dance music. (In fact, when the two-step was introduced in Europe, it was known as "The Washington Post," since this was the tune with which the dance was associated.) Sousa, of course, was the greatest of all march composers, and he was thus able to profit by a coincidence of fashions. He was able to tour profitably with his band, taking it to Europe no less than four times, and even making a round-the-world tour in 1910-11. There was hardly a town in the United States that had not heard the Sousa Band. A typical Sousa program is this one:

GRAND FAREWELL CONCERT
Sousa and his Band
Mr. John Philip Sousa, conductor
Metropolitan Opera House
Sunday, April 22, 1900
8:15 P.M.
Soloists: Miss Blanche Duffield, soprano
Miss Bertha Bucklin, violiniste
Mr. Arthur Pryor, trombonist

1.	Overture — "Imperial" (new)	Haydn-Westmeyer
2.	Trombone Solo — Air and Variations	Pryor
	Mr. Arthur Pryor	
3.	a. Slavonic Dance No. 2	Dvořák
	b. Hungarian Dance No. 6	Brahms
4.	Soprano Solo — Waltz, "Maid of the Meadow"	Sousa
	Miss Blanche Duffield	
5.	"Capriccio Italien" (new)	Tschaikowsky
	Intermission	
6.	Idyll — "Ball Scenes" (new)	Czibulka
7.	a. "Ronde de Nuit" (new)	Gillet
	b. March — "The Man Behind the Gun" (new)	Sousa
8.	Violin Solo — Adagio and Moto Perpetuum — Third Suite	Ries
	Miss Bertha Bucklin	
9.	Fantasie — "Good-bye"	Sousa

This concert took place on the eve of the Band's departure for a European tour (the first) which included the Paris Exposition of 1900.

[133]

Contemporary with Sousa, and enjoying to some degree the same prosperity, were a number of other famous bands. No less a person than Victor Herbert succeeded Gilmore with the Twenty-Second Regiment Band. Herbert led this organization from 1893 to 1897, playing at various resorts and places of popular entertainment. Herbert also wrote at this time a number of excellent marches, among them one for the inauguration of President McKinley. Other famous bands of the time were those of Alessandro Liberati, Frederick Innes, and Thomas Preston Brooke. The Seventh Regiment Band was prosperous under the leadership of C. A. Cappa, and slightly later the bands of Patrick Conway and Giuseppe Creatore enjoyed wide popularity. Arthur Pryor, who had acquired a wide reputation as trombone soloist and assistant conductor with Sousa, formed his own band in 1903, and was the first of the well-known bandmasters to make recordings.

What did they play? These are two representative programs:

The Mall, Central Park
Sunday, September 16, 1906

Seventh Regiment Band
George L. Humphrey, Bandmaster

Part I
Star Spangled Banner

1. Grand March — Rakoczy		Berlioz
2. Overture — Der Freyschuetz		Weber
3. Spanish Dances		Moszkowski
a) Valse Lente	b) Bolero	
4. Cornet Solo — Theme and Variations — Carnival of Venice		Levy
Mr. Chester W. Smith		
5. Selection from Romeo and Juliet		Gounod

Part II

6. Rapsodie — Espana No. 1	Chabrier
7. Morceau — Salut d'Amour	Elgar
8. Fantasia — Reminiscences of Scotland	Godfrey
9. Intermezzo from Cavalleria Rusticana	Mascagni
10. Ballet Music from Opera Feramors	Rubinstein

Doxology

*   *

*

[134]

BAND MUSIC IN AMERICA

August 4, 1918

Frederick Innes, conductor

1. Anglo-Americana, Folk Song Fantasy	Baetens
2. a. Offertory in F	Battiste
b. For Flag and Country	Innes
(New — First Time)	
3. Cornet Solo — Showers of Gold	Clarke
Ernest Pechin	
4. Second Hungarian Rhapsody	Liszt
5. a. Cavatine, Op. 85, No. 3	Raff
b. Minuet, Op. 14	Paderewsky
6. Aria for Soprano, from Faust — The Jewel Song	Gounod
Ethel Richardson	
7. Overture, Poet and Peasant	Suppé

These are good examples of band programs from 1870 to 1918. Of all the bandmasters, it is perhaps Gilmore whose programs showed the greatest imagination and initiative and contained the smallest amount of bad *Kapellmeistermusik*. Both Gilmore and Sousa had remarkable soloists. It is perhaps not generally remembered that Lillian Nordica started her career as soloist with Gilmore, who also employed Maude Thursby and Parepa-Rosa, as well as his galaxy of fabulous cornetists. Sousa featured Arthur Pryor on trombone, Herbert L. Clarke on cornet, and a variety of vocal soloists, the best-known of whom was Estelle Liebling.

The next, and present, period in American band music begins approximately at the end of World War I, when many changes and developments took place. Both the United States Army and United States Navy bands were formed at about this time, as was the last of the great professional civilian bands, that of Edwin Franko Goldman. The Sousa Band continued until Sousa's death in 1932, but the heyday of the professional touring band had passed. The last band concert at Willow Grove Park in Philadelphia took place in 1926, and other resorts, such as Manhattan Beach and Asbury Park, changed in character and no longer featured band music. Jazz and a new type of dance orchestra replaced the band as popular entertainment. Somewhat later, the advent of talking pictures (the movies had already begun to make a dent in the popular entertainment field) and then of radio changed the picture entirely. The band no longer had an open field to itself, and it was necessary for it to find new social functions.

The most important development of the past forty years has been the growth of band music in the schools and colleges. Many American schools had had instrumental programs as well as vocal (going back, of course, to Lowell Mason), but in the 1920s the growth of the instrumental programs (aided by instrument manufacturers) was phenomenal. Such pioneers as A. R. McAllister of Joliet, Illinois, and Joseph Maddy began organizing school bands of extraordinary proficiency, and their example was emulated throughout the country, particularly in the Midwest. Contests and festivals of school bands attracted much attention, and soon the entire movement was efficiently organized, with the aid of many associations and groups of educators. The college football band also began to develop ideas of grandeur, and we now have hundreds of "symphonic" wind bands in colleges and universities. The band today is primarily this type of amateur organization, and supports a music industry of great economic importance. It is estimated that there are at least 20,000 bands in the high schools and colleges; these purchase music, instruments, and uniforms, and contribute substantially to the health of the "music business." So far as music itself is concerned, these bands too, in several ways, have responded to changing conditions; in many ways they have replaced the old town or community bands, and provide a form of light popular entertainment as well as music for parades. Their repertory is for the most part conventional and limited in scope: the amateur band rehearses long hours to master a few programs during the course of a year. There has also developed a new repertory of easy music for the high school or junior high school band, a type of *Gebrauchsmusik* that is as a rule more profitable to play than to listen to.

But in the professional band field, and in the finest work of the university bands such as Michigan, Illinois, and others, an entirely new concept of repertory has developed. This is largely the result of the efforts of one man: Edwin Franko Goldman. Early in his career, Goldman saw that the band concert as it had existed before World War I was in many important respects a thing of the past. The growth of popular orchestral concerts was beginning to render much repertory available in its original form. (Later radio, and later still, the LP record, made this situation clear to everyone.) It

[136]

therefore seemed to Goldman that the repertory of the band needed the work of experienced professional composers if it were to command any interest. This interest, of course, had also to be predicated on a standard of professional performance of the highest kind. What has happened since the initial efforts of Dr. Goldman is, of course, band history.

It had been forgotten that composers of the 18th and 19th centuries had ever written band music. There is no evidence that Gilmore or Sousa (or any European bandmasters, for that matter) had even given a thought to "original band music," except for occasional pieces by bandmasters, and always excepting, of course, the glorious contribution of original marches, especially Sousa's. As for new works, the nature of band concerts did not require them. In the 20th century, a very rare example of "original band music" was provided by the two suites written for band by Gustav Holst in 1909 and 1911. But there is no record of these works having been performed in the United States before the 1920s.

Dr. Goldman's efforts commenced in a comparatively small way. Beginning in 1918, Percy Grainger began to compose some works, notably his children's march, *Over the Hills and Far Away*, for the Goldman Band. In 1919, Dr. Goldman offered a prize for the best original band work, the judges being Grainger and Victor Herbert. The prize was awarded to Carl Busch for his composition, *A Chant from the Great Plains*. This was a pivotal point in band history, and a point that has perhaps not sufficiently been recognized. For from that time on, principally through Dr. Goldman's efforts, more and more composers of skill and reputation began to see the possibilities in writing for the modern wind band. By the time of Dr. Goldman's death in 1956, many of the great composers of Europe and America had written band pieces, many of them directly for Dr. Goldman and his band, and many others as a result of the impetus given the work by Dr. Goldman's propaganda and performances. Schoenberg, Milhaud, Respighi, and Roussel, among others, wrote works for Dr. Goldman, while the list of American composers includes almost everyone of note from Henry Hadley to the young hopefuls of 1961.

The drastic change in the band repertory is amply illustrated by the program of a concert of works composed for band given by the

League of Composers in Carnegie Hall on January 3, 1948, in honor of Dr. Goldman's seventieth birthday. The program, of course, was selected for a special occasion, but the variety of works included, and the international representation of their composers, give an indication of the scope and size of the original band repertory by then available.

PROGRAM

1.	Toccata Marziale (1924)	R. Vaughan Williams
2.	Suite Française (1945)	Darius Milhaud
3.	Theme and Variations for Wind Band, Opus 43-a (1942)	Arnold Schoenberg
4.	The Power of Rome and The Christian Heart (1947-8)	Percy Grainger
5.	Shoonthree (1941)	Henry Cowell
6.	Canto Yoruba (1941)	Pedro Sanjuan
7. a.	La Marche sur la Bastille (1937)	Arthur Honegger
b.	Prelude (1937)	Albert Roussel
c.	Le Palais Royal (1937)	Georges Auric
8.	Symphony No. 19, for Band (1939)	Nicholas Miaskovsky

The work initiated by Dr. Goldman continues. There are now many commissions, awards, and competitions for band compositions, and the repertory of interesting original music continues to grow. At the same time, most of the interesting band music by composers of the 18th and 19th centuries has been revived, from the charming pieces by Gossec, Méhul, and Catel through the pieces by Mendelssohn, Hummel, Spohr, Grieg, the great *Funeral and Triumphal Symphony* of Berlioz (first performed in the United States in 1947 by the Goldman Band), and others. The band repertory today even has a history, small but respectable, and one not in direct competition with that of the orchestra.

With this new repertory has also come a revolution in the publication of music for band. Prior to 1900, little band music was published, except for marches and other small pieces. Arrangements of larger works were generally made for a given band by its conductor or a staff arranger, and were performed from manuscript. Full scores were all but unknown. A cued piano part, or a synthesized three-line score, were considered, until recently, more than adequate. For many band arrangements, a first cornet or clarinet part was all that the conductor had to guide him. (It must be noted in this respect that in the publication of band music both England and Germany were ahead of the United States.) Today, however, most important band works are published in full score, with careful editing; and even minor works are decently printed, with adequate conductor's scores and carefully calculated distribution of parts.

The character of the band concert, however, has altered only to a degree. The new literature has given it a certain musical interest it did not have before. But the staples of the repertory are very similar in kind to the popular favorites of one hundred years ago. Overtures of Rossini, Suppé, and others, cornet solos, operatic potpourris, marches, and assorted specimens of *Kapellmeistermusik* (mostly patriotic) are still with us. But there is unquestionably more variety than there once was, and although the character of activity has changed considerably, there is no doubt that band music remains as much as ever a flourishing branch of popular musical culture in the United States.

Popular Music from
Minstrel Songs to Rock 'n' Roll

By ARNOLD SHAW

The history of popular music from the death in obscurity of
Stephen Foster to the widely lamented passing of Oscar Hammerstein II is a tale of creative aspiration and doctrinaire neglect, of
condescension and prejudice, of dedication and payola, of talent,
trash, and many turns of taste, but in an over-all view, of the development of an amazingly varied and appealing body of song that has
gradually moved away from the cliché towards a more realistic
and artistic expression of human values. It is a more vulgar, but
also a more vital, body of song than the genteel arbiters of taste
would have it — and its influence abroad is so great precisely because it has been so spontaneous and unashamed in embodying the
romantic dreams, the anxieties, the fulfillment and the frustrations,
as well as the crazy fads and playful moments, of the American
people, or, more specifically, of each courting and dancing generation of the American people.

When *Old Folks at Home* appeared in 1851, the title page
indicated that it was "written and composed by E. P. Christy,"
impresario of the famous Christy Minstrels. So strong was the prejudice of "refined people" against "Ethiopian melodies" that the

real composer was at first ashamed to be associated with it. (A contemporary of Stephen Foster likened its melody to "a morbid irritation of the skin.") More than a century later, the latest type of "Ethiopian" song likewise is the subject of rancorous condemnation. These are significant historical markers, not only because 1961 is the year of the Civil War Centennial in the era of desegregation, but because the position of the Negro in American popular song is pivotal.

Harmonically, popular music is a product of the European "classical" diatonic system. Rhythmically, however, it stems largely from Afro-Cuban sources, and melodically, it is based on the Negro "blues" scale — what I would describe as a ten-note scale in which both the flattened third and seventh have been added to the regular major scale. The characteristic sounds and "feeling-tones" of many ethnic groups are to be heard in our popular music — the sadness of the Jews, the tender nostalgia of the Irish, the Italian love of soaring melody, the Latin American leaning towards contrapuntal rhythms. But the influence of no group has been as pervasive and as decisive, or as frequently denied and depreciated, as that of the American Negro. Whether one considers minstrelsy, ragtime, Dixieland jazz, swing, or rock 'n' roll, the Negro community has been the source of styles and forms that have given different eras their distinctive sound.

Unlike concert music, the development of popular music has been constantly affected during the past hundred years by changes in the media of entertainment. As the major means of song exposure shifted from the minstrel show to vaudeville, from radio and talking pictures to dance bands, from vocalists to records and disk jockeys, the character (also the life expectancy) of songs changed. During the latter half of the 19th century, the most popular form of entertainment was the minstrel show with its white man in blackface, its banjos, tambourines, and bones, its Negro dialect and plantation melodies, its semicircular arrangement of performers (the Interlocutor in the center and Mr. Tambo and Mr. Bones as endmen), and its varied specialty acts (olio) and finale (walkaround) Out of this original and uniquely American type of theater came three important song-writers: Daniel Decatur Emmett, the Bryant Minstrel who wrote *Dixie* as a walkaround; James A.

Bland, the Negro minstrel who wrote what is now the Virginia state song (*Carry Me Back to Old Virginny*) and who has only recently been rescued from obscurity; and, of course, Stephen Collins Foster, our first major song-writer.

The feeling for native material shown by these was not fashionable. So much of the song-writing of the day was modeled on an alien tradition that two early historians of our music, Frédéric Louis Ritter in 1884 and Louis C. Elson in 1904, both concluded that we had no "national people's music." They were wrong. Work songs, hollers, shouts, chain-gang songs, blues, spirituals, and gospel songs were being created by a hard-working folk. But limited transportation facilities and the immobility of a poor and enslaved people kept this music locked in the regions where it was created. Not until 1871, for example, when the Jubilee Singers of Fisk University went on a fund-raising tour, did the country as a whole, and Europe too, become aware of the existence, and then of the beauty and expressiveness, of the Negro spiritual.

The Civil War brought to the fore the considerable talents of two song-writers who were competitive to Stephen Foster. Both continued to write sacred songs and maudlin ballads into the seventies, long after Foster's improvident and lonely death in a New York hospital, and both were associated with the pioneer Chicago publishing firm of Root and Cady. George F. Root, whose brother founded the firm, was responsible for two of the war's great marching songs, *Battle Cry of Freedom* and *Tramp, Tramp, Tramp*, while Henry C. Work accounted for the equally stirring *Marching Through Georgia*. The liberation of the Negro from slavery not only opened the door to the industrialization of the United States; it also helped to free song-writing from the alien tradition with which it was saddled during the first half of the 19th century.

Less important to the post-Civil War song-writer than minstrelsy were the forms of musical entertainment known as the extravaganza and burlesque (then a theater of caricature and parody). *The Black Crook*, the big extravaganza of 1866 that ran for sixteen weeks, nevertheless contributed significantly to the development of musical comedy by its exposure of the female figure and the battle of the sexes (*You Naughty, Naughty Men*). Other signposts of the future are to be found in the satiric song sketches of Harrigan and Hart

(The Mulligan Guard), popular through the eighties, and in the burlesque comedy of Weber and Fields. By 1881, when New Yorkers were flocking to Tony Pastor's Variety Theatre on East 14th Street, vaudeville (the French term for variety) had evolved from the "olio" of the minstrel show and the variety performance whose main business had been to sell liquor. The song-writer had a new and more flexible vehicle for his wares.

* *
*

Song publishing began to take shape as "music biz" and eventually as Big Business in the 1890s. In Milwaukee, Charles K. Harris, who wrote *After the Ball*, the decade's biggest hit, advertised "Songs written to order." In Chicago, publisher Will Rossiter went from store to store demonstrating his songs at music counters. In New York, Edward B. Marks and Joseph Stern "contacted" a hundred beer halls and variety houses a week, plugging *The Little Lost Child* with the aid of singing waiters, colored slides that illustrated the lyric, and a whistler who distributed "chorus slips" bearing the words. Paul Dresser, a true apostle of sentimentality (and brother of the novelist Theodore Dreiser), left *The Banks of the Wabash* to come to New York, for Union Square with its cluster of music halls and new, aggressive publishing houses had emerged as the entertainment center of the country.

The so-called Gay Nineties was a period of two depressions, bank failures, nation-wide strikes, workers' marches, and bloodshed — not to mention a war memorialized in *There'll Be a Hot Time in the Old Town Tonight*. Oblivious of much of this, the song literature of the era was soaked in saccharine sentiment. Its point of view was largely that of the best-selling ladies' magazine of the day, Godey's *Lady's Book;* its basic concern the homely virtues; its aim, to touch the heart of the female discreetly. The major piece of furniture of a lady's parlor was still the piano, which she played and around which her beaux clustered in close harmony. (The pianola and divan came later.) The tenor of the weeping waltz-ballad tradition is suggested by songs like *Take Back Your Gold, She Is More to Be Pitied than Censured,* and *After the Ball*, which sold over two million copies and proved the big hit of the Chicago World's Fair.

It was at the Fair, held in 1893, that Americans in general first heard ragtime, as played by Scott Joplin and other Negro keyboard interpreters. Visitors were also thrilled by the band of John Philip Sousa, who was soon to write his masterpiece of patriotic fervor *Stars and Stripes Forever* and was well on his way to recognition as The March King. As later Paul Whiteman, so-called King of Jazz, was to give the dance band a concert sound, so Sousa gave the marching brass band a "symphonic" sound.

One of the things that made the Nineties gay was the "coon song." The number of tunes that used this opprobrious epithet — *All Coons Look Alike to Me* was written, not without later remorse, by Negro song-writer Ernest Hogan — indicate that it was a craze. Insofar as these songs helped perpetuate a stereotype evolved by the minstrel show and later exploited by the movies, one must view them with regret. But it seems clear from contemporary attacks by genteel publications like *Musical Courier* that they had an earthiness and vitality that made them popular as a reaction against the sentimental and moralizing ballads of the day.

*   *
*

America cakewalked and turkey-trotted into the 20th century to the syncopated rhythms of ragtime. Song publishers moved up to 28th Street between Fifth and Sixth Avenues, where Tin Pan Alley acquired its name. Ballroom dancing had its beginnings, while vaudeville, a staple of the American entertainment scene until the advent of the "talkies" in the late twenties, now became the song-writer's showcase as minstrelsy once had been. (Boys who served water during intermission, among them Willie Howard, were drafted as song pluggers.) Out of vaudeville came hits like Gus Edwards's famous song *School Days* (1907), which sold over three million copies. Publishers eagerly courted singers on the main circuits (Orpheum, Loew's, etc.), paying for scenery, arrangements, etc. Placing a song with an entertainer like Bert Williams, Eddie Leonard, Anna Held, or Nora Bayes meant a forty-week plug, with orders for sheet music pouring in from one city after another played by the touring act. Many of the decade's hit song-writers were famous vaudevillians, e.g. Joe Howard *(I Wonder Who's Kissing Her Now)* and Cole and Johnson *(Under the Bamboo Tree)*.

[144]

The years between the Spanish-American War and World War I were years of jangling optimism. Marked by a sense of "manifest destiny," they found ebullient expression in the personality and work of that Yankee doodle dandy, George M. Cohan. His ascent to the role of song laureate of World War I *(Over There, Give My Regards to Broadway,* etc.) was as natural as it seemed inevitable. If Cohan, born appropriately on the 4th of July, projected the feeling of patriotic nationalism that swept the land of Teddy Roosevelt, there were still the pens of Victor Herbert, Reginald DeKoven *(Robin Hood),* Gustave Ludens *(Prince of Pilsen),* Karl Hoschna, later Rudolf Friml and the early Sigmund Romberg, to continue the tradition of European operetta, *opéra bouffe,* and *opéra comique* in derivative American form.

A versatile and prolific contemporary of George M. Cohan was Harry Von Tilzer. Not unlike Monroe H. Rosenfeld (prototype of the song-writer as Broadway character), who is remembered less for his songs than his invention of the name "Tin Pan Alley," Von Tilzer, in whose office the cognomen was coined, became the prototype of the commercial writer, able to embody the mood, fad, or expression of the moment in a hit song. *A Bird in a Gilded Cage* continued the lachrymose waltz tradition. *Down Where the Wurzburger Flows,* which Nora Bayes plugged with Von Tilzer as singing stooge in a stage box, was a drinking song. *Wait Till the Sun Shines Nellie* became a "gang-song" favorite. *What You Goin' to Do When the Rent Comes 'Round* capitalized on the "coon song" craze while *Good-Bye Eliza Jane* was a ragtime adaptation.

The ballad tradition of Paul Dresser *(My Gal Sal)* and Charles K. Harris found more expansive and polished expression in the songs of Ernest R. Ball, whose first hit was characteristically called *Love Me and the World Is Mine.* Curiously, this song and another Ball perennial, *Till the Sands of the Desert Grow Cold,* employ a triplet figure that was to become a staple of rock 'n' roll. Trained at the Cleveland Conservatory, Ball worked as a staff writer at Witmark and produced, along with such hits as *Let the Rest of the World Go By,* a group of Irish ballad favorites, including the inescapable *Mother Machree.*

Towards the end of the decade a song-writer appeared who combined the versatility of Von Tilzer and the polish of Ball, and who

[145]

brought song-writing to a level of expressiveness that has made him the most successful writer through more than forty years of popular music. A self-educated product of Tin Pan Alley, Irving Berlin worked as a singing waiter in a Chinatown saloon, plugged Von Tilzer's songs in the balcony of Tony Pastor's Music Hall, and has remained unable to play piano in more than one key to this day. Yet he was able to change with the many shifts in taste from 1910 to 1955 and to write both words and music for hits in many different genres, including the screen and Broadway (*Annie Get Your Gun, Call Me Madam,* etc.). The most performed song-writer of our time — he stood at the top of ASCAP's charts for years with, but above, Cole Porter — Berlin launched his long list of best-sellers in 1911 with two ragtime hits.

Because of the persistent popularity of *Alexander's Ragtime Band* and *Everybody's Doin' It,* people sometimes assume that ragtime began with these songs. But in actuality the style was a regional Negro music all through the nineties with roots in the syncopated rhythms of banjo minstrelsy and colored marching bands. By 1897 it began to assume the proportions of a national craze. Two years later, the first big ragtime hit made its appearance in a piano piece, *Maple Leaf Rag,* named after the Sedalia (Mo.) club where Scott Joplin, its composer, performed. After the turn of the century, the craze leaped the Atlantic and caught Europe up in its jangling dissonances and rhythms. Soon it found expression in the flashy personality and pianistics of Mr. Jelly Roll Morton of New Orleans and, later, in the clowning and the compositions of Thomas "Fats" Waller *(Honeysuckle Rose).* For almost twenty years (1897-1917), the rag occupied a central position in popular music, inflaming even the imaginations of many august composers. Igor Stravinsky composed *Ragtime* in 1920.

At the height of the craze, attempts were made to deny Negro musicians their role in fathering the style. Critics either found that it was not new or tracked its sources back to Scottish tunes, Cuban dances, Hungarian gypsy music, etc. Ben Harney, a white pianist who wrote *Ragtime Instructor* (1897) and whose performances at Keith's in New York helped trigger the craze, frequently billed himself as even his headstone reads, "Creator of Ragtime." But on at least one occasion, Harney admitted that the style was "the contribution of the graduated Negro banjo-player who cannot read music ... [and who] is playing two different times [rhythms] at once."

That ragtime caught and expressed the bouncy, "muscular" spirit of the pre-World War I period now seems unquestioned. But at the turn of the century, it roared into the arena of popular music, upsetting the arbiters of taste much as did the group of writers castigated by Theodore Roosevelt as "muckrakers." At the very beginning of the craze, *Musical Courier* chided the "fashionable idle folk" of Newport for their shocking interest in "degenerate music" (meaning ragtime) and the "sex dance" (meaning the cakewalk). Using epithets like "vulgar," "filthy," "suggestive," and "nigger music," the *Courier* stated: "It is a well-known physiological fact that a superior race may not mingle with an inferior without causing degeneration, debasement." Two years later, in 1901, *Metronome* announced that "ragtime had come to the end of its rope." This was not the last time that predictions regarding the demise of a musical style were, like notice of Mark Twain's death, circulated prematurely. The vogue of ragtime persisted until America's entry into the War in 1917, which was also the year that the "King of Ragtime Composers," Scott Joplin, died. But the impact of ragtime was to be felt into the twenties, when Zez Confrey produced resounding hits in *Kitten on the Keys* and *Stumbling*. And echoes of its rhythms are to be heard in young George Gershwin's first enduring hit, *Swanee*, introduced by Al Jolson in *Sinbad* in 1920.

*   *
*

In the year that America entered the War and women began knitting socks and sweaters for the boys over there, King Oliver and his trumpet migrated up the Mississippi to Chicago — he was joined later by Louis "Satchmo" Armstrong — while the Original Dixieland Jazz Band went from Chicago to Reisenweber's on Columbus Circle, there to launch the noisy era of hot jazz. It was the age of "the lost generation" and Sigmund Freud, of speakeasies and gang killings, of Rudolph Valentino and the Red Scare, of *Yes, We Have No Bananas* and e. e. cummings, of Ernest Hemingway, the hip flask, and the hijacker. F. Scott Fitzgerald, who drank and danced the disillusioning days away with the best of them, called it The

[147]

Jazz Age. It was a golden age of literature and popular song.

If American fiction acquired new dimensions through the works of Dreiser, Sinclair Lewis, Sherwood Anderson, Willa Cather, etc., so song-writing rose to new creative heights with the work of Vincent Youmans, Cole Porter, the Gershwins, Otto Harbach, Oscar Hammerstein II, Jerome Kern, and Rodgers and Hart, who began their careers as the American Gilbert and Sullivan in 1925. The musical theater flourished as it never has since, producing hit after hit *(Tea for Two, The Man I Love, Who, What Is This Thing Called Love,* etc.), delving into new American themes *(Show Boat* and *A Connecticut Yankee),* building towards the first Pulitzer Prize musical *(Of Thee I Sing* in 1931), and pointing the way towards the integrated musical plays of the forties and fifties. There were more revues on Broadway than at any other time, with Earl Carroll, George White, the Shuberts, and the great Ziegfeld all striving to glorify (and undress) the female figure to the accompaniment of bright music, high kicking, and low comedy. But there were also little revues like *The Grand Street Follies, The Garrick Gaieties,* and *The Little Shows* that were fired by the intellectual non-conformism of H. L. Mencken and his satiric thrusts at the American "booboisie."

Popular-song production outside the theater also flourished as Paul Whiteman, Eddie Cantor, Harry Richman, Vincent Lopez (of *Nola* fame), Sophie Tucker, the last of the red-hot mamas, and Al Jolson, the first and the greatest of mammy singers, became important "plugs" and hitmakers. The gap between show music and Tin Pan Alley (whose locale had moved uptown above Times Square) was not as great as it has been since. The team of De Sylva, Brown, and Henderson produced hit songs in the theater *(Good News)* and in the movies *(Sonny Boy),* as well as outside both media *(Together).* So did Irving Berlin, who came up with an amazing succession of ballads *(All Alone, Always, What'll I Do, Blue Skies);* so, too, did the new giant of the hit ballad, Walter Donaldson.

Little known to the general public, although he had quite a reputation as a "character" inside the business, Donaldson was responsible for *Little White Lies, You're Driving Me Crazy, At Sundown, Yes, Sir, That's My Baby* (with prolific lyricist Gus Kahn), *My*

[148]

Mammy (the great vehicle of Al Jolson in blackface and on one supplicating knee), and *My Blue Heaven* (which yielded, in Gene Austin's Victor disc, one of the first million-copy sellers). Another major producer of hits was Richard Whiting, whose career began with *Till We Meet Again* (1918) and whose output included such characteristic songs of the twenties as *Ain't We Got Fun, Ukulele Lady,* and the still popular torch ballad *She's Funny That Way.*

Harlem became a mecca for young whoopee-makers, as Duke Ellington held forth at the Cotton Club and drummer Chick Webb, who later wrote *Stompin' at the Savoy* with Benny Goodman, kept the flappers jumping at the Savoy Ballroom. The middle generation danced to the "Mickey Mouse" bands of Wayne King and Guy Lombardo, who played what the swingsters soon were to deride as "the business man's bounce" and whose brand of corny music made a million-dollar TV attraction of Lawrence Welk in the fifties.

This was the beginning of the era of "the No. 1 plug," when each publishing house selected the one song of many that was to be promoted into a hit by concentrated plugging and when ASCAP, founded in 1914, began to make song-writing a remunerative and an honorable profession. In 1921 ASCAP made its first distribution, paying out a total of nearly $82,000. By 1955 Irving Berlin was alone to collect more than that sum as part of the annual melon, which in 1959 totalled twenty-four million dollars and was divided among a membership of 5,500 composers and authors and 1,500 publishers. Since the competing performing rights society, BMI, distributed eleven million dollars among its 4,400 writer members and 3,400 publishers in 1959, the total performance take had risen to thirty-five million dollars.

The twenties were a dazzling era when song-writers became imbued with a desire, not only to create hits, but to grow and produce lasting works. While Aaron Copland, George Antheil, Louis Gruenberg, and other "serious" composers used the rhythms and colors of jazz, George Gershwin (and Ferde Grofé in his *Grand Canyon Suite*) struggled manfully to avail themselves of the resources of classical form and the symphony orchestra. The historic Paul Whiteman concert of February 12, 1924, for which Gershwin wrote his world-famous *Rhapsody in Blue,* projected him in a direction that soon yielded the more ambitious Concerto in F, commissioned for the

New York Symphony Orchestra by its conductor, Walter Damrosch.

Whiteman's "Experiment in Modern Music," which was hardly a resounding critical or financial success, served two other purposes. Despite the frigidity of many critics, more than a passing question was raised as to the legitimacy of the hard distinction between popular and "serious" music, since erased many times but still not completely eliminated. This was a positive contribution. But the Whiteman program also served to promulgate a confusion between jazz and popular music that has persisted with some historians right up to the present moment. A contemporary critic suggested that Whiteman made a lady of jazz, while another credited him with adding sophistication to her. It was not an unnatural confusion, since the Whiteman band on stage included a number of outstanding jazzmen. But the truth is that the so-called "King of Jazz" had given concert polish and dimension, through the arranging genius of Ferde Grofé, not to jazz, but to popular song and ballroom dance music.

Jazz as such was to be heard in the "unbuttoned" two-beat music played by small Dixieland combos like Red Nichols and His Five Pennies and Louis Armstrong's Hot Five. It was happy music, spontaneously improvised, whose characteristic sound came from the independent interplay of three melody instruments — cornet, clarinet, and trombone. This was the music that was characterized by Daniel Gregory Mason of Columbia University as "a commotion without purpose" and attacked by the Rev. John Roach Stratton from his pulpit as "music of the savage, intellectual and spiritual debauchery, utter degradation." "Flaming youth" paid little heed to such fulminations, dancing out its new-found freedoms and postwar frenzies to the rhythms of the Charleston, the Shimmy, the Black Bottom, and the Varsity Drag.

A major song-writer in the Dixieland tradition was Spencer Williams, who began his keyboard career in one of New Orleans's licensed bordellos — later celebrated by him in the well-known *Mahogany Hall Stomp* — and who manned "the eighty-eight" at Bricktop's fashionable club in Paris in the twenties. Born on the jazz street that he remembered in *Basin Street Blues*, "The Blue Boy of New Orleans" was responsible for such great Dixieland standards as *Shim-Me-Sha-Wabble, I Found a New Baby, Everybody Loves*

My Baby, and *Twelfth Street Rag.*

The northward migration of Negro musicians, which turned into a flood in 1917 with the Army's closing of Storyville (New Orleans's center of legalized prostitution), brought not only two-beat jazz into the mainstream of American popular music, but also the blues. The now classic *St. Louis Blues* of W. C. Handy had appeared in 1914. In 1918 Spencer Williams wrote *Tishomingo Blues* and the following year, *Royal Garden Blues.* But it was not until the twenties that white writers began to make use of the twelve-bar form and chord sequence. In view of the feelings of despair, disillusionment, and dislocation that marked the era of the lost generation, it is not strange that the blues took hold. For the blues — whether self-pity is present as the historian John Tasker Howard claims or absent as the semanticist S. I. Hayakawa asserts — are, above all, songs of endurance. Their appeal is in the combination of major-minor modes, and, as has not been pointed out, in the bi-polar expression of courage in the face of despair, hope in the face of frustration, determination in the face of defeat, the two moods playing one against the other.

What the Negro musician did not bring to the north, white folklorists and recording executives went south to find. Columbia began its series of "race" records with songs by the famous Empress of the Blues, Bessie Smith, while Ralph Peer made on-the-spot recordings for Victor of rural blues singers like Blind Lemon Jefferson and railroad brakeman Jimmie Rodgers, regarded as the pioneer of white country singers. Between 1918 and 1926 no less than twelve collections of Negro spirituals were put into print, and in 1927 Carl Sandburg published *The American Songbag,* the first of many folksong anthologies to make the general public conscious of its rich heritage. (The valuable collections of the Lomaxes came mainly in the forties.) While it was an era highly productive of new talent, many collectors sought to mine the golden ore of the past.

* *

*

During the depression years, popular music suffered a dislocation that was not economic so much as geographical. For almost forty years, even though the focus of plugging had changed several times and publishing offices had gradually moved uptown — they were now almost all concentrated in one building, the Brill, at 49th and Broadway — Tin Pan Alley meant Manhattan. Now, electronics created two new hit-making media, which shifted the fulcrum of activity westward.

In 1927 a pretty waltz, *Charmaine*, interpolated in the film *What Price Glory*, became an almost overnight hit. The following year, the screen accounted for a flock of bestsellers while in '29 Nacio Herb Brown alone had screen hits in *Singin' in the Rain, You Are My Lucky Star*, and *Pagan Love Song*. As the stock market crashed in October, the Hollywood Gold Rush was on. One well-known song-writer after another rushed to the coast, attracted by offers of large guarantees and high salaries. Some writers like Jimmy McHugh and Dorothy Fields (who wrote the all-Negro hit revue *Blackbirds of 1928)* and Harry Warren *(Cheerful Little Earful*, etc.) settled permanently in the movie capital. George Gershwin himself died in Hollywood in '37 while at work on *The Goldwyn Follies*. Publishers began to open Hollywood offices as the prices paid by the movie companies to interpolate music (synchronization fees) rose. In turn, the picture companies began buying up Broadway publishing houses. Three of the oldest catalogues, Harms, Remick, and Witmark, were purchased by Warner Brothers while M-G-M took over Leo Feist, Robbins, and Miller Music. Although the Alley was beginning to disperse geographically, control of the music market (the number of publishers with hits) seemed to tighten in this era. The nation's golden songs came regularly from such "silver screen" teams as Kalmar and Ruby *(Three Little Words*, 1930), Gordon and Revel *(Stay as Sweet as You Are*, 1934), Robin and Rainger *(Thanks for the Memory*, 1938), and Burke and Van Heusen *(Swinging on a Star*, 1944, and a flock of Bing Crosby hits).

Despite the westward trek of song-writers, the Broadway musical theater made significant forward strides. Early in the thirties a new edition of *The Garrick Gaieties* brought to light the double-barreled talents of Vernon Duke, who was born Vladimir Dukelsky and who had begun his career as a "serious" composer. Duke was to continue functioning in the symphonic-concerto-ballet field for which study at the Kiev Conservatory had prepared him, at the same time that he wrote such hits as *Autumn in New York*, the polytonal *April in*

Paris (from *Walk a Little Faster*), and the jazz perennial *I Can't Get Started With You*. In 1931 Broadway theatergoers saw *The Bandwagon*, an imaginative revue which offered the best score of Howard Dietz and Arthur Schwartz (*Dancing in the Dark* and other hits). In 1934 Cole Porter produced what is frequently regarded as his masterpiece, *Anything Goes*, bringing a rare talent for clever lyrics and fresh, sophisticated melodies to a new peak of perfection. The original production of *Porgy and Bess*, the great achievement of George Gershwin's musical majority and now universally recognized as "America's greatest piece of stage music," came in 1935. In '36 Rodgers and Hart's *On Your Toes* became the first Broadway musical to use genuine choreography (in place of Radio City high kicking): it incorporated ballet sequences by George Balanchine to advance the story line.

Top hits of the thirties, without benefit of either the screen or the Broadway stage, included Hoagy Carmichael's perennial *Star Dust*, originally composed as a ragtime piano piece but furnished with lyrics by Mitchell Parish; *Blue Moon*, the only "pop song" written by Rodgers and Hart, with a chord line that became a basic framework of rock 'n' roll ballads; and *Deep Purple*, a haunting Peter de Rose tune to which Mitchell Parish added purple lyrics.

The dispersion of Tin Pan Alley in the thirties was promoted by another development — the rise of the radio networks. NBC was formed in '26 and CBS in '27. Together with the film theme song, the coast-to-coast network show now became the crux of the publisher's plugging activity. The new gods of popular music were Bing Crosby (co-writer of his radio theme song *When the Blue of the Night Meets the Gold of the Day*), Kate Smith (co-writer of *When the Moon Comes Over the Mountain*), Russ Columbo (co-writer of *I'm Just a Prisoner of Love*), and Rudy Vallee (co-writer of *I'm Just a Vagabond Lover*) and his megaphone. In the heyday of vaudeville, publishers had bought scenery for touring acts. In the twenties, various bandleaders were reputedly on the payrolls of leading publishing houses. In the thirties, one heard more and more of the "cut-in," of vocalists with network shows who contributed second verses, à la Jolson, to songs that did not have them.

By 1932 the Palace, the mecca of vaudeville acts the world over, had become a movie house; the song plugger was becoming a "contact man"; and many publishers supported offices in Chicago and other key cities to make direct contact with local bands that had become exposure media through "remotes," programs picked up locally for network circulation. The first Oscar for a screen song hit was awarded in '34 and *Your Hit Parade* began a twenty-year run on radio in '35.

Although it has been maintained that the history of a country is written in its popular songs, American song-writers have not been too responsive to sociological developments, except, perhaps, for wars. The depression, however, found expression in songs like *Brother Can You Spare a Dime* (E. Y. Harburg and Jay Gorney) and *I've Got Five Dollars* (Rodgers and Hart); also in several musicals, *The Cradle Will Rock* by Mark Blitzstein and *Pins and Needles*, a revue produced in 1937 by the Ladies Garment Workers Union, which ran for a record-breaking 1108 performances and launched Harold J. Rome on his show-writing career.

A development perhaps not unrelated to the tensions of the depression was the formation in 1931 of the Songwriters Protective Association (now the American Guild of Authors and Composers). An initial membership of 50 has grown through the years to over 2,000 as more and more publishers (now close to 1,000) have agreed to use the contract, highly advantageous to the song-writer, developed by the Guild.

The thirties brought an influx, too, of Latin-American songs and dances, which acquainted us with the works of Agustin Lara out of Mexico and the Cuban Ernesto Lecuona of *Malagueña* fame. In 1929, with Lecuona's *Siboney*, Americans took up the rhumba, initiating a tendency to turn southward for new dance rhythms. The following year *The Peanut Vendor* of Moises Simon and *Mama Inez* of Eliseo Grenet became the first big Latin hits. Maria Grever was later responsible for *What a Difference a Day Made*, a song that went through several revivals. By 1937 the conga, a Cuban carnival dance introduced by Desi Arnaz, was popular with American dancers and in the forties, bandleader Perez Prado helped make a hit of the mambo, also from Cuba. During the middle forties the samba was brought from Brazil by Carmen Miranda and went through a short-lived popularity. More recently, we have imported the merengue from the Dominican Republic and the cha-cha-cha from Cuba, the latter currently enjoying the favor of teen-agers in the form of the "rock-cha-cha."

In actuality, the tango was the first Latin dance to become an American craze. It was in the pre-World War I era of the Dancing Castles, when Negro bandleaders Jim Europe and Ford Dabney were writing *The Castle Walk, The Castle Classic Waltz,* and *The Castle Tango.* Americans heard the distinctive rhythms of the habanera (out of Havana) in W. C. Handy's *Memphis Blues* (1912) and in the more famous *St. Louis Blues* (1914). In the twenties the tango enjoyed a revival when Rudolph Valentino magnetized American women with his dancing in *The Four Horsemen of the Apocalypse.* But the tango was too stately and, like the samba, too demanding to catch on, as did the rhumba and cha-cha-cha. The reasons why this Latin strain persists in our music, other than the influx of musicians like Xavier Cugat, Noro Morales, and Machito and the attractiveness of Afro-Cuban rhythms to our jazz musicians, are a subject for future research.

*   *

*

It was a coast-to-coast NBC show, *Let's Dance,* that ushered in the swing era, helped make Benny Goodman the King of Swing, and launched a dance craze that led to the proliferation of as many as a hundred big dance bands. As with ragtime and Dixieland, the impetus for the chugging, blasting, four-beats-to-the-bar music came from Negro musicians. Long before the white bands of the decade ('36-'45) made a type of jazz into the popular music of the nation, the bands of Chick Webb, Jimmy Lunceford, Fletcher Henderson, Count Basie, and others were playing swing. In fact, the very arrangements Fletcher Henderson made for his own comparatively unsuccessful band became the basis of the Goodman library. The swing era was also the era of the New Deal — the connection between the two needs study — and a growingly optimistic generation of bobby-soxers and jitterbugs added the Shag and the Big Apple, a circular "square dance," to the bouncy Lindy.

In 1937 the appearance of Benny Goodman at the Paramount brought frenzied dancing in the aisles. Soon there were the bands of Larry Clinton with *The Dipsy Doodle,* Tommy Dorsey with *Marie,* Artie Show with a double-faced hit recording of *Begin the*

[155]

Beguine and Glenn Miller with *In the Mood*. Out of the Goodman band itself — which broke down the color line in public appearances — came the bands of Gene Krupa, Lionel Hampton, Teddy Wilson, and Harry James. (Cloak-and-suiters even today use the expression "a Benny Goodman" to mean a maneuver in which employees go into business for themselves.)

Taking off from a "lick" that Goodman's high-flying trumpeter Ziggy Elman used, Johnny Mercer wrote *And the Angels Sing* in 1939. It was the beginning of a period in Mercer's career that produced such hits as *Blues in the Night, That Old Black Magic,* and *Ac-cent-tchu-ate the Positive,* all written with the able Harold Arlen, whose feeling for Negro folk music found climactic expression in the hit musical *St. Louis Woman* (1946), also a Mercer-Arlen collaboration. The same period saw the emergence of Kurt Weill, a German emigré whose scores for *Knickerbocker Holiday, Lady in the Dark,* and *One Touch of Venus* yielded brooding hits like *September Song* and *Speak Low,* and paved the way for the aspiring but less than successful musical drama *Street Scene* (1947). Weill was one of the rare composers of Broadway musicals who orchestrate their own scores.

Along with swing, 1936 brought the revival of a form of piano blues known as boogie woogie. Popular in Chicago during the twenties — "Pine Top" Smith recorded his famous *Boogie* in 1928 — boogie woogie is marked by the use of an eight-to-the-bar ostinato figure in the left hand. Four men made it into a national craze during Franklin D. Roosevelt's second term. Three were pianists: Pete Johnson of Kansas City, who had accompanied blues singer Joe Turner; and Albert Ammons and Mead Lux Lewis, both of whom had played Chicago "rent parties" to prevent evictions. The fourth was jazz impresario John Hammond, important in the careers of Benny Goodman and Count Basie, who went searching for Ammons and Lewis as the result of an old record. Lewis was working in a Chicago garage when Hammond located and brought both of them to New York. Overnight, they became the rage of Café Society.

During the swing era ASCAP and the country's broadcasters came to a showdown, which kept ASCAP music off the air for most of 1941 and saw the formation of a competing performing rights society, Broadcast Music Incorporated. By that time France had been invaded by Hitler, and Oscar Hammerstein II and Jerome Kern had written the enduring *The Last Time I Saw Paris*, America's entry into World War II was a matter of months, and before long the troops at home and abroad had made a smash of Irving Berlin's *White Christmas* (1942). The same year brought *The White Cliffs of Dover* and *When the Lights Go On Again*. The biggest record and sheet music seller of the following year turned out surprisingly to be *There's a Star Spangled Banner Waving Somewhere*, a patriotic number with a distinct hillbilly flavor. It foreshadowed the postwar emergence of country music into the main stream of popular music.

In 1944 Benny Goodman signalized the end of an era by dissolving his band. The kids were no longer dancing; instead, they just hung aimlessly around the bandstands. Now one swing band after another went down like ninepins in a bowling alley, partly as a result of wartime shortages of cars and gas, which kept customers at home and bands off the road, also presumably as a result of the wartime shortage of men, which kept the girls off the dance floor.

* *

*

The shift in taste that came with the end of the war was indicated by a change in record label credits. Whereas in the swing era labels read: "HARRY JAMES and HIS ORCHESTRA. Vocal by F. Sinatra," now the billing was to be reversed. The Paramount Panic of '43, in which bobby-soxers squealed and swooned over The Voice, revealed that the era of the big, blasting bands was at an end. Soon song pluggers were "romancing" not the bandleaders, but romantic crooners like Perry Como, Dick Haymes, Eddy Howard, Vic Damone, Nat "King" Cole, et al. Accompaniment was provided by large, string-dominated orchestras, led by schooled arrangers like Axel Stordahl, Percy Faith, Gordon Jenkins, Mitch Ayres, and Hugo Winterhalter.

The Voice added a new dimension to the art of popular singing but he also helped give new dimensions to the craft of popular song-writing. Severely critical of lyrics, as was Bing Crosby before him, he sang with an expressiveness and a feeling for words that was both a joy and a challenge to post-war song scribes. Among others, Frank Loesser, Sammy Cahn, Paul Francis Webster, Johnny

[157]

Burke, Jack Lawrence, Ray Evans, walking in the footsteps of the literate Hart, Harbach, and Berlin, brought lyric writing to a new level in sensibility while melodies revealed a new richness and depth (*Tenderly, Laura,* David Rose's *Holiday for Strings*). Sinatra early showed a sensitivity to the changing vocal colors and the pulsating phrasing of jazz singers like Ella Fitzgerald and Billie Holiday, which led him after a period of decline to re-emerge in the middle fifties as one of the great song stylists of our time — a jazz-oriented singer's singer who "swings with strings," and whose influence is to be felt in the orientation even of new teen-age idols like Bobby Darin. But during the forties he dominated the vocal scene with romantic ballads, sung at slow tempos to soft, a-rhythmic backgrounds. *All or Nothing at All* and *You'll Never Know* were his first hits, followed by a series of Sammy Cahn-Juley Styne ballads, among them *I'll Walk Alone* (while the soldiers were away) and *It's Been a Long, Long Time* (after they returned).

Just about the time that Sinatra appeared on the music scene, one of the country's most brilliant lyricists and one of its finest melodists died, and an outstanding new songwriting team was born. The melodist was Jerome Kern, whose death in '45 ended a career of hit-writing that included *Smoke Gets in Your Eyes, Ol' Man River, The Way You Look Tonight, Long Ago and Far Away,* and an amazing list of unforgettable melodies. The lyricist was Larry Hart, whose eighteen-year collaboration with Richard Rodgers had helped make an American Gilbert and Sullivan of Rodgers and Hart, and whose level of artistry as a creator of witty, deftly-rhymed verse was to be approached only by Cole Porter. The new-born team was Rodgers and Hammerstein, a collaboration begun in '43 just before the death of Hart with the hit-laden score of *Oklahoma!* (the second musical to win a Pulitzer Prize) and destined to yield such exciting achievements of the musical theater as *Carousel, South Pacific,* and *The King and I.*

Between '47 and '50 Broadway saw at least three other shows that were high-water marks of the musical theater. The romantic fantasy *Brigadoon* revealed the capacious talents of Lerner and Loewe, later responsible for *My Fair Lady* and the Academy Award winner *Gigi.* Another fantasy, *Finian's Rainbow* by E. Y. Harburg and Burton Lane, offered a tuneful treatment of racial discrimination and

[158]

proved its point by using a mixed cast. *Guys and Dolls*, likewise a musical with more than the customary complement of hit songs, was Frank Loesser's masterful projection of the oddball world of Damon Runyon.

In 1943 Duke Ellington, regarded by many as the foremost figure in jazz if not one of the most original minds in American music, gave the first of a series of Carnegie Hall concerts. The Duke, whose song hits include inventive melodies like *Sophisticated Lady, Mood Indigo*, and *Caravan*, had previously attempted excursions in the field of extended form (*Black and Tan Fantasy*). The annual Carnegie Hall concerts from 1943 to 1950 led to the writing of a series of long works, the most interesting and expressive of which is *Black, Brown and Beige*.

By 1947 the vocal pendulum began to swing from the soft crooners to the hard "belters." It was the year when a demonstrative singer named Frankie Laine arrived on the scene with *That's My Desire*, a song whose sensual lyric (written in 1931) heralded the coming of a new era of realism. By the fifties, veiled references to romance via nature imagery yielded to the actuality of sex, the artificial dramatics gave way to true tension and conflict. The school of belters included female vocalists like Teresa Brewer (*Music, Music*) and Georgia Gibbs (*Kiss of Fire*), as well as male vocalists like Eddie Fisher and Johnny Ray, of whom the last-mentioned carried Laine's muscularity to a new peak of exhibitionism with a song called *Cry*.

In '47 the outlines of a new medium of plugging songs also became apparent. Soon the record would be the thing and music business would lavish most of its promotional budget on a new figure known as the disk jockey. As more and more local stations shifted to a format of spinning records between dull news reports, inaccurate weather forecasts, and bellowed or singing commercials (radio networks also went thataway when the big ad budgets went to TV), vocalists and the recording companies themselves became dependent on the whims of the Knights of the Turntable. (The free professional copy and stock orchestration, so necessary in the era of the No. 1 plug, virtually disappeared as control of the music market shifted from the publisher to the record company, and the contact man began to carry a disc instead of a printed copy.)

The post-war years also saw the spread of a type of song whose vogue was originally limited to the southeast and the midwest corn-belt. Nashville, Tenn. (Tin Pan Valley), tended to be the center of this music, largely because of *The Grand Ole Opry*, a program launched on WSM in 1925 and still be heard every Saturday night. The movement of rural people to urban areas, accelerated by the war, apparently helped create a nationwide market for Nashville singers like Marty Robbins, Eddy Arnold, Red Foley, Elton Britt, Roy Acuff, Hank Snow — also Hank Williams, whose short-lived career included song-writing of a high order (*Cold, Cold Heart, Your Cheatin' Heart*). The rise of country music was also promoted by the growth of Broadcast Music, Inc., for its older competitor ASCAP was not well represented either in this area or in rhythm-and-blues. After '53 these two types of song merged to create the popular music of a new generation of record buyers.

Along with the vogue of country music there was a revival of folk music through the efforts of singers like Burl Ives, Richard Dyer-Bennet, and a group called The Weavers, who made a hit of a Leadbelly waltz, *Good Night, Irene*. The folk tradition was to persist in popular music, later attaining new levels of artistry with the calypso songs of Harry Belafonte (*The Banana Boat Song*), the banjo-twanging Kingston Trio (*Tom Dooley*), and the collegiate Brothers Four (*Green Fields*).

As the forties came to a close, the jazz field was torn by at least two schisms. The new jazz fans, reacting to their elders' love for revived Dixieland, castigated them with the epithet "moldy figs." And a new school of Negro jazz artists, disillusioned by the war, their lack of opportunity, and the ability of white artists to capitalize commercially on their creations, sought to develop a style that "the whites could not steal." A music of surprise accents, "flatted fifths," and new polytonal chords, it became known as be-bop or simply bop. Bird, Diz, and Monk — i.e., Charles Parker, Dizzy Gillespie, Thelonious Monk — were its high priests. Louis Armstrong called it "the modern malice." Like its antithesis, cool jazz, it was played in clubs devoid of even postage-stamp dance floors, where the new fans came to "dig," not dance. Non-functional, it had either no beat or a very complex one. Together with the "beatless" vocal music of the time, it helped prepare the ground for the change of taste that occurred in the middle fifties. A new generation of youngsters that wanted to dance had to go elsewhere for its music.

          *   *

      *

They found it in what became known as rock 'n' roll, a type of vocal music which, like ragtime and swing before it, first developed within the Negro world. There it was fully grown by the 1940s and, carrying the marks of gospel music, was known as "rhythm and blues." Although white artists were harbingers of the development (Bill Haley and his Comets with *Rock Around the Clock* in '53, the Crewcuts with *Sh-Boom* in '54, and Elvis Presley with *Heartbreak Hotel* in '55), it was a period unlike the swing era, in that Negro artists did not turn over their product to whites but were themselves made welcome in the major white markets. Of equal significance, it was an era of teen-age buyers who were generation-conscious as no generation before them had been and who had enough spending money to enforce their young tastes.

Just as they questioned the authority of their elders, so the new buyers were quick to reject the older generation of singers. The hit-making powers of vocalists like Tony Martin, Jo Stafford, and Vaughn Monroe evaporated almost overnight. Young artists, some with limited voices and crude deliveries, became the rage. Small rhythm combos superseded the large string orchestras of the crooners and belters. Whining and twanging guitars replaced singing strings. Repetitive triplets became standard figuration and chords beyond the simple triad became suspect. Along with the hitmakers who had dominated the music scene, the older generation of arrangers, publishers, record manufacturers, and song-writers found themselves facing an uneven challenge in young competitors who talked and "felt" the musical language of the new generation. A group of established ASCAP writers, in fact, brought a still unsettled lawsuit charging monopoly and unfair competition against BMI, with whom most of the new writers and publishers had become affiliated. Major record companies began purchasing outside masters and retaining independent producers when their own well-schooled A & R (artist and repertoire) staffs proved unable to produce hits.

[161]

It was an era of major dislocation for music business. Soon, it was apparent that the music market was sharply split three ways: an older generation that bought nostalgia (in LP's made by artists of its courting days); a college generation that bought either hard bop (Sunny Rollins, John Coltrane) or cool, cerebral, chamber music jazz (Dave Brubeck, Miles Davis, the Modern Jazz Quartet); and the teen-agers who were buying their own togetherness in the new rock 'n' roll single discs.

Rock 'n' roll brought with it a further dispersion of writers and publishers that virtually removed Tin Pan Alley from New York. Now, publishing houses, recording companies, recording artists, and, of course, writers were to be found spread out all over the map of the United States. But there was also a movement towards centralization. The major film companies, some of whom had previously entered the publishing business, now went into the recording business en masse. Paramount bought Dot Records of Tennessee, while Warner Brothers, United Artists, and 20th Century-Fox all formed their own record companies. At the same time, Music Corporation of America, the biggest of the talent agencies, and Desilu, the biggest of the TV studios, established publishing outlets through which they could control the theme songs and background music of their TV productions. These developments, along with the mounting sales of LP albums in a market that saw dwindling single record sales, suggest that popular music may be headed towards a package business not unlike the rest of American industry.

From an esthetic standpoint, the sharp shift in taste has its positive as well as negative aspects. One can dismiss the usual animadversions against the corrupting influence of rock 'n' roll. More acceptable is the claim that this is an era of the recording engineer rather than the recording artist, when tape reverb, echo chambers, the overdub, and tape splice electronically create performances that can never be duplicated alive. Yet it is hard to question the vocal artistry and possibly enduring showmanship of such young stars as Bobby Darin, Ray Charles, Johnny Mathis, Brenda Lee, Brook Benton, Connie Francis, also Paul Anka, who, like Fats Domino, has written all of his own song hits (*Diana, Lonely Boy, Put Your Head on My Shoulder*, etc.). Nor can one readily discount the songwriting talent of the new, young team of Jerry Lieber and Mike

Stoller, whose numerous hits include that probing expression of teen-age rebellion, *Yakety Yak*. It is interesting to note that rock 'n' roll brought with it a destruction of the thirty-two-bar form which had dominated popular song-writing since the turn of the century; also that just as contemporary European concert music has explored odd-numbered patterns and rhythms, so the new rock 'n' roll song forms and rhythm patterns increasingly employ odd-numbered formations. Unquestionably, this is an era of primitivism, when crudeness is accepted as an indication of deep feelings and sincerity. But it is also an era in which song-writing has been stripped almost completely of all vestiges of Victorianism and has moved towards the directness of expression, the precise imagery, and the realism of folk literature.

Nor can one question the esthetic fitness of a period that has seen not only the amazing development that jazz has undergone, but such productions as *Fiorello!*, the fourth musical to win the Pulitzer Prize and the work of a new team of writers, Jerry Bock and Sheldon Harnick; *My Fair Lady*, perhaps the most literary and best integrated musical that has appeared on Broadway; and that triumph of contemporary ballet and juvenile tragedy, *West Side Story*. Mention of the last-named reminds us of the presence on the popular music scene of the remarkably versatile conductor of the New York Philharmonic Orchestra, Leonard Bernstein, responsible with Betty Comden and Adolph Green for such Broadway successes as *On the Town* and *Wonderful Town*. In considering the popular musical picture, some critics would obviously prefer to separate the work of Bernstein from the teen-age songs that jostle his *Maria* (as recorded by Johnny Mathis) on the airwaves. However, it would seem clear that just as the world of "serious" music must accept George Gershwin, the Tin Pan Alley song plugger who contributed at least two major works to its repertory, so popular music, snobbish in its own inverted way, must accept the symphony conductor and composer who represents the process in reverse.

*　　*

*

The effort to keep music compartmentalized and to establish two separate streams, one popular and the other "serious," concert, or "classical," is one of several destructive tendencies with which the development of popular music has been beset. As far back as 1930 Isaac Goldberg sounded audacious in asking: "How far removed from the spirit of a classical scherzo is a good rag?" Even earlier, in November 1923, Eva Gauthier devoted a section of an Aeolian Hall concert to songs by Berlin, Kern, Walter Donaldson, and Gershwin, and used the last-named as her accompanist. Nevertheless, in his study of *Our American Music* published in 1939, John Tasker Howard concluded: "The line between popular music and art music remains sharply drawn, even after the many fusions of the two styles that have been made during the last twenty years."

Today, the wall between the two fields still remains standing, although there are widening cracks in it. Recently, Douglas Moore observed that "Europeans who have always liked our popular music have discovered that we have several composers in the serious field well worth their attention . . ." It is hard to discover the purpose of the separation, although in the minds of those who seek to perpetuate it there is probably the same fear of the hybrid as among those favoring segregation. Fortunately, this snobbery has prevented neither Gershwin from moving "upward" nor Bernstein from moving "downward." But there are serious consequences for scholars, historians, and critics, many of whom pay little heed to developments in popular music and consequently blunder when they feel compelled to deal with it.

A related destructive tendency is the condescension that has surrounded the field of popular music. Popular song has suffered from the stereotype, which has made loose ladies of actresses, dope addicts of jazz musicians, and drunkards of reporters and song-writers. More significantly, the craft, the profession, the art, and the average song-writer have all been constantly on the defensive. "We depend largely on tricks, we writers of songs," wrote Irving Berlin in 1916. "There's no such thing as a new melody." Ten years later Paul Whiteman confided to readers of his book on jazz: "Do you not know that more than half of the modern art of composing a popular song comes in knowing what to steal and how to adapt it — also, that at least 9/10 of modern jazz music turned out by Tin Pan Alley is frankly stolen from the masters?" In 1930, when Isaac Goldberg wrote an early history of Tin Pan Alley, he subtitled it: "A chronicle of the American popular music racket [!]" While this was an attempt to capitalize on a word that had much currency at the time, it also represented a concession Dr. Goldberg felt called upon to make to a public enjoying Ring Lardner's salty satire of popular music, *June Moon.*

Today, our attitude towards popular music is much changed. It had changed by 1945, when Sigmund Spaeth wrote in a revised edition of *Read 'em and Weep:* "In the past twenty years America's popular music has made such definite advances that it no longer deserves either a patronizing or a pitying approach." Since '45 popular music has made even greater strides. Yet it lingers in public esteem much behind its symbiotic sister, jazz, which has, within the past decade, been warmly received at home after a long and honorable sojourn in Europe. Within the past ten years American scholars have in growing numbers accorded jazz the objective and dedicated research that will eventually yield a full picture of its genesis, growth, and changing form.

To the historian, the biographer, the musicologist, and the student of theory, popular music today still offers almost unlimited areas and subjects for investigation. Among popular composers, only Gershwin, Foster, Duke Ellington, and Harrigan and Hart have been well researched. Biographies or autobiographies are available also on Berlin, Richard Rodgers, Kern, James Bland, Paul Dresser, Vernon Duke, Hoagy Carmichael, Harold Arlen, W. C. Handy, and Harry Ruby (scheduled). (Books abound on jazz vocalists and instrumentalists.) Among popular singers, there are published biographies or autobiographies only on Crosby, Vallee, Sinatra, Billie Holiday, Ethel Waters, and Lena Horne. Except for autobiographies by Charles K. Harris, Edward B. Marks, and Isidore Witmark, the growth of American song publishing is an uncharted field, nor has the relationship of publishing as a business to the development of the music been fully explored. Even the facts surrounding the coining of the name Tin Pan Alley have never been fully investigated. While there are several good accounts of the development of the record industry, the history of popular records still remains to be written.

The art of the lyric writer has been neglected even more than the work of the composers. Although collections of the lyrics of Hammerstein, Ira Gershwin, Cole Porter, and Larry Hart are available, historians and critics of the music pay scant attention to lyrics, while students of light verse seem to consider them outside their domain. Even the present paper has bypassed the novelty hits of each era — nonsense songs like *Flat Foot Floogie with the Floy Floy*, children's ditties like *Mairzy Doats*, sound-gimmick songs like *Open the Door, Richard* (knock, knock), which rely basically on an exercise of the lyric writer's craft and imagination.

In many ways the forgotten man of popular music is the arranger. From the days of Paul Whiteman onward, arrangers of "stock orks" like Arthur Lange, Frank Skinner, and Archie Bleyer, of piano parts like Albert Sirmay and Helmy Kresa, and of show scores like Robert Russell Bennett and Phil Lang have played a vital part in developing the harmonic and rhythmic elements of popular song. In fact, the texture and ultimate sound may well be attributed to the interplay between schooled arranger-conductors and intuitive author-composers. In addition, the song plugger, the disk jockey, the A & R executive have all played key roles in making the continuing repertory of popular music what it is. There is no documented history that fully presents the interrelated contribution of all of these, nor are there even studies of the major figures in each area.

Although the musical theater and minstrelsy have been the subject of a number of good historical studies, the development of vaudeville requires further documentation. Recent books trace the development of the brass band, but there is no extended study of the growth of the dance band. Nor has anyone probed the contribution of the cabaret, the dance hall, and the night club to popular music.

"Songs are history," according to John Tasker Howard. And Sigmund Spaeth has said: "The history of American manners, morals, tastes and absurdities is largely written in our songs." But Mr. Spaeth's *History of Popular Music* is less an integrated and analytical history than an accurate and extremely useful chronology, year by year and decade by decade, of the songs, their writers and their sources. John Tasker Howard's study of *Our American Music*, despite its eclectic point of view, focuses mainly on "serious" music and makes well-intentioned blunders in dealing with popular music, e.g., as to the characteristics of swing music. Recent books by Elliot Paul and David Ewen are popular histories, sketchy and with their complement of careless errors. Earlier anecdotal books

[166]

by Isaac Goldberg and Douglas Gilbert lack the scholarship of Howard and Spaeth, but are more effective in relating the songs to the times. Only Gilbert Chase's recent book on *America's Music* (1958) approaches the subject with the assumption that "folk-popular" music is "the most important phase of America's music" and attempts to relate "these idioms to one another and to the whole cultural development of the United States." Musicological and sociological scholarship still faces a challenge in providing a rounded work that will correlate the development of our popular music with changes not only in our culture, but in the temper and conditions of American life. For that matter, considering the number of songs that must be examined, studies of major periods are probably necessary before an over-all history can be written.

While Tin Pan Alley has generally meant New York, it is quite apparent that the Alley as such has long been non-existent and that many other cities have contributed to the growth of popular music. There is a need for regional studies of Memphis (birthplace of W. C. Handy and Elvis Presley), Philadelphia (which has nurtured an unusually large number of vocalists, including Eddie Fisher, Fabian, etc.), Cleveland (which, for many years, was the city that "broke" the hits), Chicago (important in the development of Dixieland jazz, boogie woogie, and the blues), Kansas City (out of which Count Basie and other jazzmen came), Nashville (the center of hill-billy music and the habitat of country writers like Hank Williams, Boudleaux Bryant, and Don Everly), and Hollywood (whose many talented arranger-composer-conductors of screen and, more recently, of TV music — Nelson Riddle, Hank Mancini, Elmer Bernstein, Miklos Rosza, Dmitri Tiomkin, Max Steiner, Morris Stoloff, etc. — constitute a vast and frequently neglected outpost of popular music).

No adequate study is available of the interrelationship between popular music and jazz. Despite doctrinaire attitudes, particularly on the part of "purist" jazz critics, the repertory of jazz music comes in large part from popular music, and jazz musicians rely on "pop" recording dates, dance bands, and TV and movie studios for part of their income. Conversely, popular music has turned periodically to jazz when it needed fresh sounds and new rhythms for dancing instead of melodies for singing. Passing references to jazz in existing surveys of popular music and passing (albeit condescending) references to pop music in the many studies of jazz do not reflect the true debt of one to the other or the interplay between them. An increasing number of colleges, universities, and conservatories are giving courses in the history of jazz. One would have to look far and wide to find a curriculum that includes a course in the history of popular music as such.

Our popular music deserves better treatment, not only because it is a body of material that has a relevance, fitness, and richness of its own, but because its influence reaches far beyond our own shores. The tumultuous reception of *Porgy and Bess* in Moscow, of Dizzy Gillespie in the Middle East, of The Platters in South America, all suggest the high esteem in which our popular music is held abroad. Moreover, the hit lists of many foreign countries constantly contain American records in the original English-language versions by American artists. In other words, it is not an exaggeration to say that the popular music of our country has become a significant part of the popular music of the world. Whatever our prestige as a political, military, or space-exploring nation, our standing in the field of popular song is at an all-time peak. Paradoxically, our popular music has still to attain a similar prestige in its own land.

The Business of Music

The Dilemma of the
Music Publishing Industry

By RICHARD F. FRENCH

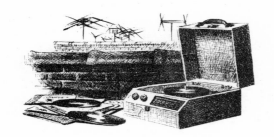

> The new modes of expression, when they have attained the
> maximum degree of perfection, will certainly eliminate
> everything that will have become superfluous, encumbering,
> without artistic or practical utility. But no mechanical in-
> vention can ever prevent the musician from lingering often
> over the pages that form the basis of his culture or his
> technical skill. No mechanical invention can ever cause the
> disappearance of the great editions that are the fruit of long
> and patient researches of musical scholars and do the
> greatest honor to a civilized nation. No mechanical inven-
> tion can ever destroy the beauty of a rich and precious
> musical collection and the joy that it brings to its happy
> possessor.

If the music publishing industry holds up a mirror to the century
of its activities that is celebrated by the publication of this volume,
it does not deceive itself when it sees that it has done more than
everything that society could have asked of it. Its music is everywhere — music accompanies our eating, sleeping, working, it travels
on the road, in the air, and under the sea. Our national appetite
for music cannot be satisfied; we have more orchestras than the

rest of the world put together, our instrument manufacturers are selling merchandise in greater quantities than ever before, our churches and schools are buying and using music at an undiminished rate. Our choice of repertory may be made from resources more extensive than at any other time in history. We have music for every use, we can obtain virtually every current edition of a foreign work, the music of our composers is known throughout the country and abroad. The publishing industry has accomplished all this, and if congratulations are in order, the industry has reason to believe that it is entitled to receive them.

What the industry has accomplished is more interesting and even more remarkable when we see it against the background of the world in which it happened. The musical world of 1961 bears almost no resemblance to its counterpart of a century ago. In 1931, at the International Congress of Publishers in Paris, Carlo Clausetti of Ricordi, Milan, delivered a report on the subject: "The Diminution of Sheet Music Sales and Its Causes." In the passage that stands at the head of the present essay, Clausetti was referring particularly to the effect on sheet music sales of one element of the new world, the invention and use of the phonograph record. But his basic concern was not merely this, but rather more broadly the sum of political events, social changes, and inventions that had come tumbling out of history at the beginning of this century and whose forces seemed to be combining to threaten the welfare of the industry and possibly the very nature of music itself. His rhetoric helps to raise his hopes and calm his fears, but his remarks, nevertheless, leave a lingering doubt. Will our editions, he seems to be asking, be used in the future as they have in the past? Will our industry, if it continues to do what it has done so magnificently, ultimately discover that it has done something that people no longer care about? Will the industry as it is presently identified be eliminated by the new modes of expression as something superfluous, without artistic or practical utility?

The speed of change in musical society in the last century can be measured by the fact that if Clausetti's questions were of theoretical interest in 1931, they are much more than that now. At the end of a brief span of thirty years, the industry finds itself on the threshold of a new world whose artistic attitudes and demands are without precedent. The industry may not die, but to remain alive it must first try to see the present for what it is and prepare to deal with the future. As it searches out the new, it may learn much about itself, about society, and about music.

The music publisher of the 19th century worked in a society that used and regarded music in a very special way. We tend now to view the musical activities of that period with particular reverence and nostalgia and to assign to its prominent figures an authority and distinction that we deny to our own, as if the old world had disappeared and nothing of value had come to take its place. The musical world of the 19th century is far behind us, it is true, and not merely because the calendar has turned beyond the year 1900. But concern with value must not blind us to the special qualities that characterized the music of that time.

To identify the special nature of music in that society, we can begin by recognizing that in order to have any music at all a century ago, either of two conditions had to be met: either people had to make it themselves, or they had to come within earshot of others making it. In this respect, the people of the 19th century differed in no way from their ancestors of the 18th, 16th, or 14th centuries, or indeed of any other period of historical time. They differ only from us.

This society whose members had to make music in order to have it at all, needed and used the sets of directions for making music that the publishers provided. The 19th-century publishers were primarily printers, printers of multiple copies of musical scores, sets of directions for making music set down by composers, engraved, printed, and sold by publishers. The commercial operations of music publishers in the middle of the 19th century did not differ in nature from the kind of commerce in printed music carried on since the invention of music printing towards the end of the 15th century. By the middle of the last century, however, musical society had come to organize itself around three sets of assumptions that defined the special nature of the musical society and the primary role in it of the music printer.

The first of these assumptions was that the ability to read music was a criterion of musical literacy. People had to read music in order to make it sound, and those who wanted to make music alone or with others accepted as normal and natural the need to acquire reading skills. Since the musical scores of the times were sets of directions for doing something, for going through certain physical motions, the criterion of literacy was naturally extended to include the ability to sing, or to play an instrument. The professional musician had no monopoly of these skills — no one could make music without acquiring them.

Since music as sound could not exist apart from music-making, and since no one could hear such sounds unless he found himself within earshot of the music-makers, people assumed that to gather together and hear music was a natural and necessary condition of music's existence. Concert life existed because it was a necessity of the times: if an orchestra or a singer or any combination of individuals wanted to make music for others, people had to present themselves at the place of performance while the performance was going on. Some of these people, naturally, were illiterate in the sense in which the word has been used here, but they could not have the sound of music in any form without seeing others play it and realizing that the reading and playing of music were natural and necessary. The literate members of the audience had learned to read and play by studying a musical literature composed for their more private use in the home — because they could have music in their homes only if they made it themselves. What they brought to the performances of others by way of an ability to participate vicariously in such performances is breathtaking for us to imagine. The composer's imagination was limited only by the need to compose music that others could read and play, music whose sounds proceeded directly and simultaneously to the ears of everyone within hearing.

The third set of assumptions relates to the directions for performing, to the score. Since the score had to be used in musical performance, since its existence at the moment of performance was indispensable, the score itself acquired a symbol of status — it symbolized the status of the composer as a professional, and the music to be played from the set of directions as worthy of professional and public consideration. Furthermore, the composition of music came to be regarded as virtually synonymous with writing it down; to exist, this music had first to be made precise in written form. To demand, however, the written form of music as a condition of recognizing its existence, to demand a high degree of precision in such written form, to refuse to recognize the existence of music itself apart from such a written form placed a very severe and special limitation on the nature of music itself. For if a composer had to convey his ideas precisely in written form, he had to use a notation that may or may not have been adequate to convey the ideas but that itself conditioned their nature and shape. The fact that the musical idea should have been so conditioned, that such a limitation was accepted by composers, performers, and all members of musical society was, I think, the most distinctive characteristic of music itself a century ago.

For the printer-publishers, of course, such conditions and the assumptions derived from them provided a field of operations as near to the ideal as publishers of this particular kind could ever have. Their security and strength derived from the fact that they offered the public a musical product — the printed score — that was indispensable to all forms of music-making, public and private, secular and religious, and to every step of the educational process in music. No matter how the field of operations might expand, the publishers thought, music could not be music without the printed score.

Particularly in the United States, the field of operations did expand, and mightily. The establishment of our important performing organizations, the entire history of music in our schools, the virtual explosion in the field of church music, are among the developments of the last century. The industry explored these fields eagerly and effectively. Sometimes with reluctance, often without enthusiasm or understanding, but always with good intentions, the industry printed the great bulk of works by American composers. It made available the works of European composers and the great historical editions of the European tradition by print, reprint, and importation, and European publishers who established branch operations in the United States often turned to American composers for sacred, educational, and concert materials. The supply of printed music in the United States is massive, polynational, polycenturied.

This is the record the country knows, this is the picture the industry sees. It is to be congratulated, and with reason, and the more remarkably for the fact that what it has done, brilliantly and responsibly, it has done under conditions without precedent. For during this time, the technological developments that have produced the long-playing phonograph record, radio, television, and magnetic tape have made it possible for the first time to preserve and reproduce the sounds and sights of live musical performances at another time — any other time — and another geographical location — any other location. Or to put it another way, to have music today, people no longer have to make it themselves (LP record, magnetic tape) or come within earshot of others making it (radio, television). The perfection and almost universal adoption of these inventions have produced a new public for music, a public of individuals who come to music and use music without regard to the necessary limitations of the 19th century.

Consider, for example, the significance of the LP record, one of the brilliant developments of the last thirty years. The natural first impulse of the recording and publishing industries was to use the LP record to preserve the sounds of the standard printed literature. As a result, anyone in the United States can now own, hear repeatedly, and come to know intimately the major works of several centuries of European and American music. A century ago, the professional musician and the literate amateur could not find such an extensive literature even in printed form. But it is not the professional musicians and the literate amateurs who have made the market for recordings; it is, on the contrary, a new public, much of it initially illiterate in the 19th-century sense, that has provided a substantial portion of the new market on which the recording industry now lives.

For a member of this public, the assumptions of 1861 are preposterous. He sees no necessary link between the ability to read musical notation or play an instrument and the availability of musical literature. The recording permits him to bypass the need to acquire these skills, to proceed directly to the sound at his pleasure, to become learned in the literature of sound without regard or concern for it as a set of directions for performance by others. He knows that concert life is not a necessity, and if he continues to attend in large numbers, it is, in part, because his interest in music has been stimulated by the new inventions themselves.

But although his capacity to participate vicariously in the techniques of performance may be altered, and what he gives and takes away is of quite a new order — and may often include a comparison of what he hears with what he already knows — he is nevertheless aware that what he hears is a special kind of music, music that is played from scores in a room with an audience. He even calls it by a special name — "concert music."

Most important of all, music cannot be definable to him in terms of something written down. He may recognize that one kind of music has this attribute, but the written form of music — the conventional printed set of directions — is irrelevant to the ways in which music may come to him and he to music.

Clausetti defined the new public as a public of auditors and performers — people who hear music without having to read or play (and, we would add, without having to be within earshot of those who play), and people who play and are still literate in the old sense. The auditors have no need, Clausetti saw, for printed materials, their ideas of music are not conditioned by the traditions of written music, they are disdainful of obviously outmoded canons of literacy. This new public of auditors, created by inventions whose significance finds historical parallel only in the invention of music printing itself, has given the industry its greatest opportunities, its greatest difficulties. I believe that the effect of the new public on the industry and on music will be profound, and that the need to understand this is imperative.

This effect derives notably from three elements: the abrupt change in the size of the musical public, how music now comes to it, and how it now comes to music.

At the moment when Clausetti was seeking to discover the reasons why sheet music sales were declining and were providing a decreasingly satisfactory income from what had always been a traditional source, the new technological developments were rapidly providing the industry with the first mass market in its history. This market is a fact of the present and the foreseeable future, and how to understand its nature and satisfy its demands is the knottiest problem facing the publishing industry today.

Traditional economics, so often a fascinating compromise of habit with expediency, may no longer be relevant. The new market

[177]

initially uses music in recorded or broadcast form, but the money accruing to the publishing industry through the licensing of mechanical rights even now bears an odd relationship to the kind of product being sold. The statutory fees payable to the copyright proprietor for the grant of a license to record music are still based on the playing time of the 78-rpm record, a device that most responsible business people would agree may not have a brilliant commercial future. Now that the market buys principally 45-rpm and LP (33 1/3-rpm) records, publishers and record manufacturers have generally disregarded the statute to settle upon what they regard as a more reasonable rate of payment under the new conditions, and this new rate has the added advantage of flexibility, lending itself to changes up or down according to the degree of pressure or strength of bargaining position of either party. But the industry has never really faced fundamental questions raised by the sales of records in high volume to a mass market. Is the level of the present rate really fair (does it represent a reasonable levy on the record manufacturers and provide a reasonable return to authors and composers) under present circumstances, or should it be set by reference to both playing time and quantity as a matter of course? Should the recording of a 12-minute piece earn a mechanical royalty three times that of a 4-minute piece, or six times, or only twice? Should the royalty on so-called serious or concert music be higher or lower than that payable on popular music, and can such a distinction usefully be made? These are not idle questions in a day when sales in volume of all kinds of recorded music can have such a great impact on the economics of record manufacturers and copyright proprietors alike. An assembly of interested persons convoked to debate such matters would produce a violent struggle opening with large salvos fired from prepared positions, but it would at least have the advantage of forcing into the open problems that the interested parties may now prefer to ignore for not wholly disinterested reasons.

A curious anomaly also exists in the way in which the mass market pays for the pleasure of listening to broadcast or televised musical performance. At the present time it pays nothing directly, not one cent for all the music it can receive by radio and television every hour of every day. Whether the public should or should not pay directly is a matter for the future to decide (and it will have

[178]

to decide), but the anomaly of the present lies in the amusing fact that the vast number of people who use—who hear—broadcast or televised performances has no direct bearing on the money paid by the broadcasting facilities to the performing rights societies for the right to play music. The broadcasting facilities pay fees based on their gross annual incomes, whose principal source is of course advertising revenues. The performing rights society, therefore, receives income not because the public may listen to its music, not because the public may buy soap, not because the manufacturer may make more soap or sell less soap, but only because the manufacturer buys time from the broadcasting facility to try to persuade the public to buy his soap. However equitable—and however fancy—may be the arrangements between the performing rights societies and authors and composers for the sharing of funds received, the fact remains that the pool of these funds rises or falls largely according to advertising revenue. The present situation may be inevitable, it may be the best arrangement under the circumstances, or it may be just plain laughable. For certain, it cannot remain as it is for the next century, and the publishing industry will have to play a positive and responsible role in the changes that are sure to come.

A more serious question is the industry's relationship to the formation and influencing of a public musical taste. Never before have the conventions of musical taste suddenly become subject to the pressing responses of so many people. Music may have always been for the comparatively few, and the standards set, maintained, and altered by enlightened despots of various kinds may have found acceptance among a relatively small number of enlightened subjects. But now and in the future music is available to everyone, and public musical taste will be an important force in establishing musical standards. We like to think that our society can establish and re-define these standards on some free and objective basis, giving full rein to innovation on the one hand and continuity of tradition on the other, and we shrink from solutions by political decree that we think we see in other lands. But we must not also shrink from the misuse of instruments of mass communication, which lend themselves to the manipulation of musical taste so easily that very frequently what our public wants by way of music can be what it has been made to want by skillful and expensive propaganda. The publishing industry and the communications media can take—and have too often taken—the low road of artistic safety and commercial security, giving the public products that evoke a calculated enthusiasm, or at least a minimum of complaint. But the capacity of the new public to accept and even to stimulate artistic innovation has hardly been tested, and to sell short its capacities in these directions in the hope that its standards may fall—or be made to fall—to that of the lowest common denominator will be to risk artistic and financial disaster.

The fact that music can come to the public in packaged form or by broadcast has consequences of major importance. The purchase or playing of a record may be the principal point of contact between the new market and the musical work, and for an industry that has necessarily been concerned throughout its entire history with the need to prepare printed materials as a prelude to such contact, the effect of the new mass market means something more than a sudden disclosure of additional sources of income. The hunger and limitations of the new public not only tend to make obsolete the production of printed materials, with all its attendant and traditional fussiness. They stimulate as well the appearance of new publishing companies for whose success the traditional rites are unnecessary, and they force all publishers to decide whether in fact the printed materials are necessary, and whether the existence of a recorded version of a work may be a tool now indispensable to promote the sales and use of the work in any other form. The right to licence recordings, and success in obtaining them, may have become the most important commercial assets of the music publishing industry.

Tradition dies hard, and composers are often reluctant to relinquish demands for the production of printed materials and thereby release monies for perhaps more profitable investment. The prestige of the printed score is still high, and of course in some areas its existence is still indispensable as a starting-point for any promotion. To assume a prior need for it, however, may lead to wasteful expenditure, and not to question its indispensability or, more importantly, not to calculate when and how, in the long sequence of publishing events, it appropriately enters as a promotional factor or performance tool is to ignore a flexibility easily inferred from the new conditions.

The recording and broadcasting industries have also brought the new public a musical repertory broader and more varied than any imaginable programs of even the most ideally endowed and situated concert ensembles—a repertory of composers, pieces, and styles encompassing our entire Western musical tradition and gradually reaching out to include the cultivated and primitive musics of our own and other cultures. What a feast of music we have on records! The young men and women of our day are members of the first generation for whom an evening's program — any evening's program — may include Gershwin, Machaut, Bach, Burl Ives, Wagner, five different recordings of Beethoven's Fifth, and so on almost *ad infinitum*. The extraordinary and quite novel aspect of all this is that our entire musical past has become their musical present, free of the stylized limitations of concert programs and rules of concert behavior, often in total disregard of historical sequence, continuity, or development and in total ignorance of musical notation or instrumental techniques. This is the new breed, alert, insatiable, often scorned by the traditionalists who comfort themselves with the thought that it cannot "know" music as they do. But the public nevertheless continues to revel in its literature of sonorities.

The effect of all this becomes clear at the point where the new generation makes contact with traditional operations of the industry —in school, and in the concert hall. The private teacher, who has been the traditional first point of contact with music and to whom music in this country owes a very heavy debt—the private teacher finds herself no longer being the initiator or bearing the burden of musical education, and the musical literature that has been so important to her work cannot now be of such relatively great commercial importance to the industry. She has, of course, to a degree rendered herself obsolete, by having worked so well and so indefatigably that the school systems have seen the value of bringing the beginnings of musical education into the classroom. Where these were once available only to the more curious and the more fortunate, they have now become a generally accepted part of our curricula at all levels.

[181]

The music publishing industry has not reacted to the consequences of this important change. To teach groups of children, for example, to read and make music requires materials and techniques as specialized in their way as the piano literature for private beginners was in its—recognizing the sheer numbers of people involved, teachers and pupils, is of basic importance in developing new materials, which must often perform the dual role of instructing teacher and pupil alike. Publishers cannot be content to continue the supply of the usual graded pieces, instructional methods, and collections of jolly songs, leaving it to the teacher to select from this miscellany a program of pieces to form the basis of musical instruction. The teacher may not be equipped to do this, she may not be able to read music easily, her pupils may not be able to read it at all, and both she and they may have heard a variety of musical styles outside the classroom in contrast to which the folksy school materials may seem unusually impoverished. Here a new effort of imagination is called for, and it is a pity that the music publishing industry should have lost the initiative in this area to the textbook publishers, whose activity and commercial success is a tribute to their ability to study the novel needs of a field whose peculiarities should be more easily recognizable by everyone. If music publishers are content to remain behind the line traditionally separating their operations from those of the textbook publishers, the latter can only smile, but they will not be deterred from crossing the line themselves into the area of instructional methods and perhaps even into the area of music publishing if they find that the carefully planned materials that they can offer in book form meet current needs. Even textbook publishers, however, must not fear to ask themselves whether the pupils of today at all levels really need to learn musical notation, or whether there may be other modes of approaching all music that may be as rewarding in their own way as the traditional and heretofore necessary approach via notation, and that may yield remarkable insights of their own not otherwise available. It is just here that the wisdom and experience of the music publishing industry might be brought into a fruitful collaboration.

Accustomed as it is to music everywhere around it, when the new generation goes out to the concert hall it is making contact with music in, for it, a very special way. It is difficult for us to imagine that the experience may be awkward, fatiguing, unpleasant. Proximity to others in a formal situation may be an annoyance, the need to pay attention and to sit quietly may be intolerable restrictions that cannot, under the circumstances, be relieved by movement or conversation. That the sound always comes forth from one point, or that the repertory is limited by the forces of the performing ensemble may be no more than unpleasant reminders of the pleasant musical liberties in the world outside.

If attendance at live musical performances has become a special and perhaps even an odd way of having to hear music, the industry must dare to accept the fact and try to see its implications. First comes the need to imagine whether a special kind of music composed for such conditions might have a wide circulation—a music that in some way celebrates the act of going out and being together, a kind of festival music employing large and novel combinations of forces in sonorities and effects the full comprehension of whose complexity and variety demands the physical presence of the auditors. A public becoming more and more familiar with stereophonic sound will naturally expect that the concert hall be more adventurous: why must our new music employ forces playing from only one position in the hall? Perhaps the collaboration of architects is needed to encourage the design of halls and even outdoor areas giving full scope to the new elements of sonorous novelty and surprise to which the public has become accustomed. Public pressure may also be exerted in the direction of a more varied concert repertory than is ordinarily provided by our concert ensembles. The future will find nothing sacred in the string quartet, the brass ensemble, or the symphony orchestra as concert media. There is already some small sign that ensembles able and willing to present programs of works in a variety of instrumentations are gradually finding public favor, and composers and publishers alike can profit from this apparent partiality for a variety of sonorous experience. With all this, however, there will still remain a need to maintain and somehow to support live musical performances of conventional works. If performing organizations as we know them now take on thereby something of the quality of museums, may that frankly be their quality and may its virtue be recognized.

The raw materials of the publishing industry are, of course, music itself, and to discover and develop composers of all kinds has been basic to publishing operations and will remain so. The present is a particularly difficult time in this respect, and perhaps one without parallel. Our schools and colleges have almost universally adopted programs of instruction in musical literature and composition, with the astonishing result that there have never before been so many people claiming the distinction of being composers as there are today. Perhaps we are a far more musical nation than we could have dreamed; perhaps, on the other hand, our techniques of instruction have developed to so high a point that learning to become a composer is far easier than it ever has been before. There is still, however, a very fine line dividing the technically imitative from the inventive, the inventive from the imaginative, and the imaginative from the communicative, and mere quantity of composers qualified in the first respect does not invalidate these distinctions. If our crop of young composers has never been so promisingly large, neither has the industry ever had so great a responsibility to know its materials and the uses to which they can appropriately be put. In all this no part of the future can be foreclosed, no basic assumptions go unchallenged. Even the proposition that the musical composition—no matter how long or how short—must be apprehended in its entirety to be understood will be open to challenge with the coming of the electronic score, which, freed from all limitations of human performance, may be in shape spiral and therefore endless, and may be designed to be heard in alternating periods of attention and inattention, presence and absence, thought and reverie. Who dares to say that our new public is not ready for this new music?

For music, and for the music publishing industry, there can be no return to the beautifully articulated consistency of the 19th century. Musical society is rapidly being altered by technological developments, and its musical demands are becoming vastly greater, more varied, and more subtly interrelated. How to foresee their impact on the entire musical scene will demand the best talents and skills of an industry that has sometimes had too little respect for both. The electronic composition, for example, may completely alter traditional notions of how we hear sounds, how music is organized and identified, what constitutes a musical idea or a musical texture. The industry cannot afford to be ignorant of this field, but it needs energy, imagination, and intelligence to inform itself, and great business acumen to see the need. It may choose, of course, to abandon commercial exploitation of electronic music to more specialized companies, because the new products differ so radically from those that the industry has learned to handle. If it does so, it forfeits a responsible participation in the full enrichment of our musical life that will come from the simultaneous cultivation of the new and the old, with possibilities of cross-fertilization that only professionals have come to suspect.

The next century, indeed, will ask new standards of professionalism of the industry—a new sense of responsibility to music and to society, new techniques of market research, a renewed respect for tradition and technology, and an excited curiosity. The industry cannot survive merely by improvisation and compromise, merely by being canny, resourceful, and flexible. It can re-assert its position as a major cultural force only if it combines a sense of history with an adventurous estimate of technological possibilities to form an effective view of the present and the future. The opportunities were never more abundant, the hazards never greater, and the greatest risk will be assumed by the least venturous. "Merely to sound the alarm is of no use," wrote Clausetti. "The march of science is like the course of a river which must inevitably rejoin the sea. We can give it as a motto the verse of Dante: Non impedir lo suo fatale andare."

Music on Records

By ROLAND GELATT

The phonograph was invented by Thomas Edison in 1877; it became a musical instrument in 1902. Between these dates lay a quarter-century of missteps and slow development. The new invention flourished briefly as an exhibition novelty, next as a dictating machine, then as a nickel-in-the-slot dispenser of short marches and ditties, and finally (towards the end of the 19th century) as a device for home entertainment — but nobody in all that time seriously considered it a musical instrument. Well, almost nobody. We know of one pioneer — a young Italian-born resident of New York named Gianni Bettini — who made cylinder recordings of several Metropolitan Opera singers in the 1890s, but his was a small, custom-order business, so small that not one Bettini cylinder seems to have survived. Otherwise the level of recorded music rose no higher than *La donna è mobile* played on the cornet.

During this quarter-century of limping progress, two media of recorded sound vied for public favor — the wax cylinder (an outgrowth of Edison's original tin-foil invention) and the flat shellac disc. The disc record player, or gramophone, had been invented by Emile Berliner (an American of German birth) in 1887 and by the end of the century was fast overtaking Edison's cylinder phonograph. Perhaps if Edison had been a shrewder businessman and a person of some musical sophistication, the cylinder would have made a better showing, for it had certain clear technical superiorities. But marketing acumen, promotional imagination (for example, the picture of a fox terrier listening to "His Master's Voice," the world's most famous trademark), and musical taste were all on the side of the disc.

The musical taste manifested itself first in Europe, where the flat disc had been introduced by the London-based Gramophone Company. In 1901 this company's Russian branch took the unprecedented step of recording certain celebrated singers from the Imperial Opera and issuing their performances in a special series of high-priced discs bearing red labels. News of the profitable venture in Russia was soon forwarded to the head office in London, and plans were made to extend the program of celebrity recording to all of Europe. In March 1902 the company's talent scouts in Milan heard a young tenor, Enrico Caruso, win an ovation at La Scala. A few days later Caruso recorded ten arias for the Gramophone Company's new Red Label series. The discs were an immediate success, both artistic and commercial. And technically they set a new standard. Caruso's strong, slightly baritonal voice somehow triumphed over the crude recording techniques and the grating surface noise of the early discs. Even on the inadequate reproducers of the time, his records sounded rich and vibrant; and in addition they offered singing of great artistic refinement.

A year later, Caruso's Milan recordings — as well as others made in Europe by Calvé, Battistini, and Plançon — were issued in the United States by the Gramophone Company's American associate, the Victor Talking Machine Company. Meanwhile, Victor's chief competitor, Columbia, enlisting the talents of Edouard de Reszke, Marcella Sembrich, and Schumann-Heink, had issued the first celebrity discs of American origin. Victor responded by initiating a celebrity recording program of its own based in America. For the convenience of musical artists, a room in Carnegie Hall was rented and converted into a recording studio; and there on April 30, 1903, the first Victor Red Seal recording session took place.

For another twenty years the recording of famous opera stars continued in high gear. Every singer of note was lured before the huge acoustic recording horn — Patti, Melba, Nordica, Sembrich, Eames, Tetrazzini, Galli-Curci, Calvé, Homer, Schumann-Heink, Tamagno, Caruso, McCormack, Maurel, Battistini, Chaliapin, Plançon, De Reszke, the entire Who's Who of the Golden Age. The emphasis on opera singers was understandable, for they were the most glamorous and highly paid entertainers of the day (the Hollywood movie star was yet to come). In addition, the human voice was the only musical instrument to which pre-1920 recording techniques could do even partial justice. On the acoustic-mechanical recording and reproducing apparatus of that epoch, orchestras sounded thin and feeble, pianos jangly and quavering; only the voice could be captured with some semblance of fidelity.

Across America, in towns where opera companies had never set foot, a growing clientele for standard arias and ensembles was to be found patronizing Victor's ten thousand authorized dealers. It would be hard to say how much of this trade derived from a genuine desire for good music. There was considerable snob value attached to Red Seal records. A collection of them established one as a person of both taste and property; and along with leather-bound sets of Dickens and Thackeray, the Victor Red Seals became a status symbol of the refined American parlor. To some extent at least they served to educate a generation (the average American of 1920 might never have attended a symphony concert, but he was apt to know *Caro nome* and *Celeste Aida*) and they served also to perpetuate for us a legacy of inimitable vocal performances. Inimitable is the word. Whether the art of singing in 1910 was "better" than in 1960 is a question best avoided here, but there can be no doubt that it was different, and from the hundreds of vocal recordings made in the first two decades of this century we can reconstruct a style of operatic performance that has vanished from the contemporary stage.

After 1920 the orchestra began to assert itself. Again the initiative came from Europe. In a sense, the European record industry was forced by economic circumstances to explore this area of recorded repertory, for the New World's fabulous royalty payments had persuaded most of the famous opera stars to sign exclusive contracts with American companies. But economics only partially explains the drift to orchestral recording that gathered momentum in Europe from 1910 on. Just as the pioneering operatic records had resulted from the European record buyers' desire for something more elevated than sentimental ballads and Sousa marches, so did the pioneering orchestral records derive from a desire for something more substantial than vocal sweetmeats. In 1913 the first uncut symphonies on records, the Beethoven Fifth and Sixth, were brought out in Germany, and by the early 1920s a profusion of orchestral and instrumental works were being recorded in England and on the Continent.

Unfortunately, the phonograph still could not reproduce the sound of a full orchestra with anything like its full dynamic volume or frequency range. The acoustic recording process invented by Edison had been enormously improved and refined over the course of the years, but at its best it was limited to a range of 168-2,000 cycles (as compared to a range of 20-20,000 cycles audible in the concert hall). America now stepped in with a tremendous technological assist. The Bell Telephone Laboratories initiated research on an electrical method of recording sound in 1919, and by 1924 the problem had been solved. The new electrical method of recording brought about three striking improvements in sound reproduction. First, the frequency range was expanded by two and a half octaves to encompass 100-5,000 cycles. Second, the "atmosphere" surrounding music in the concert hall could begin to be simulated on records (for musicians were no longer forced to work in cramped quarters directly before a recording horn but could play, thanks to the use of microphones, in spacious halls with proper reverberation characteristics). Third, records were louder and free from blast.

The electrical recording system, quickly made available to all companies, gave fresh impetus to the record business. Victor's recordings of the Philadelphia Orchestra under Leopold Stokowski set a world standard for exciting recorded sound. In general, however, European companies continued to pay more attention to orchestral and instrumental repertory (as witness, for example, the 1927 recording of Beethoven's nine symphonies under Weingartner's direction, instigated by the British Columbia firm). In quick succession all the standard, and a good many non-standard, works

[189]

found their way onto records, and people who had formerly dismissed the phonograph as an unmusical toy began to look upon it with new respect. One of these was the critic Ernest Newman. "Those who have heard these [electrical] records for themselves," he wrote in 1926, "will have probably felt, as I did at my first hearing of them, that at last it is possible for the musician to sit at home and get the thrill of the real thing as he knows it in the concert hall. The records have their weaknesses, but they seem trifling in comparison with the great mass of their virtues."

One major problem remained. Records still had to be changed every four minutes. The short playing time of the 78 rpm record had been no hindrance with *Caro nome*, but it was decidedly vexing in Beethoven's Ninth Symphony. In 1931 the RCA Victor Company (successor to the Victor Talking Machine Company) announced the development of a long-playing record capable of reproducing "the longest movement of a symphony without interruption." Unfortunately, the records themselves made a rather poor impression on the few people who bought them; they sounded tonally constricted, wore out quickly, and required expensive reproducing equipment. The "bugs" could eventually have been ironed out, but in the early thirties the American record business found itself in dismal circumstances. Suddenly, the country had stopped buying records (sales dropped from 104 million discs in 1927 to 6 million in 1932), and as a consequence Victor's long-playing record was allowed to expire without a struggle. By the time the record business came to life again in 1940, the world had more important technological fish to fry.

At the end of the war, the Columbia Broadcasting System set up a laboratory for various lines of experimentation under the direction of Peter Goldmark. To Goldmark and his staff went the task of developing a practical long-playing record for the CBS subsidiary Columbia Records. In 1948 Goldmark could report that the job was accomplished: the laboratory had devised a recording head capable of cutting hair-width grooves consistently, a pickup that would track them easily, and an electronic equalization system able to compensate for an otherwise disturbing loss of fidelity in the inside grooves. Columbia's LP Microgroove Record turned at 33 1/3 rpm and played for twenty-three minutes per side.

After a preliminary period of confusion brought on by RCA's advocacy of the 45 rpm disc (the so-called War of the Speeds), the LP record firmly established itself as the preferred medium for classical music. The LP boom of the early 1950s coincided with two other important developments. One was the spread of interest in high fidelity reproduction and the emergence of quality equipment — amplifiers, speakers, turntables, pickups — far in advance of anything previously available. The other was the use of magnetic tape at recording sessions. Tape was not only a far more flexible recording medium than anything known before, but it was also remarkably cheap. As a result, many small entrepreneurs with high musical ideals joined the American record industry. They took tape recorders to Europe (where musicians were plentiful and low-salaried), recorded great amounts of little-known music, transferred the tapes to LP discs, and — back in the United States — issued a flood of fascinating repertory on various "independent" labels. The large companies, of course, also expanded their production, and before long the comprehensive Schwann Long Playing Record Catalogue bulged with a fabulous array of recorded musical literature — cantatas by Bach and operas by Handel, concerti grossi of the Italian Baroque, Mozart's piano works *in toto*, Beethoven's music to *Egmont* and Schumann's to *Manfred*, resurrected operas by Bellini, Rossini, and early Verdi, the complete songs of Mussorgsky, the symphonies of Mahler, the lifework of Webern.

The list could go on and on. Performances were by no means all first-class, and the documentation often merely demonstrated how much indifferent music had been composed in the last three hundred years, but nothing could detract from the excitement of fresh discovery and the delight of an unexpected *trouvaille*. The ordinary music listener no longer had to rely on scholars to learn about Gesualdo and Vivaldi, Satie and Ives, early Haydn and late Strauss. It was all on records. Nothing like this had occurred in the history of music, and the credit for it was due in large part to American technology and enterprise.

In time the bubble began to burst. The "independents" sailed into foul weather, hit by rising costs, cut-throat competition, and a saturated catalogue. By 1957 many of the small record producers were either out of business or fast on the way, and the larger companies were concentrating increasingly on merchandising standard repertory through huge mail-order record clubs. The situation temporarily worsened with the advent of stereophonic records in 1958. Stereo represented a step forward in the technique of reproducing sound, but it required additional expenditure for both the record producer and the record listener, and the effect was to discourage further the kind of untrammeled enthusiasm that had enlivened the early years of the LP era.

Predictions that sales of classical records in the United States would snowball indefinitely have proved to be overly optimistic. The boom has leveled off; and though the market for good music continues to grow, it is clear that the consumer is becoming more and more demanding. The success of certain productions (London's *Das Rheingold,* for one example) has shown that well-conceived and imaginatively executed recordings still find a ready welcome, but pedestrian efforts no longer even pay back their cost, and the industry in future is certain to concentrate on fewer and (let us hope) better ventures.

It is curious that in an age of technological break-throughs the preferred medium of recorded music should continue to be the flat, grooved disc — essentially a 19th-century contrivance. No one can say how long its hegemony will last. Magnetic tape, invented in Germany during World War II and further developed in the United States since then, may some day replace the venerable grooved disc in our homes. Tape can lay claim to some unquestionable advantages. It is less prone to distortion than the disc (for example, there is no deterioration in sound at the end of a tape, as there is at the end of a disc) and repeated playings do not affect the fidelity of the sound (though this benefit is somewhat offset by the questionable longevity of tape's plastic base).

These advantages have already persuaded many listeners to convert to tape. Their needs are catered to by most of the large record companies, which regularly issue tape versions as well as disc versions of important new recordings. However, the cost of tape (still considerably higher than the disc equivalent, despite recent reductions in price) and the bother of threading tape from reel to reel have conspired to keep the tape market a relatively small one. The answer to these objections is the tape cartridge, or cassette, which —

according to its proponents — promises to be as versatile and inexpensive as the disc. America's two largest record companies, RCA Victor and Columbia, have tape cartridges under development for eventual commercial exploitation, but it nevertheless seems safe to predict that the flat disc will be with us for a good many years to come.

One great difficulty still awaits solution. During the past sixty years the record industry has produced a vast documentation of musical performance, but only a fraction of it remains in print. The work of illustrious singers, instrumentalists, and conductors, authoritative readings of their own scores by composers, unique realizations of esoteric music are continually being deleted from the catalogue to make room for newer merchandise. This recorded legacy must be made available to the serious student and the curious music-lover. At present it is not. No satisfactory reference archive of recorded music exists in the United States. There are, to be sure, depositories for records (notably at the Library of Congress and the New York Public Library), but lack of funds, personnel, and equipment prevents them from being of much general use. Now that America's philanthropic foundations have begun to support the music of the future, we may hope that they will soon look with favor on perpetuating the music of the past.

Neither Quick Nor Dead:
The Music Book Paradox

By R. D. DARRELL

It is easy to diagnose the health of musical literature in the United States today — *if* you can be satisfied with the evidence of surface symptoms and you are not disconcerted by its promptly leading you to two equally persuasive, yet almost completely contradictory, conclusions.

At first glance, the patient patently is glowing with vitality. Throughout the last hundred years there has been a more or less steady growth both in over-all production and the proportion of books originating in this country (rather than merely re-issued or translated from overseas sources). Lately the "paperback revolution" has begun to bring many standard works in bargain-priced reprints to the attention of markedly expanded audiences, as well as to restore some celebrated older ones to active circulation, and to extend the useful life of some specialized studies which had gone prematurely out of print in hard covers. There also have been impressive increases in both the number of participating publishers, paced by hitherto-musically-inactive university presses, and the scope of subject-matter — ranging from scholarly theses at one extreme to mass-public primers at the other, and with exceptionally enhanced attention to such peripheral and tangential fields as those of folklore, jazz, high-fidelity and stereophonic sound reproduction, ballet and the dance. Most promising of all, of course, has been the mushrooming expansion of potential readership, embracing the incalculable audience of "new" listeners whose interest has been galvanically stimulated by a phenomenal rise in recorded and broadcast, as well "live," music-making.

At second glance, however, even the most optimistic diagnostician is likely to be shocked by an equal profusion of alarming syndromes. The *rate* of growth in music-book publication has not kept pace with that of the publishing industry as a whole and lags still farther behind that of our expanding population. The paperback catalogues are haphazardly spotty, too exclusively confined to reprints only, and plagued with grave distribution difficulties. There has been a disproportionate increase not only in ephemera and frank potboilers but also in books of bogus authority and pseudo-scholarship. Sales of more serious and substantial works are largely confined to institutional libraries, and too many of them that are not officially prescribed for school textbook use are allowed to go out of print within only a few years. Publicity for music-books is notoriously inadequate — at once a reason for and consequence of their failure to "move" more than sluggishly even in specialized bookstores. Worst of all, the potential new readership stubbornly refuses to realize its potentialities: today's record-buyers, broadcast-listeners, and concert-goers still have to demonstrate sustained interest in reading — to say nothing of buying — books on their favorite subjects and composers.

Of course there is no lack of ready explanations for even so startling a paradox as that which faces us here. Psychologists and sociologists are quick to identify the dichotomies and ambivalences characteristic of our whole era; intellectuals find ample further incentive to continue berating our educational system for permitting, if not encouraging, the rise of a "new illiteracy"; business men mark the failure of editors and merchandisers to revise outmoded techniques on the basis of up-to-date motivational research; men-in-the-street simply protest that while listening to music may provide a blessed relief from the harsh realities of their lives, there are far too heavy demands on their time, energies, and pocketbooks to permit their "studying" it.

Yet while there may be undeniable truth in all these appraisals or apologiae, none of them really explains why musical literature has become impaled on the horns of its present dilemma or how it may escape them. To accept any or all of them as "answers" would be only to indulge in that "remarkable tendency" Wolfgang Köhler has ascribed to mankind, "to be soothed and satisfied whenever a problem, instead of being solved, has merely been located somewhere."

RUECKBLICK: FROM CIVIL WAR TO WORLD WAR I

The logical next step, towards if not a full solution at least a better understanding of some of the present basic problems, normally would be to examine in closer detail the case-history of the patient. Yet here, too, we immediately encounter another paradox. Although the early record of music-book publishing in this country was contemporaneously chronicled, there never has been (so far as I have been able to discover) any comprehensive survey or extensive specialized study[1] — distinct, that is, from those dealing with the publication of music itself or with the development of music-education in general. Without a laborious search through the dusty files of early periodicals, there are apparently only three prime sources of pertinent information:

1) the 25-page fine-print "List of Modern Musical Works Published in the U. S. A." included as a supplement to J. W. Moore's *Dictionary of Musical Information* (Oliver Ditson, Boston, 1875).

2) the 19-page music section (by Krehbiel) in R. Sturgis's and H. E. Krehbiel's *Annotated Bibliography of Fine Art: Painting, Sculpture, Architecture, Arts of Decoration and Illustration, Music* (American Library Association, Boston, 1897).

3) the 15-page "musical literature" section (based in part on the Krehbiel list above) in L. H. Hooper's *Selected List of Music and Books About Music for Public Libraries* (American Library Association, Chicago, 1909).

Moore's list is dubiously helpful for our present purposes, since few of his entries are dated, most of them are collections of music

[1] There is, however, an invaluable small-scale model for such a study: Kurtz Myers's 12-page paper, *Music Book Publishing*, in the July 1958 issue of *Library Trends*. Brief as it is and primarily concerned with the record of only the last dozen or so years, its illuminating statistical and policy analyses provocatively suggest both the usefulness and need for the full-scale investigation which Myers is well qualified to undertake.

only, and the majority of the few books about music and musicians are imported or re-issued overseas publications. This last is also true to a lesser extent of the bibliographically fuller (and descriptively annotated) Krehbiel and Hooper recommendations for music librarians. But from these three sources, eked out by a hasty search through various standard author and subject bibliographies, there is at least sufficient material to construct a working chronological synopsis which can serve — *faute de mieux* — as an exemplary-sampler of music-book publication prior to the better-known activities of more recent times.

From our arbitrary starting-point of 1861 up to the landmark year of 1866, when the first substantial work of American musical scholarship appeared (Vol. 1 of Thayer's *Life of Beethoven* — significantly only in a German translation, from a Berlin publisher, which, although completed with Vol. 3 in 1879, had to wait until 1921 for publication in English), our sampler has only two entries:

1861. White, R. G.: *National Hymns* (Rudd & Carleton, New York).
1864. Hutchinson, Enoch: *Music of the Bible* (Gould & Lincoln, Boston).

But the fuller record of the next twenty-four years confirms the natural expectation that the post-war music-book concerns of a young nation, more absorbed in establishing its own industries and pushing back its frontiers than in the cultivation of the arts, should be largely parochial and imitative. Yet the constant interest in distinctively native musical aspects and artists, however superficially it may have been expressed at this stage, is significantly prophetic as well as less obvious than it may seem nowadays, when we are likely to forget how completely the dominant influences on serious music in 19th-century America were shared by the church on one hand and imported European operatic and concert artists on the other.

1867. Allen, W. F.; Ware, C. P.; Garrison, L. M.: *Slave Songs of the United States* (A. Simpson & Co., New York).
1868. Kemp, Robert: *Father Kemp and His Old Folks* [Concerts] (The Author, Boston).
1869. Nason, Elias: *Our National Song* (J. Munsell, Albany).
1870. "Hensel, Octavia": *Life and Letters of Gottschalk* (Ditson, Boston).
1871. Moulton, Mrs. Charles: *Sketch of Her Musical Career* (Baker & Goodwin, New York).

1872. Seward, R. F. (ed.): *Jubilee Songs, as Sung by the Jubilee Singers of Fisk University* (Bigelow & Main, New York).

1873. Salisbury, S.: *An Essay on the Star Spangled Banner and National Songs* (C. Hamilton, Worcester, Mass.).

1874. Ritter, F. L.: *History of Music,* Vol. 2 (Ditson).

1875. Barton, E. M.: *History of the Worcester Choral Union* (West & See, Worcester).

1876. Ritter, Mrs. F. L.: *Woman as a Musician* (E. Schuberth & Co., New York).

1877. Whittle, D. W. (ed.): *Memoirs of Philip P. Bliss* (A. S. Barnes, New York).

1878. Garbit, F. J.: *The Phonograph and Its Inventor, Thomas Alva Edison* (Gunn Bliss & Co., Boston).

1879. Cheney, S. P.: *The American Singing Book, with Biographies of 40 Composers of Sacred Music in America* (White Smith & Co., Boston).

1880. Staples, S. E.: *The Ancient Psalmody and Hymnology of New England* (C. Jillson, Worcester).

1881. Gottschalk, L. M.: *Notes of a Pianist* (Lippincott, Philadelphia).

1882. Bell, N. R. E. (N. D'Anvers, *pseud.*): *Elementary History of Music* (Scribner & Welford, New York).

   Note: Theodore Baker's dissertation, *Ueber die Musik der Nordamerikanischen Wilden,* published in Germany (Breitkopf & Härtel, Leipzig).

1883. Ritter, F. L.: *Music in America* (Scribner).

1884. Krehbiel, H. E.: *Notes on the Cultivation of Choral Music, and the Oratorio Society of New York* (Schuberth).

1885. Mathews, W. S. B.: *Therese Carreño* (P. L. Hanscom, Chicago).

1886. Upton, G. P.: *The Standard Operas* (A. C. McClurg, Chicago).

1887. Upton, G. P.: *The Standard Oratorios* (McClurg).

1888. Brooks, H. M.: *Olden-Time Music: a Compilation from Newspapers and Books* (Ticknor & Co., Boston).

1889. Mathews, W. S. B. & Howe, G. L. (eds.): *A Hundred Years of Music in America* (G. L. Howe, Chicago).

1890. Spillane, Daniel: *History of the American Pianoforte* (D. Spillane, New York).

Although so cursory a sampling ignores the concurrent growth of interest and activity in public-school music, the rise of a musical-periodical press, and the floods of "methods" as well as natively published music for many media (but especially those of solo voice, chorus, and piano), it still does reveal several notable trends: the emergence of Chicago as a musical center; the first appearance of specialist authors (Ritter, Krehbiel, Mathews, and Upton); an increased concern with history; and — in the Upton entries — the début of the "program-annotation" guidebooks soon to become and to remain so prominent in musical literature addressed primarily to the listener rather than to the student or executant.

The next decade's sampling is even more revelatory, since it not only confirms the trends just cited but marks the rise of prolific professional specialist-writers on music (now including authoritative scholars, of whom Krehbiel was the pioneer, as well as more or less well-informed journalists); since it features more frequently works that remain (some of them of course in revised editions) in active use today; for its evidence of a lively concern with the then ultra-radical music and theories of Wagner; and for its first (surprisingly reputable!) examples of that soon-to-be triumphantly omnipresent *genre* — the "appreciation" book.

1891. Krehbiel, H. E.: *Studies in the Wagnerian Drama* (Harper, New York).
1892. Krehbiel, H. E.: *The Philharmonic Society of New York: A Memorial* (Novello, Ewer & Co., New York).
1893. Finck, H. T.: *Wagner and His Works* (Scribner).
1894. Apthorp, W. F.: *Musicians and Music Lovers, and Other Essays* (Scribner).
1895. Baker, Theodore: *A Dictionary of Musical Terms* (G. Schirmer, New York).
1896. Krehbiel, H. E.: *How to Listen to Music* (Scribner).
1897. Chadwick, G. W.: *Harmony: a Course of Study* (B. F. Wood, Boston).
1898. Henderson, W. J.: *What is Good Music?* (Scribner).
1899. Elson, L. C.: *National Music of America and Its Sources* (Page, Boston).
1900. Baker, Theodore: *Biographical Dictionary of Musicians*, 1st ed. (G. Schirmer).

In the early years of the new century there was such a marked increase in published music-book quantity and diversity that the present sampler-entry chronological synopsis now becomes less and less adequately exemplary. Even so, however, it does imply a further, orderly progression of the same trends as well as exhibiting a still larger proportion of works that remain in active use today.

1901. Mason, William: *Memories of a Musical Life* (Century Co., New York).

1902. Dickinson, Edward: *Music in the History of the Western Church* (Scribner).

1903. Hughes, Rupert: *The Musical Guide* — later to become *The Music Lovers' Encyclopedia* (McClure, Phillips & Co., New York).

1904. Elson, L. C.: *The History of American Music* (Macmillan, New York).

1905. Thomas, Theodore: *A Musical Autobiography* (A. C. McClurg).

1906. Mason, D. G.: *The Romantic Composers* (Macmillan).

1907. Surette, T. W. & Mason, D. G.: *The Appreciation of Music* (Gray, New York).

1908. Upton, G. P.: *The Standard Concert Guide* (A. C. McClurg).

1909. Burton, F. R.: *American Primitive Music* (Moffat Yard & Co., New York).

1910. Cooke, J. F.: *Standard History of Music* (Presser, Philadelphia).

1911. Huneker, J. G.: *Franz Liszt, a Study* (Scribner).

1912. MacDowell, E. A.: *Critical and Historical Essays* (Arthur P. Schmidt Co., Boston).

1913. Faulkner, A. S.: *What We Hear in Music* (Victor Talking Machine Co., Camden, N. J.).

1914. Krehbiel, H. E.: *Afro-American Folk Song* (G. Schirmer).

1915. Elson, Arthur: *The Book of Musical Knowledge* (Houghton Miflin, Boston).

1916. Miller, D. C.: *The Science of Musical Sounds* (Macmillan).

1917. Surette, T. W.: *Music and Life* (Houghton Miflin).

THE EBULLIENT RECENT PAST: WORLD WAR I TO THE PRESENT

At this point it is obvious that the illuminatory usefulness of our exemplary-sampler has been largely exhausted. And since most of the more substantial later publications are well known, at least by reputation, it may be more profitable merely to summarize some of the more influential developments in several vital areas.

In Scholarship: The establishment of *The Musical Quarterly* (1915); that of the first chairs of musicology at American universities (for Otto Kinkeldey at Cornell in 1930 and for Paul Henry Lang at Columbia in 1933); and that of the *Journal of the American Musicological Society* (1948). In quite recent years a prolific younger generation of musical scholars has demonstrated increasing freedom from the pedantries of the long-dominant German influence yet without relaxing the latter's invaluable disciplines and thoroughness. American presses — which already had sponsored Gustave Reese's great medieval and Renaissance studies and the native fruits of the last years of Alfred Einstein, Curt Sachs, and Manfred

Bukofzer — are to be credited with such notable works as Ralph Kirkpatrick's *Domenico Scarlatti* (1953), H. C. Robbins Landon's *The Symphonies of Joseph Haydn* (1955; published first in England, to be sure, as his projected full-length biography probably will be), Alfred Mann's *Study of Fugue* (1958), D. K. Wilgus's *Anglo-American Folksong Scholarship Since 1898* (1959), and W. S. Newman's *The Sonata in the Baroque Era* (1959). It is also noteworthy that this domain has not been walled off as the exclusive province of professional specialists only but has profited by such "invasions" as those by Jacques Barzun (*Berlioz and the Romantic Century*, 1950; paperback abridgment, 1956) and Minna Curtiss (*Bizet and His World*, 1958), and increasingly — if more tentatively — by a number of the more serious historian-analysts of those peculiarly American musical-sociological phenomena: jazz, ragtime, and the blues.

In Bibliography and Music-Library Guidance: The publication of the National Schools of Music *List of Books on Music* (1935, with supplements through 1957); the Music Library Association's quarterly *Notes* (formally begun in 1943); *The Music Index* (begun as a periodical in 1949, with annual cumulations); and my own "practical" bibliography (so called because it is confined to books in English and in print, and supplies prices), *Schirmer's Guide to Books on Music and Musicians* (1951).

In Encyclopedic Reference Works: The publication of an American Supplement to *Grove* (1920); the first comprehensive one-volume American work of this kind (W. S. Pratt's *New Cyclopedia* of 1924) and the largest to date (Oscar Thompson's *Cyclopedia* of 1939 and later editions); the complementary subject and biographical works, Willi Apel's *Harvard Dictionary of Music* (1944; abridgment 1960) and Nicolas Slonimsky's complete revision of *Baker's Biographical Dictionary of Musicians* (1958); and a diverse miscellany of more specialized dictionaries and encyclopedias — of opera, musical comedy, jazz, ballet, phonograph records, etc.

More broadly influential and less easy to document as specifically are various general trends which add (at least at first glance) impressive further evidence of substantial progress in comparatively recent years:

1) The perhaps slow but certainly steady increase both in the

number of comprehensive and specialized music libraries and in the size and scope of their collections — notably augmented by the diffusion of incunabula, rare out-of-print books (and manuscripts), doctoral theses, etc., via microfilms.

2) The still erratic yet gradually cumulative rise in factual accuracy (following the precipitous decline in standards during the twenties and thirties) in "popularized" biographies, histories, and appreciation books. Even the mass-production-line hack authors now tend to glean their data from the more reliable recent editions of standard reference works, which themselves have been largely cleansed of long-perpetuated errors thanks to the herculean labors of Slonimsky and other precisionists. Then, too, the hacks no longer enjoy a near-monopoly of this field, into which the dual magnets of potential opportunities and rewards have again drawn writers of greater authority (including such composers as Copland and Bernstein) and wider practical teaching experience.

3) The marked visual improvements in printing, layout, and reproduction of both pictorial and musical illustrations that characterize all but a dwindling proportion of present-day music-book publications, but that are perhaps most prominent in school textbooks and the so-called "class" (i.e., higher-priced) paperbacks.

4) The less consistently and successfully achieved, but nevertheless bravely attempted, efforts by authors to enhance the appeal of their sheerly musical materials by providing expanded historical backgrounds, correlations with the other arts, and in some cases pertinent illuminations from concurrent studies in sociology, general esthetics, acoustics and electroacoustics, psychology, and even clinical psychiatry. Probably more directly helpful, however, is the increased emphasis on complementing reading itself with active listening experiences of the music discussed — an emphasis that in most books can only be fruitful, of course, if the individual reader or classroom teacher makes actual use of the discographical recommendations, but that in the case of occasional publications is made more conveniently possible by direct tie-ins with specifically illustrative recordings.

5) The vastly increased if still too often superficial general familiarity of potential readers with the more prominent musical personalities of our day and at least the names, and some of the works,

of many composers outside the once narrowly limited pantheon of "classic masters." Television, radio, records, and periodicals not only have made national heroes of a Bernstein and a Cliburn, but have introduced many other performing artists and commentators (including folk-music and jazz specialists) to incalculably larger and more diversified audiences than they ever could command in the past. Record collectors and habitual listeners to the so-called "good music" broadcast stations have been afforded rich opportunities for making a closer and more often repeated acquaintance with the non-standard (old and new) as well as the standard repertories and interpreters; occasionally, at least, the disc-jacket and broadcast commentaries include some pertinent bibliographic references.

Yet, under more skeptical reexamination, many of these ponderable achievements and promising trends must be balanced against —and seem sometimes contradicted by—their prohibitive cost or their failure to date to attain more than partial fulfillment of the hopes they raise.

The growth in musical scholarship and research facilities has been influential largely within institutional circles only; the best of its book manifestations have won relatively scant attention from even seriously musically interested laymen. The non-specialist college student seldom is obliged (or urged) to venture outside a limited range of diffuse elementary musical appreciation and history textbooks. He, and a few unusually energetic laymen, may have learned to consult more scholarly works on occasion, but all too seldom are these added to personal libraries or even read in full; reading as a chore all too seldom metamorphoses into reading as pleasure. Steadily the eternal gap between scholar and layman widens; increasingly the latter seems content with whatever second- or third-hand scholarship may trickle down through the few popularized books he does read; more and more widespread becomes the miasmic delusion that "learning" comes to a dead stop with the end of one's formal education.

Not all the fault may be the timid reader's only: it is a rare musicologist who is also a skillful and engaging writer, and on lower levels it is a rare musical specialist of any kind who can make his own interest enthusiastically contagious or who does not too often confuse a presumed public need for information with a private itch to impart it. To whatever extent the visual and content improvements in textbooks may aid their classroom usefulness, they still seldom disguise or transcend their sugaring-the-pedagogic-pill enticingly enough to win many readers-for-enjoyment-only. Not so many years ago much of the most stimulating writing on music was to be found in the frequent collections of far-ranging, authoritative yet always lively, essays by men experienced in all the arts—masters of the provocative phrase, sparkling wit, and revelatory insight—like Carl Engel, Philip Hale, H. T. Parker, James Gibbons Huneker, Paul Rosenfeld, *et al.*, in this country; Ernest Newman and many others in England. Surely that breed has not died out entirely! Yet if not, their successors' writing is now almost exclusively confined to periodicals: essay collections are rarely published nowadays, and when they are their sales record lends scant encouragement to repetitions of the experiment.

The economic factor indeed limits the general circulation of all music-books, but particularly that of the more extensive reference works and those of exceptionally handsome format and lavish illustrations, which with very few exceptions (usually printed abroad) are nowadays dismayingly—if not unjustifiedly—high priced. It is extremely unlikely that even so widely appealing a one-volume encyclopedia as Percy Scholes's *Oxford Companion to Music* could repeat its spectacular sales success if it appeared for the first time today with the $25.00 price tag of its current ninth edition — as contrasted with the modest $6.50 cost of its original 1938 version. All too often the only currently successful publications in the higher-price brackets are the "picture-histories," fancily decorative songbooks, and the like, which are deliberately designed and merchandised as "gift" books to be skimmed through or merely to lie in state—admired but unused—on conspicuous display in living rooms.

The apparent solution of this problem, the paperback volume, has yet to prove that it can be a complete or conclusive one. Its most evident weakness is the still excessively erratic and limited choice of (almost invariably reprinted) materials, but it is more basically handicapped by the lack, to date, of adequate advertising, reviews, and other means of enticing the attention and support of potential readers. And this handicap is of course only one of the many stigmata of a general music-book promotional failure—the responsibility for which cannot be laid exclusively on publishers' and reviewers' shoulders. For it must be remembered that the amount of advertising any book is given is conventionally allotted primarily on the basis, first of expected and later (after publication) of actual sales. Similarly, the number and length of reviews published (outside highly specialized periodicals at least) is conventionally dependent on the amount of general book advertising accorded individual journals or columns — although such rough space budgeting always can be expanded if sufficient review-readership interest is demonstrated. Unfortunately, it seldom is: scanty as music-book reviews and news may be in general, literary, and even music and record journals, there are actually more published than can be justified on the basis of advertising received or the results of "readership-interest" questionnaires. Not surprisingly the consequence is that reviews are mainly confined to "prestige" works, those of optimum real or supposed "human interest," and those concerned with maximally "newsworthy" personalities.

Perhaps most disappointing of all has been the lack of expected success both in tying in specific books with related recordings or broadcast series and in more generally capitalizing on the musical interests of record and broadcast listeners. In the former case, the awkwardness of common book-and-album packaging and the scarcity (outside the larger cities) of combined book-and-record merchandising facilities have usually resulted in each medium's having to make its way alone. In the latter, a few exceptional hits (a printed collection of Leonard Bernstein's TV appreciation talks, an occasional pioneering record or hi-fi guidebook, some heavily plugged program-note anthologies, etc.) have done little to compensate for the general failure of reproduced-music listener-aids to reach more than a small fraction of their potential audience.

But it would be pointlessly cruel to continue bedevilling an already confused and exhausted patient merely to fatten our case-history files with further—and ever more puzzling—evidence of his ambiguous malaises. More than enough is already available to justify our isolating a, if not *the*, prime factor. Surely, it must be the pervading incapacity to realize its own presumed potentialities that most saliently characterizes musical literature's present loss of

nerve and orientation, its whole current dilemma of uneasy existence in a state of what is not so much suspended animation as it
is one of frantic energy expended in a near-vacuum, of reactionless
action, of vital strength neutralized by a sense of inadequacy or
even impotence. Here, too, is the most glaring contrast between the
seminal role played by the relatively few music-books published
prior to World War I and the ambivalent, if still far from wholly
sterile, contributions to contemporary American life by the geomet-
rically expanding musical literature of more recent years.

In Default of a Nostrum . . .

When it is foolhardy for even the most assured diagnostician to
promise—or even suggest the possibility of—a simple cure for a
complex real or imaginary disease, the best he can do is to cheer
up the patient and his family with the traditional and not entirely
comfortless reassurances: that the malady is a common one and has
yet to prove fatal, that time is the great healer, that regular exercise
and occupational therapy often help, and that in any case it is too
early to make any sure prognosis of the malady's future course.

For myself, I dare venture little further, except to suggest that
we all may have been too prone to confuse linearly cumulative
"progress" with the cyclic generation/degeneration/regeneration
processes of organic life. Perhaps this has deluded us into expecting
more of musical literature than it ever could—or can—be capable
of achieving. Possibly its current predicament is less abnormal than
it seems in too close perspective, or perhaps it is the temporary,
inescapable fate of any art in an era as completely abnormal by all
familiar standards as our own. At any rate, it strikes me as un-
reasonable to hold music-book authors, publishers, and readers
exclusively responsible for the uncertainties of a whole culture and
way of life in which the arts in general and that of music in
particular play, after all, so relatively minor—however vital—a part.

In larger perspective, is it unnatural that the music-book's youth-
fully rapid and purposeful growth should be followed by a "plateau"
period (common to all kinds of human experience) where the apparent halt in further progress actually provides the needful incuba-
tion time for new forces to evolve and mature, to gather strength
and orientation for the next leap forward? Or, shocking as it may

seem to those of us habituated to a dependence on books, isn't it possible that the new mass-listener's present disregard of reading may be an inevitable corollary of his still adolescently omnivorous appetite for direct raw musical experience? We may legitimately hope that what begins as escapist entertainment may lead eventually to deeper study and understanding, but are we justified in expecting it to do so rapidly or in every individual case?

At any rate, I suspect that we won't find satisfactory answers to our present problems until we begin to ask more searching questions than any that have been propounded so far. The whole case of our "ailing" musical literature cries for more thorough and thoughtful —and dispassionate—reconsideration; and if that forces us to concede the lack of any "miracle" cure, surely we can then more profitably concentrate on finding and utilizing *practicable* therapeutic measures. Some of those implied in the foregoing diagnosis may seem roundabout (like the need for a comprehensive study of the history, statistics, and policies of music-book publishing which would amplify the provocative preliminary investigation by Myers), quixotic (like the suggestion that scholarship can profit by livelier "readability," more infectious enthusiasm, and bolder adventures into traditionally non-academic domains), or unduly commercial (like the concern with more effectual publicity and merchandising). Yet can we afford to neglect or disdain any possibility of better understanding and reanimating the role of books and their makers in contemporary musical life?

I am not one of the disillusioned intellectuals who has fatalistically resigned himself to the inevitability of reading's obsolescence and supersession by other, more streamlined, modes of learning and entertainment. But none of us who refuse to abandon the most versatile and powerful intellectual tool we have inherited can afford to deny the existence or promise of newer ones; nor can we blind ourselves to the clear prospect that books must increasingly compete for the favor of younger generations as yet skeptical or unsure of the immediate as well as the eventual rewards to be found in the printed page. If Johnny can't read, surely it is only because he hasn't been properly taught how; if he won't read, is the fault only his own mulish recalcitrance, or that of his mentors and parents in failing to provide sufficiently stimulating and persuasive incentives?

If the fearful reports of the music-book's impending demise still seem grossly exaggerated, the many evidences of its vitality certainly are dangerously weakened by its current squeamish reluctance to acknowledge our new responsibilities and to respond vigorously to new challenges. Yet "neither quick nor dead" is an intolerable paradox which cannot be sustained indefinitely: if the critical resolution is not achieved voluntarily, it is only too sure to be arbitrarily —and not necessarily favorably—enforced upon us.

Music as a Field of Knowledge

Music Education:
An American Specialty

By ALLEN P. BRITTON

In the United States the term *music education* almost invariably refers to the teaching of music in public and parochial elementary and secondary schools. Music educators themselves, those who do the teaching, generally understand the term in a dual sense, taking it to imply not only instruction in music but also a more general, extra-musical education through or by means of music, thus by a bit of word magic providing school music with a nomenclature embodying its own special justification. In view of the necessity historically felt by school music teachers to justify the expenditures of public monies on their behalf, such a term had to be invented. While the love of music for its own sake must be considered the basic reason for the place that music holds in American schools, a place quite unique among educational systems of the world, extra-musical values have always been advanced in support of music education for the benefit of that part of the public for whom beauty is not enough of an excuse.

Whatever the term may imply, it stands for a musical activity of vast scope and sublime purpose. The purpose is nothing less than to provide an education in music for all children everywhere in the country — "Music for every child, every child *for* music," as Karl Gehrkens phrased it in 1923 in a statement that has been used as a motto ever since by the Music Educators National Conference. The scope has so far never quite matched the purpose, but, of the thousands of junior and senior high schools supported by the public across the whole breadth of the continent, almost every one maintains a choir and a wind band conducted by professionally trained musicians, and hundreds have symphony orchestras in addition. These secondary school groups are the end-products of an extensive music program offered in the elementary schools, beginning in the kindergartens, where children are taught to sing and to engage in other musical activities appropriate to their ages, and where instruction in instrumental music is begun. The so-called vocal music program (it is much more than that, but singing is the heart of it) is available to most school children through the sixth and usually the seventh and eighth grades. This program is most often taught under the supervision of professionally trained musicians who assist the classroom teachers in selecting music and in organizing the work generally. In many school systems, however, the musicians themselves do the actual teaching. The quantity of teachers, textbooks, instruments, rehearsal rooms, printed music, and miscellaneous equipment needed to keep the entire program in operation involves a huge and continuing monetary investment by financially hard-pressed local school districts and, in the case of the parochial schools, by parishes and congregations the members of which also pay taxes for the support of public school programs.

How did so extensive a system come into existence? What can be said with regard to its quality? What does the future hold for it? These questions are not as disparate as they might at first appear. The answer to each is to be sought in the nature of the American experience and in how that experience conditioned the development of American culture, if we may speak now of such a culture, taking it to be the amalgam of all the cultures brought to this land during the past four and one-half centuries.

Historians of American music now know that the founding fathers of New England loved music as much, at least, as did the general run of Englishmen of their day. However, although they were drawn from the rising mercantile classes, their Calvinistic religious convictions made them critics rather than imitators of the conventions of social classes higher in status, and they never emerged as patrons, in the European sense, of music or of any other art. Such music as they had they made themselves, fitting it into the normal religious and recreational aspects of their lives. The function of music in the society they created has ever since required that the music be understandable to the majority, a situation that has fostered the development of popular forms but that has provided little encouragement for the growth of a high art.

Characteristically, the first social efforts towards instruction in music were directed towards solfaing the simple psalm tunes of the Puritan churches. According to the Reverend Thomas Symmes, a nephew of the scholarly Cotton Mather, this art was taught at Harvard College during the earliest years of its existence. The practice had long been discontinued by the 1720s, however, when Symmes and many others put their best efforts into the establishment of singing schools for the laity. Such schools (actually, evening classes convened at any convenient hall) are known to have existed as early as 1712, but by 1721 they were flourishing in New England. In that year the Reverends John Tufts and Thomas Walter each produced a textbook for them. The two works, modeled after similar works already being produced in England, were the progenitors of hundreds of singing school textbooks, popularly referred to as tunebooks, the publication of which reached its height during the first half of the 19th century and continues in a small way today in the South.

Almost everything about the singing school is characteristic of American music education today, if one looks to its basic aspects rather than to externals. In the first place, the singing school was popularly supported; not, of course, through tax funds, but directly through fees paid by student to singing master. In the second place, its teachers, peripatetic as they might have been, were nevertheless drawn directly from the society in which they worked, and, for the most part, were only a short step ahead of that society in musical taste and education. Most of them had learned all the music they knew in the type of school they served. In the third place, the music taught was generally popular in nature and of immediate social usefulness. Both students and teachers possessed an immediate and common aim, that of learning to handle the singing voice and to read music at sight sufficiently well to participate in the simple religious activities of the village and city choirs. In the fourth place, although from the very first singing school teachers showed an interest in improving the methodology of teaching and constantly produced "plainer and easier" techniques, for and about which they debated and propagandized, on the other hand, in what can, I think, be called typically American fashion, they remained eclectic in practice, never adopting one method completely but utilizing bits and snatches of all.

In the fifth place, the singing school produced its own body of textbooks and its own music, so that it functioned largely as an independent musical entity. In the sixth place, the singing school always aimed at a certain moral and social and musical uplift. Tufts and Walter avowedly sought to improve the quality of music in the churches as well as to provide innocent recreational opportunities for the young, and such aims certainly continue in full force with music educators today. The atmosphere of reform has permeated American music education as it has all other aspects of American culture. From the musical standpoint, because of the essentially popular nature of the singing school and the system of music education derived from it, the reforms sought have always been comparatively simple in nature—an improvement in such things as voice quality, sight-reading ability, and, more importantly, but in ways more difficult to understand, in the quality of music used.

American music teachers have always talked about the importance of utilizing "better music," but, when one surveys the historical developments, just what better music seemed to be presents some peculiar puzzles. For Tufts and Walter and their immediate successors, using better music meant substituting for a well-loved improvisatory style of congregational singing one in which the traditional psalm tunes were sung note for note according to the book. By 1838, when Lowell Mason succeeded in introducing music to the public schools, music teachers found to be better music the blander and, to modern ears, more insipid music of English and third-rate Continental composers, and such music was gradually adopted, at least in the North, to replace the virile native product of the days of early sovereignty. Throughout the 19th century and too well into the 20th, compilers of school singing books have found better music to be almost anything song-like so long as it possessed no indigenous flavor, excepting only a few patriotic airs and the most popular tunes of Stephen Foster. Perhaps the heart of the matter is this, that once the music of the Revolution had been done away with, American music teachers have tended to seek for better things outside their own culture, but, having had little opportunity to develop refined tastes for music of other cultures, have often settled for the appearance of things, satisfied, for example, with a Croatian folksong or a posy from some German textbook, regardless of intrinsic merit and deliberately regardless of appeal to American children. One result has been that music education, although created and nurtured by a popular love of music, has nevertheless always operated at a certain distance from the well-springs of American musical life, both popular and artistic. Music education in the United States has tended to create a world of its own with its own people, music, and thought patterns. While individuals can and do move between this world and the world of popular music and of art music, the transitions are self-consciously made and special efforts are required to function comfortably in more than one. Since folk or popular music has been considered to lack gentility, and since the highly artistic forms of European art music have been little understood by the public, the music educator has found himself in the position of trying to find understandable music that could be taken as "classical." The term "polite" is perhaps as good as any other to characterize much of the music utilized in schools from the time of Lowell Mason to the present day.

But politeness is what Americans have wanted from their schools. This is what they have needed most of all. American families, generally speaking, have sent their children to school hoping to open a better way of life for them; not, in other words, to train them for an accepted way of life, but to prepare them for entrance into the life of the next higher social class, however the latter might be conceived. An education in music has always been considered somehow to be genteel, and the prospect of being able to follow a musical career has, traditionally for most Americans, seemed to represent a decided social and cultural advancement. The ranks of the American teaching profession have traditionally been filled by persons for whom comparatively low salaries were significantly augmented by a sense of increased prestige, of having become a member or, at least, an associate of the genteel classes. To such people the forms of politeness have a special importance for reasons that are obvious enough, and the polite music of the schools, dissociated as much as possible from the music of the city streets and open countryside, fulfilled and still fulfills a need created by the very nature of American life.

Putting the matter in this way represents an attempt to explain something of the intellectual climate within which music educators have been obliged by circumstances to pursue their vocations. The attempt is intended as a basis for a defense of music education and the music educator as well as a basis for predicting what the line of future developments will be. When we have taken this special climate into consideration, the accomplishments of the music education profession in this country should appear all the more remarkable.

Among the most remarkable aspects of American music education is the fact that it has stemmed entirely from the combined efforts of the teachers themselves and of the general public. No governmental fiat placed music instruction in American schools or determined what forms it should take. Very few of our distinguished composers, performers, or critics have ever contributed to its development. American schoolmen in general have, on the whole, displayed a similar lack of interest, except when they have paused to wonder about this strange thing that grew up in their midst.

The typical process by which music was introduced to the thousands of independent school districts that are immediately and almost solely responsible for American public education may be illustrated by the events surrounding the inauguration of music instruction in Boston. It was not the school board that suggested the idea, nor the superintendent of schools, but a singing-school teacher whose name was Lowell Mason. The story of the difficulties he encountered has been perceptively told by Birge in his *History of Public School Music in the United States*. In the end, Mason was forced to donate his services for an experimental year, during which he provided his own textbooks and equipment. With the sanction of the school board, Mason taught music to the pupils at the Hawes Hall school during the school year 1837-1838. According to the masters of the school, who submitted an official report regarding the instruction on May 25, the results were quite satisfactory, and the school board thereupon engaged Mason and four assistants to institute a program of vocal music in the grammar schools.

During the remainder of the century, music was introduced in much the same way all across the country. By 1900 it was an accepted item of instruction almost everywhere. Always entirely practical in nature, the instruction resolved into two principal endeavors, one to teach the children to sing as many songs as possible by what Birge calls "a sort of rote-note process," the other to teach them how to read music at sight. The only aim of a higher nature was that the children later might be able to participate in the numerous choral societies and church choirs which existed in every population center.

All of the early school music teachers were secured from the ranks of the singing-school masters. During the 19th century most of them continued with both types of activity, but as more and more secured permanent positions, they gave up their wandering ways, and the singing school began to pass from the American scene. For the most part, singing-school teachers had been trained in the singing schools they served as well as by private tutelage. During the latter years of the century, however, more formal means of education became available. In addition to the musical "conventions" first instituted by Lowell Mason, the normal schools and the liberal arts colleges began to offer courses in the methodology of teaching school music. The tunebooks of the singing schools were converted into textbooks for the public schools.

By the year 1900, then, all of the basic elements of the present system had been laid down. A body of school music teachers existed, together with a textbook literature, a system of teacher training, and a methodology. The entire system had been created without the aid, without even the knowledge, one might say, of the most highly trained musicians of the country. The latter consisted almost entirely of new immigrants from Europe and of native Americans who had been trained by Europeans, either here or on the Continent. These people lived in their own musical world, apart from that of the school music teacher, and like the school music teacher, apart also from the world of American folk or popular music (two terms the writer chooses to consider synonymous).

Some idea of the present scope of the music education program has already been given in the opening paragraphs of this essay. During the sixty years that have passed since the turn of the century, a considerably more complex and well-rounded system of instruction has evolved. On this account, how to describe present activities presents a rather difficult problem. Perhaps it will be best to begin with the most typical activities in which school music teachers engage. To oversimplify just a little, school music teachers now fall into two major categories: vocal music teachers and instrumental music teachers. However, each of these categories itself divides into two groups. Vocal music teachers tend to specialize in the work of the elementary schools or in conducting high school choral ensembles. Instrumental music teachers are for the most part clearly differentiated as band directors or orchestra directors. In actual practice, of course, and especially at the beginning of their teaching careers, many teachers operate in two or more areas. Sopranos conduct bands, trumpet players teach strings, everyone may try his hand with the high school choir or junior high school general music class. In the main, however, the curriculum in music is largely defined by the four principal areas of activity, and most of the practical and philosophical problems of teaching school music may be related to one of them.

In many ways the most important, probably involving the greatest expenditures of time, effort, and money, and certainly the least known outside the profession, is the music program of the elementary schools—the so-called vocal music program with which music education began. Although practices vary somewhat, generally speaking this program is taught by the regular classroom teachers under the supervision of music specialists, as the latter tend to be called. In a more or less typical situation illustrated by a local school system, for example, 125 minutes a week are allocated to music instruction by the school authorities — 25 minutes a day. The classroom teacher conducts the lesson four of these days, and the music specialist comes in on the remaining day. Depending upon the facilities available, the children may receive the instruction in the classroom or may go to a special music room.

MUSIC EDUCATION: AN AMERICAN SPECIALTY

Despite the facts that individual classroom teachers may frequently be quite unskilled as musicians, that the music specialist may visit any individual classroom only at intervals, and that the total amount of time available is none too great in the first place, the declared aims of the instruction are complex. A recent statement of purposes and goals prepared by Lilla Belle Pitts, one of the most authoritative spokesmen in this field, and published in the April-May 1958 issue of the *Music Educators Journal*, declares: "We must provide a balanced and interrelated program of music, beginning in the elementary school, which includes an integrated total of singing, expressive bodily movement, dramatic interpretation, playing instruments, discriminating listening, enabling skills, and creative activities." These are not merely words. Concerning each of the activities proposed there has grown up a vast body of methodological literature and of instruction materials — books, recordings, films, melody and percussive instruments, and so forth. An analysis of the activities desirable in implementing this program has been made by Jessie L. Fleming and reported in the Spring 1953 issue of the *Journal of Research in Music Education*. Fleming found 83 activities considered to be essential by music educators, ranging from "singing rote songs with accompaniment" to "viewing motion pictures and other visual aids based on music and musicians." She also found that the regular classroom teacher, in order to supplement the program, should possess a total of close to a hundred specific competencies!

Fleming's findings, although not intended to do so, represent a *reductio ad absurdum* of the notion that the average elementary school teacher can be expected to acquire the musicianship necessary to teach music. On the other hand, authors of college textbooks for use in courses designed to provide it have been much less demanding. A few years ago one very prominent textbook writer was almost read out of the music education profession, in a manner of speaking, for seeming to suggest in such a work that the less one knew about music the better able he (she) would be to approach the child with understanding and thus to teach him to love and appreciate the art.

Were music educators to deny that the average classroom teacher can teach music and to insist that all music be taught by musicians, there would be very little music taught in American classrooms, for

[219]

there would not be enough musicians to go around, even if school boards could be inveigled into employing them. So the situation remains that, while a few school districts do employ enough specialists to teach all the music, perhaps a majority provide only supervisors to come in occasionally, leaving the classroom teacher responsible for most of the instruction. Tragically, many school districts do not even employ supervisors, and what music is taught depends upon the propensities of individual teachers.

But thousands of school districts over the whole breadth of the land employ sufficient elementary music specialists to supervise or teach as much music as can reasonably be fitted into an increasingly busy school day. A serious problem still exists in these numerous instances with regard, first, to whether the proposed complex program is a practicable one and, second, whether its purpose is valid. It may be quite possible, for example, to teach third, fourth, and fifth graders to read simple music at sight by spending about a half-hour each school day on the matter, providing the teacher is competent and the music beautiful enough to furnish a sufficient motivation. But whether this can be done under the teaching conditions that generally prevail remains doubtful, especially when the children do not in fact devote one half-hour a day to it but spend most of the time singing rote songs, making up new songs, inventing bodily movements (dancing) to fit songs they sing or music they hear played for them, listening to items from the standard concert repertory everybody ought to know, and engaging otherwise in a variety of undoubtedly worthy musical activities including attending concerts by the local symphony orchestra or by groups from their own school system.

Until recently, when a remarkable book appeared under the title *Basic Concepts in Music Education* (University of Chicago Press, 1958), little attention had been given by music educators to the esthetics of music. The subject is subtle and difficult, of course, but some attention to it might have brought a quicker intellectual appreciation of the necessity of utilizing in education only music of great intrinsic appeal. To do anything else can hardly be calculated to induce the love and appreciation of music that periodic resolutions of the Music Educators National Conference put forth as the principal aim of instruction. This aim, the validity of which cannot be questioned, seems to have been misunderstood by compilers of school music books as well as writers of methodological treatises.

The latter works rarely ignore the basic purpose entirely but generally tend to subordinate it in a kind of rush to describe the type of activities in which children are to engage. Writers speak in terms of "using music as a part of the experience of the daily life of the child" and of "helping boys and girls to enjoy music" but rarely if ever in terms of what specific music might be most esthetically satisfying to know. That music educators usually refer to the songs they use as "material" probably indicates that they do not think of these songs primarily as music. The capacity of young children to enjoy music is well enough known, but the enjoyment normally stems as much from concomitant activities and circumstances as it does from the purported music. Vocal music programs that place a primary emphasis upon extra-musical considerations tend to lose appeal rather quickly. In the upper years of the elementary school a certain ennui seems to set in — at the time when a paucity of musical vitality cannot longer be concealed by hopping, skipping, and dancing. A perennial complaint of elementary-music specialists is that the capacity of children to respond with creative bodily movements and the like seems to dry up somehow with advancing years. A constant admonition runs through the literature —to try to preserve as much as possible of their freedom in music and song as they grow older. Despite all the talk about *growth* that fills educational literature, the fact remains that teachers of the very young seem not really to believe that children should in fact grow up. Or so it would seem when one sees constant attempts to carry into the higher grades and secondary schools the methodologies and esthetic materials of the primary grades.

The vocal music program continues into the first and second years of the junior high school in most instances, in the form of general music classes. Without any doubt at all, such classes are universally recognized to be the most difficult to teach. A few music educators seem to have a knack for doing so, but most would rather do almost anything else, and the classes are often assigned to new teachers, those with the least seniority. A special problem also faces these teachers. By the time students have reached junior

[221]

high school age, most of them with musical proclivities have already taken up an instrument and are playing in the school band or orchestra, or they have joined one of the school choral ensembles. The general music class is typically reserved for all the rest, the least talented or interested on the whole. In addition, if the teacher is at heart an elementary school specialist, he will tend to use methods and materials appropriate for elementary schools. If he is at heart a choral director, he will tend to try to make the general music class into a kind of choral ensemble. At this date, the problem of the general music class remains unsolved at the junior high school level, except in individual instances.

Before leaving this topic some attention must be paid to the textbooks used in the elementary schools. These take the form of complete series of books, each series consisting of a book for each year of school from kindergarten through the eighth grade. The publication of such series is as competitive as the automobile business, and the number of publishing companies in the field is correspondingly small. At the present writing, four firms have complete series on the market, another firm has a new series started, and still another is preparing to enter the competition shortly. There is no need to go into the long history of the publication of such series, a history that began in 1861 and continued in an atmosphere of controversy over the *rote song method* or the *note reading method*. The first method was embraced by a complete series, *The National Music Course* (1870-1875), by Luther Whiting Mason, the second by *The Normal Music Course* (1883), a series compiled by Hosea Edson Holt and John Wheeler Tufts (Tufts is one of the very few prominent American musicians who have contributed significantly to the school music movement). Since that time the grade schools have never been without a number of such series from which to choose. The principal publishers of the present day have been in the business for a long time, and each of their current series is only the latest of a series of series. Music educators generally believe that planning for a new series begins as soon as the latest is well launched. Commercially speaking, the job of the sales agents of these publishers is to secure as many "adoptions" as possible. To secure an adoption means to have a series designated officially for use throughout an entire school district or, in some happy instances, throughout an entire state. The magnitude of the potential market for single copies of the songbooks equals the number of children in the public and parochial schools.

Now the point to be kept in mind here is that these series provide the basic musical content of the elementary school music program. Regardless of the skill of a teacher or of the facilities and teaching time available to her, the specific musical compositions with which her students will become acquainted will consist largely of those in the series adopted by her state or school system. A very simple question may be asked. Are all the songs in all the series worth knowing? In fairness to the publishers and to the music educators who have prepared the various series currently in use, the present writer suggests that not one of them would answer this question in the affirmative. The fact is that each of the series contains substantial numbers of songs without discernible musical attractiveness. For a variety of special reasons, the compilation of songs for a textbook series seems to be the most difficult job in music education. Copyright restrictions enter the picture, as well as the desire to have each new series different from the last (a frequent complaint is that a new series by a given publishing house invariably excludes all the most popular items from its immediate predecessor). The seeming necessity of including "reading songs" (often specially composed and designed to provide exercise material for the sight reading program) accounts for many uninteresting items, as does the desire to provide songs with texts concerning various extra-musical interests of children — horses and witches, mailmen and airplanes, for example. If the world's musical literature has somehow failed to provide us with a Halloween song, then there seems nothing to do but have such a song composed. Such songs are rarely gems.

Fortunately, the current series all contain a higher proportion of good songs than did older series, and rumor has it that one of the great publishing houses is now contemplating the preparation of a series that will contain music selected on purely musical considerations. The publishers themselves all are honestly interested in producing exactly what the profession desires. There is no forbidding reason that all of the songs in all of the series should not be musically entrancing. When they are, the place of music in the

[223]

elementary schools will be easier to hold and to advance.

The vocal music program culminates directly in the choral program of the junior and senior high schools. The typical high school, junior or senior, maintains a mixed chorus and a variety of other vocal ensembles including boys' and girls' glee clubs. The quality of these groups is generally high, and the best of them perform, capably and artistically, the finest music in the choral repertory. A large publishing industry has grown up to supply the voracious demand for music, since the amount even a junior high school chorus can perform in a given year is tremendous. Aside from a significant quantity of music composed originally for choral ensembles, most groups also make extensive use of music from other sources specially arranged for voices. Regrettably, some of the original choral music and most of the arrangements possess dubious musical worth. In recent years, choral groups have been provided with arrangements of folk and Broadway tunes done up in the style of the choruses one hears on commercial radio and television shows. This music has the advantage of being idiomatically familiar to young people and of serving to help identify the school music program with the outside world. It is defended by many as representative of a new American art form. Perhaps it is. At any rate, its widespread use in schools represents a break in the polite tradition of avoiding anything smacking of indigenous origin, and the music is at least as good as the innocuous pieces in 19th-century style turned out by church and school choral directors that still comprise too large a share of the school repertory. Very little contemporary music by serious composers is performed in our schools. Not much is available, as a matter of fact, and most of it is beyond the performing abilities of high school students. The serious American composer has shown an almost total lack of interest in school music, leaving the field clear for arrangers and composers of more modest talent.

When one thinks of instrumental music in American schools, he is almost sure to think of the high school band, that ubiquitous organization of wind and percussion instruments which plays for school football and basketball games, and for civic celebrations of all sorts, but which also carries out a schedule of serious as well as popular concerts, and which constitutes the principal avenue open to

American youth for the study of instrumental styles. Perhaps no other aspect of music education has been subjected to so much criticism both from inside and outside the profession. Hardly a *Bulletin* of the Council for Basic Education misses an opportunity to say something disrespectful about the marching band and its bare-legged majorettes. Criticism has been equally vigorous within the profession. All the world, except the band directors themselves and their students, seems to deplore the fact that almost every junior and senior high school has a band. Wholesale criticism has served to unite the bandmasters in a kind of truculent fraternity within the profession, a fraternity that participates vitally in the essential business of music education, i.e. teaching music, but that also manages to maintain a certain professional aloofness from the rest of the profession, an aloofness compacted of pride of accomplishment, singleminded attention to the business at hand, and hurt at the criticism of outsiders.

Some band directors also direct orchestras. In the main, however, the orchestra directors constitute a separate and much smaller group. For the most part they are string players whose musical backgrounds seem to have conditioned them, generally speaking, to a more individualistic outlook than is typical of the bandmaster. The high school orchestra director tends to be a little more interested in music for its own sake, and he performs, on the whole, a more highly artistic repertory. But as a class he is not so adept at attracting and holding students as is the bandmaster, nor does he possess the latter's indefatigable organizational talents. Then too, string players tend to be trained for careers as concert soloists, while wind instrumentalists are trained as sidemen. The former approaches the large ensemble with certain spiritual and musical reservations, the latter considers it the end and all of being. Certainly the bandmen have had special historical and social influences on their side. The high school band took over the place formerly occupied by the town band and so began with a ready-made social function and acceptance. On the other hand, the high school symphony orchestra was something quite new. At any rate, all of these things taken together resulted in a fantastic success for wind bands, one enjoyed by them nowhere else in the world. Given every aid by the manufacturers of wind instruments, tolerated by school administrators for their practical utility as well as for their innate appeal to a youth the administrators were trying to keep happy and amenable in school, and developed to unbelievably high standards of technical excellence in the annual band contests which first got under way in 1923, the high school band quickly outgrew the orchestra in numbers, and during the 1930s came to dominate the educational scene. Despite the promising beginnings of orchestral activity made during the 1920s, the total number of orchestras did not increase significantly during the next two decades. During the past decade, however, the orchestral movement has begun to show amazing vitality. The number of schools with strong string programs increases constantly, and the players being developed, when augmented by the excellent wind and percussion players produced by the band program, have enabled a large number of schools to organize symphony orchestras of very high quality. The new body of string teachers and orchestra conductors seems to be much more closely attuned to the practical realities of the school situation than were most of their predecessors. They are more adept at the class teaching required for success, and they are showing signs of developing the organizing techniques necessary to the development and maintenance of large ensembles. In short, the new breed of school string teachers seems at last to be profiting from the successful example set for all string teachers by Joseph E. Maddy, who first showed how the thing could be done during the 1920s. Since 1928, when Maddy organized the National Music Camp at Interlochen, Michigan, the magnificent high school orchestra he assembles there for eight weeks each summer has constituted one of the chief glories of American music education. The National Music Camp itself now attracts well over 2,000 school and college students to Northern Michigan each season, where they engage in all aspects of musical study as well as in the study of plastic and graphic arts, the theater, and the dance. Dozens of other summer camps now also provide musical opportunities of high artistic merit for the best of the thousands of young performers developed in school programs. That Maddy's high school orchestras inspired the whole development illustrates how practical-minded attention to the finest of musical expression can succeed on its own merits in America.

The success of the bands and the promise of the orchestras

reflect an extraordinary amount of hard work on the part of their conductors. Instruction in instrumental music typically begins during the later years of elementary school and is given in classes to which students are sent from their regular classrooms. On the latter account, instrumental music has always created disruptions in school schedules that are allowed to continue only by the good will of the principals and regular teachers — a good will that the instrumental teacher must carefully and continuously nourish. Excellent techniques of instruction have been devised, based upon the use of a judicious combination of technical exercises and well-known songs. After one to three years of such instruction, the student is ready to join a junior high school band or orchestra, where, in addition to the social and musical attractions of belonging to such a group, he is motivated to continue serious study by the solo and ensemble contests that form so characteristic a part of the instrumental program.

The contest movement in music education had its origins during the 1920s. Although the "music memory" contests of those days have long since vanished, contests for bands, orchestras, and choral groups still continue with undiminishing vigor. The contest idea has been attacked by many, but musical contests are at least as old as the first Olympic games, and the criticism leveled against contemporary school contests has only seemed to stimulate their growth.

One serious criticism can still be made of the contests as one generally observes them. Bands and choruses particularly, and even orchestras to some extent, that come from any but the largest schools with the most highly developed instrumental programs tend to perform a species of music specially manufactured for contest purposes. Little of it can be considered worth the time and effort spent in its mastery, except as one considers the development of the required technical proficiency to constitute a worthy aim in itself.

The problem of the contest pieces points up what continues to be a serious weakness of the band movement particularly but also of the music education program in the schools generally. The program has never been conceived as a means for the study of Western art music, for example, nor of any other body of musical literature. Rather, the ability to perform has been treated as an end in itself, an activity for activity's sake.

Almost everything said so far has been directed at the generality of things, and particularly at certain basic weaknesses of music education as it functions broadly throughout the land. The fact that it has weaknesses should be allowed to obscure neither its tremendous accomplishments nor its function as the bedrock upon which American musical culture now rests. Millions of elementary school children are being taught to sing and otherwise to enjoy music, and thousands upon thousands of adolescents are performing in high school choirs, bands, and orchestras that meet satisfactorily high musical standards, and the best of which are almost unbelievably proficient. From the ranks of these young musicians come our professional performers and teachers as well as the constantly growing audience for music of all kinds.

The music departments of American colleges and universities are largely engaged in preparing teachers for the public and parochial schools. That there are so many students in music education accounts for a large college demand for professors of applied music and of the musicological subjects. Furthermore, particularly in state-supported schools where legislative appropriations tend to be geared strictly to size of enrollments, the budget required to staff and maintain a department large enough to train the school teachers and the college teachers who will do the training is often sufficient to support a composer-in-residence or a string quartet. Thus, the tax and other monies spent directly for school music now constitute a patronage of music by the general public on a scale that dwarfs any patronage to be found elsewhere (except, perhaps, in Russia), now or in the past. To have won for music the voluntary support of the public stands out as the most magnificent accomplishment of American music education. The thing was not done with conscious forethought, nor has the accomplishment been properly appreciated inside or outside the profession.

Although the term music education has been employed throughout this essay in reference only to the teaching of music in public and parochial schools, the term is also used on occasion to refer to any music teaching whatever. There is a great deal of music teaching in the United States besides that which goes on in schools. Thousands of private piano teachers perform an inestimably valuable service in the musical education of children and adults, as do thousands of private teachers of other instruments. The departments, schools, and conservatories of music, a very few independent, most of them now integral units of colleges and universities, have established a system of musical education that seeks to combine the best of the academic and the conservatory traditions. The system is unique and as much admired abroad as it is at home — generally speaking, and with due regard for those who do not admire it very much at all. American business continues to contribute a great deal to education, with some hope of economic gain, to be sure, but nevertheless with good sense and will. The recording industry has gone out of its way to cooperate with educators in the production of educational materials. The instrument manufacturers, the publishers, and the large variety of suppliers have all done more than their fair share to help the cause according to the nature of their opportunity and capability. And from the days of Theodore Thomas, through those of Walter Damrosch, right down to Leonard Bernstein at the present time, the American symphony orchestra conductor has engaged in some semblance of educational endeavor.

We have been a nation of improvers, of uplifters, of raisers of standards. Our aims have been wholesome, our efforts great, if sometimes misdirected or uninformed. There is no reason to doubt that the average erudition and musicality of school music teachers will continue to rise, or that the enthusiastic practice of music in today's schools will become more enthusiastic in the future as its esthetic significance continues to grow.

The Taste Makers; Critics and Criticism

By EDWARD DOWNES

"As known and practiced in this country musical criticism is a department in the complicated service of the daily newspaper."

This pragmatic view was formulated nearly half a century ago by William J. Henderson, one of the best critics this country has produced, in an influential essay on *The Function of Musical Criticism*, published in Volume I, Number 1 of *The Musical Quarterly.* By and large, professional practitioners of music criticism in the United States during the past hundred years have agreed with Henderson. This in turn has determined much of the character and the quality of American music criticism.

To let the above quotation stand alone, as an implied summary of Henderson's penetrating and idealistic essay, would be a distortion. There is no doubt that Henderson put service to the art of music above service to a newspaper. Like a majority of the best American music critics, he had enthusiasms that a daily newspaper could not wholly accommodate and that overflowed into magazine articles and an impressive number of books. And like most of his distinguished colleagues, Henderson was a crusader (the great cause of his early years was the music of Richard Wagner).

Much fine American criticism, written by men who never held a position on a daily paper, has appeared in serious periodicals from *Dwight's Journal of Music* (founded 1852, Boston) and William S. B. Mathew's monthly, *Music* (founded 1891, Chicago), to the literary "little" magazines of our day and the invaluable "Current Chronicle" established in 1948 as a regular department of *The Musical Quarterly*.

Nevertheless it is true that the main stream of American music criticism has flowed through our daily press, and it is to the character of this press that we must look for some basic influences that have made criticism in this country strikingly different from the older tradition of the continent of Europe.

To a traveling American, the most arresting trait of the European press is its open partisanship. Many a famous European newspaper seems primarily a journal of opinion or the organ of a political party and only secondarily a *news*paper. This basic tendency has important repercussions. European music criticism often appears to be unnecessarily subjective, the expression of a highly specialized point of view of a given school or clique or, occasionally, of a single composer. Since the time of Berlioz in France and Schumann in Germany, composers have often been brilliant practicing critics — with all the technical and intuitive insights that implies, but also with the blind spots and sometimes openly indulged prejudice. As a group, composers have been notoriously unobjective judges of each other's music.

In contrast to the European press, American (and British) newspapers of the past hundred years have put a greater and ever increasing emphasis on sheer news. This was not, initially, the result of any great idealism, but of crass financial interest. In America it started with imitations of the English penny press. It was discovered, as early as the 1840s, that there was a mass market of American readers vastly more interested in sensational news (criminal trials, murders, sex scandals, prizefights, and the like) than it was in political opinion. This new mass of readers and skyrocketing circulation figures proved extremely profitable, and the competition in speedy newsgathering grew.

At the opening of our hundred-year period, the "Great Rebellion," as the Civil War was called by many Northern papers, gave all Americans a tragic stake in the swift and accurate gathering and dissemination of news. The ingenious exploits and heroism of many a war correspondent enhanced the moral prestige and glamor of news gathering as such. By the end of the Civil War it was apparent that news, rather than editorial opinion or political partisanship, was going to be the central strength and attraction of American newspapers.

This was to have the most profound effect on music criticism. By 1876 it led to the reporting of the first Bayreuth Festival by cable to the New York Times, a hitherto unheard-of exploit in music. But it influenced more than the mechanics of criticism. It influenced newspaper editors' attitudes towards their music departments. (The assistant critics of the New York Times are still officially classified as "music reporters.") Many of our most prominent music critics, from William Henry Fry a century ago on the New York Tribune, through "H. T. P." of the Boston Transcript and William J. Henderson of the New York Sun, to Howard Taubman and his recent successor, Harold C. Schonberg, of the New York Times— all of these men and many more have taken particular pride in their accomplishments as reporters. Henderson, indeed, is said to have had an active dislike for the titles music critic and music editor, preferring to be known as "a reporter with a specialty— music."

This emphasis on the reportorial function of the music critic led to another, more obvious difference between European and American reviews. A European review may, and often does, appear several days after the event. American reviews normally appear the next morning or afternoon. In the 19th century, when the deadline for material to appear in the morning paper might be 3 A.M. or even later, the American critic usually still had plenty of time.

Today, when the first edition of a great metropolitan daily is on the street before midnight, the critic needs to turn in his copy some time between eleven and twelve o'clock to make even the second edition. This means leaving an opera and often even a concert performance before it is over. If time is pressing, the critic will have to turn in his article by "takes" of one or two paragraphs at a time, so that by the time he has finished his review, the first paragraphs are already in type. This in turn means that there is no time for revising or rewriting an article except for a possible third edition of the paper.

There are critics to whom this is a hardship—who feel that a well-considered opinion needs a day or two to be properly matured and accurately expressed. But there are many, and these are by no means always the fastest writers, who feel that the critical impression actually is formed during the performance, is most vivid and complete when the critic leaves the hall, and only suffers in its expression if the sharpness of the original impression is given time to wear off. But this is getting ahead of our story.

In 1861 serious music did not yet bulk large enough in American life, even in the older cities of the eastern seaboard, to compel attention in much of our daily press. Symphony orchestras, which were to become the backbone of our musical life in the 20th century, were few and feeble in 1861. Only one managed to survive to our time: the New York Philharmonic Society, which was founded in 1842. More typical was the Boston Philharmonic. Inaugurated in 1855, it collapsed in 1863. Its conductor, Carl Zerrahn, like the conductor of the New York Philharmonic, Carl Bergmann, and many other influential musicians of the day, had come to this country from Germany in the wake of the political convulsions of 1848 and 1849.

Opera, still a faintly immoral entertainment, was on an even more precarious footing, although the New York Academy of Music had been brilliantly inaugurated in 1854 by Grisi and Mario in Bellini's *Norma*. But even in New York, opera seasons continued to be erratic and irregular under the constant threat of bankruptcy.

Persistent and, in the long run, successful crusaders for chamber music were among the distinguished German refugees to the country in 1849 and 1850. They became members of several chamber groups, the most prominent and long-lived being the Mendelssohn Quintette Club of Boston, which toured this country for fifty years in programs of uncompromising seriousness.

It is against such a background and within the framework of the press of the Civil War years that we must picture our musical journalism of one hundred years ago. The wonder is that serious criticism did exist not merely on the eastern seaboard but as far west as Chicago, where in 1861 George P. Upton was appointed music critic of the Chicago Tribune. His were the first music criticisms to appear in any Chicago newspaper, and for twenty-five years his criticisms were a constructive force in the development of Chicago musical life. He was, for example, an enthusiastic supporter of Theodore Thomas from the day of Thomas's first visit to Chicago at the head of his pioneering orchestra. And in 1891, although he was no longer active as a critic, Upton's influence contributed strongly to the establishment of the Chicago Symphony Orchestra with Theodore Thomas as its permanent conductor.

The father of American criticism is often said to be John Sullivan Dwight, the Boston critic and editor of *Dwight's Journal of Music*. Founded in 1852, the *Journal* exercised great influence throughout the country until its discontinuance in 1881. Trained originally for the ministry, Dwight became a leading Transcendentalist and he judged music from an exalted moral point of view. We may take him as an important representative of a strong and originally Puritan tendency in American criticism, which contributed, as late as 1907, to the horrified condemnations of Richard Strauss's *Salome* and has by no means died out today.

Musically speaking, Dwight's opinions were conservative to reactionary. He found Brahms depressing and unedifying and Wagner "the denial of music." But his idealism was sincere, his language elegant, and his influence enormous from the foundation of the *Journal* until long after its discontinuance. However, he was neither the first American critic nor the best-equipped one of his age.

In New York in 1861 William Henry Fry was already nearing the end of a brilliant career as music critic for the Tribune, the most powerful daily newspaper in the country. Fry was an eminent American composer. He acquired considerable European background as foreign correspondent for the New York Tribune before his appointment in 1852 as the Tribune's regular New York music critic.

In view of his importance in the story of American music criticism, his concept of a critic's duties, described in a letter to the *Musical World and Times* of January 21, 1854, is enlightening:

In the capacity of musical critic, I deem it inseparable from the honest performance of my duty to write, however late at night I may sit down to the task, a full notice of any musical performance of particular novelty, so that it may be spread before the readers of that journal the very morning after the performance ... For example, when *Le Prophète* ... was produced lately at Niblo's I deemed it my duty to get the full score from the manager and study every page, and on the night of the first performance when it closed near midnight, to sit down in my editorial room and write some three columns of analytical criticism—historical, vocal, instrumental and personal —of the work and of the special performance of that night—all of which appeared the next morning in print, though of course I did not get to bed till dawn. I mention this to show simply what I consider a conscientious performance of a critic's duty ...

Fry criticized in an attractively informal and rather vivid style. He was an aggressive crusader for American music, yet catholic in his taste, except for his conservatism. He believed that opera had been in an obvious decline since Bellini's *Norma*. Reviewing the United States première of Gounod's *Faust* he found it wanting in melody. Wagner's *Tannhäuser,* to him, breached "most of the established laws of musical beauty and truth," substituting "sheer ugliness and melodies so-called which even the most acute and attentive ear finds it nearly impossible to apprehend or retain."

It was long before many American dailies took the reporting of music as seriously as the Tribune. More typical, even of the most serious American press, was the procedure of the New York Times, which published a regular Monday morning column summarizing the amusements of the past week. Only opera performances rated a separate account the day after. Like most music criticism until well into the next century, these articles were anonymous.

The news outweighed criticism. "Although it rained in torrents," reported the Times of the opening of the New York Philharmonic season of 1861, "every bench of the hall was crowded." The critical comment that the conductor, Carl Bergmann, "seemed frequently to have accomplished the almost impossible task of making the orchestra play softly as well as loudly" tells us more about the Times critic than about the concert.

The national expansion of the post-Civil War years brought a great expansion of our musical life and of music criticism. One striking symptom of this was the first use of the new transatlantic cable for music criticism: five articles cabled to the New York Times on the first performance of Wagner's *Ring of the Nibelung* at Bayreuth in 1876. On August 20, after the conclusion of the cycle, the Times declared editorially: "This is the first occasion, we believe, on which the readers of any journal have seen in the morning criticism upon a musical or dramatic performance that took place the evening before in another hemisphere. Is it altogether beyond anticipation that the time may come when we shall record and judge the production of another opera in another planet . . ."

However, the Times Bayreuth series, signed "F.A.S.," was more of a reportorial accomplishment than a critical one. F.A.S. referred approvingly to Siegmund's *Winterstürme* in the *Walküre* as "a dainty love song," and he found *Das Rheingold* "musically . . . not significant," and *Götterdämmerung* on the whole a disappointment.

Again it was the New York Tribune's literary and music critic, John R. G. Hassard (1836-1888), who contributed far, far the most enlightened and complete account. By the end of the dress rehearsals Hassard had already reached the emphatic conclusion that the *Ring* was "one of the most stupendous triumphs of our age."

In the course of the detailed articles that followed he tried to communicate the flavor of individual scenes in these controversial works—for instance, Siegfried's funeral music in *Götterdämmerung:*

And so, with armed forms dimly descried through the gathering mists bearing the hero on his last journey, night falling, and the rays of the moon touching the tops of the spears and helmets, with the wondrous music, so full of memories and suggestions rising out of the unseen abyss, the scene passed away and left us haunted by its awful beauty.

During the 1880s there was a sudden increase of literate music criticism, centered in Boston and New York. From 1881 to 1903 William Foster Apthorp (1848-1913), a graduate of Harvard University and a pupil of the composer John Knowles Paine, was the music critic for Boston's most distinguished paper, the Evening Transcript. Apthorp had admired Dwight's literary style but abhorred his ex-cathedra manner. Like his Boston colleague, Philip Hale, Apthorp was influenced by what he called "the French style of personal criticism." "To my mind," Apthorp wrote, "criticism should be nothing but an expression of enlightened opinion—as enlightened as possible but never dogmatic." The critic's true position, he claimed, "is that of an interpreter between that of a composer or performer and the public. . . ."

Philip Hale (1854-1934) was educated at Yale University, in

Berlin, Munich, and Paris, where he fell in love with French civilization. He became one of the foremost proponents of Debussy in this country at a time when Debussy was almost unknown here. He also was an enthusiastic admirer of Richard Strauss. Between 1889 and 1903 Hale wrote for the Boston Home Journal and the Boston Post. From 1903 to 1933 he was music and drama critic of the Boston Herald.

In 1907 he made one of his frequent trips to New York for the American première of Strauss's *Salome* at the Metropolitan Opera. While Henry Krehbiel, then critic of the New York Tribune, found the music the "apotheosis of that which is indescribably, yes, inconceivably, gross and abominable," Hale ridiculed the moral approach. "*Salome* has been produced in New York," he wrote, "and there was no perturbation of nature, no shower of fiery, consuming rain; no fall of scarlet stars; no earthquake shock." At the end of a long and vivid report Hale concluded: "It is now possible to record only first impressions and the chief of these is that *Salome*, however distasteful the subject may be to some, is a stupendous work by a man of indisputable, if irregular and abnormal genius."

Simultaneously with the advent of Apthorp and Hale in Boston, four new critics came upon the New York scene, which they were to dominate for some forty years. Indeed, they went far towards guiding the musical taste of the nation at large. They were: Henry T. Finck (1854-1926), Henry E. Krehbiel (1854-1923), William J. Henderson (1855-1937), and Richard Aldrich (1863-1937). They were joined in 1891 by James Gibbons Huneker (1860-1921), one of the most brilliant and versatile critics this country has produced.

Henry T. Finck, music critic of the New York Evening Post from 1881 to 1924, had been educated at Harvard and was a performer on the 'cello and piano. He had borrowed money to make the pilgrimage to Bayreuth in 1876 and stayed on for four years' study in Germany. He became an enthusiastic champion of Wagner, Liszt, Tchaikovsky, Grieg, MacDowell, and Massenet. "Massenet's creations will outlive by decades the majority of Brahms," he assured his readers. And on another occasion he declared that the operas of Richard Strauss "are already moribund, whereas Massenet's are more popular than ever."

Krehbiel began his newspaper career in the city room of the Cincinnati Gazette and became a star reporter in murder cases, baseball news, and boat races while he studied music in his leisure time. In 1884 he succeeded Hassard as music critic of the New York Tribune. Conservative by nature, he inclined to be dogmatic and gave the impression that he was in possession of the unchangeable laws of music. His denunciation of Strauss's *Salome* for its "moral stench" and "the diseased and polluted will and imagination of the authors" was an echo of the stern ethical approach to music we found in Dwight's Transcendentalism. Yet Krehbiel showed strong understanding of Brahms and Tchaikovsky and other contemporary Russians. He has been praised as a great scholar as well as a journalist. But his scholarship was, to say the least, uneven. His best-known work of scholarship is his translation and completion of Alexander Wheelock Thayer's great Beethoven biography. The material that Krehbiel added to Thayer is of such variable quality that a recent review of a reprint of the book points out that "no careful student can safely accept any statement in the biography without independent verification."

The most brilliant New York music critic of this period was William J. Henderson. He has been widely regarded as the greatest American critic. A graduate of Princeton, Henderson studied piano and, briefly, voice as well. In music theory he was chiefly self-taught. He came to the New York Times in 1883 as a reporter, but was almost immediately given important musical events to cover. When the Times music critic, Henry A. Schwab, left the paper in 1887 Henderson became titular music critic. He served for fifteen years on the Times, and in 1902 went to the New York Sun, where he remained for the next thirty-five years until his death in 1937.

Henderson immediately put the New York Times in the front rank of musical authority with his lucid, pointed literary style, his acute reasoning, his broad background, his impressive and growing knowledge of the history and practice of music. The great passion of Henderson's early years was for Wagner, who was still a highly controversial figure. Henderson reviewed the first American performances of *Siegfried, Götterdämmerung, Rheingold,* and later of *Parsifal.* In drastic contrast to the Times critic F.A.S., who had taken a naive and rather confused view of the first *Ring* cycle in Bayreuth in 1876, Henderson characterized the final scene of *Götterdämmerung* after his first hearing of the work as a "fitting culmination to the most remarkable series of musical-dramatic works ever conceived by the mind of man."

Henderson was a kindly, warm, and considerate person. As a critic he exuded, particularly in his early years, tremendous conviction and enthusiasm for the works he loved. He also had a passionate hatred of sham and mediocrity, and this sometimes took the form of a laconic and devastating comment. In addition to his championship of Wagner, Henderson made himself an authority on both the technique and the art of singing and he was known also for his special aptitude in characterizing pianists. In short, he had a specialized authority in a variety of musical fields that few have equalled.

Richard Aldrich was Krehbiel's assistant on the New York Tribune for the decade 1891-1901. And in 1902 when Henderson left the Times he recommended Richard Aldrich to take his place. There Aldrich remained until his retirement in 1924. Aldrich had studied music with John Knowles Paine at Harvard and upon his graduation became music critic of the Providence Journal. Aldrich's style was fluent and agreeable, the language of a cultivated, educated man, but he never attempted the flaring brilliance of a Huneker, or the driving enthusiasm or deflating epigrams for which Henderson was noted.

James Gibbons Huneker studied music in Philadelphia and Paris and at the National Conservatory in New York, where he later taught piano. For breadth and intensity of critical activity in all the arts he had no equal here in his time. Huneker was a novelist, art critic, and musician as well as music critic. He had an insatiable curiosity about all the currents of contemporary artistic life. At a time when Richard Strauss was still a questionable figure on the musical horizon Huneker wrote of him, "He is the living issue in music today; no other master has his stature ... As the great narrator in modern prose is Gustav Flaubert, so Richard Strauss is the greatest musical narrator ... In his gallery of psychological portraiture Strauss becomes a sort of musical Dostoyevsky."

He was bowled over by Strauss's *Zarathustra:* "It is a cathedral in tone, sublime and fantastic, with its grotesque gargoyles, hideous flying abutments, exquisite traceries, prodigious arches, half Gothic, half infernal, huge and resounding spaces, gorgeous facades and heaven-splitting spires — a mighty musical structure."

While his style was sometimes purple, Huneker also could be almost epigrammatic in his condensation. "Richard of the Footlights," he called Wagner. "The last of the great romantics; he closed a period, did not begin one." Huneker began as music and drama critic of the New York Reporter, 1891-1895, and Morning Advertiser, 1895-1897. For twelve years he served as music, drama, and art critic of the Sun. During the war years 1918-19, he took Richard Aldrich's place on the New York Times. For the next two years he wrote for the New York World.

These five men, Finck, Krehbiel, Henderson, Huneker, and Aldrich, friends and colleagues, dominated the critical scene not only in New York but to a large extent throughout the country for a span of over forty years, and they exercised their power with a sense of responsibility and idealism.

Early in the 1920s two representatives of a new generation made their appearance on the New York scene. Lawrence Gilman (1878-1939), who was self-taught in music, had been music critic of *Harper's Weekly,* 1901-1913, and music, drama, and literary critic of the *North American Review,* 1915-1923. In the latter year he succeeded Krehbiel as music critic of the New York Tribune, where he remained until his death.

Gilman had wanted to be a painter before he began his career as a music critic, which may in part explain his sensitivity to visual color, and his love of highly colored prose. He was a devotee of modern poetry, as well as modern music. He was one of the most perceptive analysts of and commentators on Debussy and Richard Strauss. Of *Pelléas et Mélisande* he wrote that it was "music of twilight beauty and glamour that persuades and insinuates, that persistently enslaves the mind . . . There is passion in his music, but it is the passion of the desire, less of life than of the shadow of life."

In addition to his enthusiasm for contemporary music, Gilman felt an enormous attraction for the music of Wagner. And when the Metropolitan Opera revived *Götterdämmerung* for the first time after World War I, Gilman was shaken by that event and said so. "We are very fine fellows indeed," he wrote, "with our undiluted challenging brains and our swift, spare vital sensitive art: but one page from a score like *Götterdämmerung*—one gleam from that luminous, kindling godlike eye, one sweeping gesture of that titanic arm, is enough to remind us who and what we are and who is still lord of the eternal heavens, unvanquishable and secure."

On New Year's Day of 1924 my father, Olin Downes (1888-1955), succeeded Richard Aldrich as music critic of the New York Times, a position he held until his death thirty-one years later. For the preceding nineteen years he had been music critic of the Boston Post. He had begun music study at an early age, mastered the piano sufficiently to appear as soloist in one of the MacDowell concertos. Family financial reverses when still a young boy deprived him of conventional academic training. Despite this lack, which he felt keenly through the rest of his life, his appetite for literature and the unorthodox guidance of his own intuition and enthusiasm helped him to form a style of his own which at best was powerfully communicative and moving.

Early in his career, he fell in love with the music of Sibelius, which was then almost unknown in this country and was ridiculed by French-oriented arbiters of taste in Boston. He became an enthusiastic crusader and eventually was to play a major role in establishing Sibelius in the affections of the American concert public. In later years, when the battle had long since been won and Sibelius's popularity was for a time on a par with that of Tchaikovsky, he grew rather tired of always being labeled the champion of Sibelius.

One trait that I believe he shared with the best spirits in American music criticism and that set American critics somewhat apart from European practice was a fierce independence and resistance to any attempts to influence his critical opinion. The number of European artists new to the American scene who have sent more or less expensive gifts to American critics would seem to indicate that this was at one time an accepted practice in Europe. In cases of which I had personal knowledge the gifts were always returned courteously, sometimes to the deep embarrassment of the donor. All except one, that is. This critic, who must be nameless, kept the case of champagne, acknowledged it handsomely in the opening paragraph of his review, and proceeded to "roast" the performer.

Attempts at coercion, whether from outside powers or (very rarely) from inside the paper, generally meet determined resistance. On the one occasion when Olin Downes believed that he *was* being coerced by an official of the now defunct Post, he resigned in a matter of minutes, although no alternative employment seemed to be available. Later it was explained to him that it had all been a misunderstanding, but the matter was settled by the invitation to go to the New York Times.

Olin Downes was succeeded by Howard Taubman, a long-time associate in the paper's music department. An excellent critic, Taubman, who subsequently headed the drama department, is also a first-class newspaper man who never shrinks from an awkward situation that demands a courageous stand. He was in turn succeeded by Harold Schonberg, a younger critic, but one of considerable and varied experience and of a fresh, unhackneyed manner of writing.

With the death of Richard Aldrich and William Henderson in 1937, the last of the old guard left the scene impoverished by their disappearance. The loss was compounded by the death only two years later of Lawrence Gilman.

Gilman was succeeded on the New York Herald Tribune by Virgil Thomson (b. 1896), who used a pointed, elegant, and frequently witty style to express a subjective orientation somewhat in the French tradition. He believed that "the sole justifiable purpose of reviewing . . . is to inform the public; any other is an abuse of confidence . . . No responsible newspaper owner would consider the use of his valuable columns for a private pulpit." He did not attempt to make a private pulpit of the columns of the Herald Tribune, yet in reading his inviting reviews one often had the feeling that he represented a clearly partisan point of view. Thomson is noted as a witty and dextrous conversationalist of wide-ranging interests, and particular sympathy and understanding for many contemporary composers. This is reflected in his criticism. This facility, his professional mastery of the craft of music, his quick perceptions and strong opinions produced a highly individual style of music criticism which was widely admired and influential.

In 1954 Thomson resigned to devote himself to composition and conducting. He was succeeded by Paul Henry Lang (b. 1901). Lang brought to his criticism an eminence in the field of professional scholarship that was new to American music criticism, although familiar on the European continent. Lang's multifarious activities as editor of *The Musical Quarterly*, professor of musicology at Columbia University, president of the International Musicological Society, and a prominent member of the American Musicological Society, plus his early experience as a professional musician, give him an enviable background and perspective for his journalistic activities.

American music criticism has continued to change during the most recent half century. First of all, the number of American dailies has been sharply decreasing throughout this period. Obviously this means a smaller number of critics in any given city and a great increase of influence in the hands of those remaining. On the other hand, newspapers that employ competent critics are not restricted to the eastern seaboard. Men like Alfred Frankenstein in San Francisco, Thomas Scherman in St. Louis, John Rosenfield in Dallas, Roger Dettmer in Chicago, and a number of others, are all modern, knowledgeable critics, alert to the needs of their community and always ready to speak up. Music criticism in the general periodicals is gaining, though generally via the phonograph record reviewer. As yet few can compare with the radius Irving Kolodin, music editor of the *Saturday Review*, traverses.

As I have said, their influence is increasing, yet I do not know a single music critic who does not deplore the exaggerated importance attached to his words by a large part of the public and for a variety of reasons by artists and their managers. The shrinking number of daily newspapers has been accompanied by a shrinkage of space available for music news and criticism. During the first two decades of this century daily criticisms often averaged twice the length they do today. In the 1930s, a typical Sunday New York Times offered about two pages of music news and comment. Taking into account the smaller type of that day, this meant that the actual number of words was sometimes two to three times what is customary today.

In 1876 the Times had allowed its Bayreuth correspondent to cable criticism as long as a full newspaper column. In 1924 the

[243]

cabled review to the Times of the première of Boito's *Nerone* in Milan ran to two-and-a-half columns and was followed by a one-and-a-half supplementary cabled review the next day. Today criticisms of European performances are rarely cabled.

Along with the decreasing number of dailies and decreasing space in them has gone an increasing emphasis on the reportorial function of the critic. This tendency, which we saw at work a hundred years earlier, is related to the basic orientation of American newspapers. No one questions the value of sheer factual recording and news about music, but one may well question whether a shift of emphasis away from the critical function is desirable from the point of view of the art of music or of people seriously concerned.

One of the most recent developments in American music criticism is due to a technological achievement—high fidelity recording. The enormous market for serious recorded music has created a demand for record criticisms, not only in periodicals but in the daily press. There are musicians who believe that the character of our entire musical life may be radically altered by the recorded music and that live concert and opera performances will diminish in importance. Whether or not this comes to pass, it seems likely that record criticism may develop enormously in the immediate coming years with unforeseeable results.

The American Music Library, Past, Present, and Future

By RICHARD GILMORE APPEL

The first book printed in what is the United States, in 1640, was really a music book, a sort of libretto. Although not the first music book printed in the Western Hemisphere—that was the *Ordinarium* for Augustinian use printed in Mexico City in 1556, on a press sent over from Spain in 1539—it was the beginning of the vast publishing business and, actually, of the whole library movement in the United States. It became known as "The Bay Psalm Book," although its real title on the oft reprinted title page was *The Whole Booke of Psalmes*. It did not contain musical notation—the notation was first printed in the 1698 edition—but the names of some of the tunes are printed there and, of course, the stanzas were written for the "very neere fourty common tunes" which were included with various settings in four parts in Ravenscroft's *The Whole Booke of Psalmes*, 1621.

Except for names of biblical authors or commentators, it is of importance that the name of a musician is the only name mentioned in this first book. After the first edition in Cambridge, Massachusetts, the subsequent editions, of which there were some fifty-six, including English and Scottish editions, were entitled *The Psalms*,

Hymns and Spiritual Songs. The tercentenary of the first edition in 1940 marked the appearance of Thomas J. Holmes's *The Minor Mathers,* which contains a bibliography of all the editions known up to that time. A facsimile edition by the University of Chicago Press appeared in 1956.

At the time "The Bay Psalm Book" was printed it was the custom for the congregation, where books were scarce, to sing by ear following a precentor who "lined out" the words and tunes, a custom mentioned as still in use in New York as late as 1840 by George Templeton Strong in his *Diary* of that date. It is fair to say that America started its libraries and publishing business with a song on its lips. While the stanzas were universally decried by literary critics, the value of "The Bay Psalm Book" as an important document in the history of printing in the United States led to keen competition among antiquarians and collectors to acquire a copy of the first edition, of which there are some eleven still surviving. The last one sold for the fabulous sum of $151,000 in 1947. Along with a copy of the Bible, it constituted the sole library in many a Puritan home, and that so few copies have survived is testimony to its extensive and frequent use.

Among the first in New England to accumulate a private library, including music books, was the Rev. Thomas Prince, minister of the Old South Church, in Boston. Included in his collection were several copies of "The Bay Psalm Book," and the story of the gradual dispersal of these volumes forms a fascinating chapter in Zoltan Haraszti's *The Enigma of the Bay Psalm Book.* The Prince Collection is in the Boston Public Library on loan from the Old South Church.

Following Prince, the names of Hopkinson, Revere, Franklin, and Billings bulk large in the history of early American music. Rev. George Hood's *History of Music* lists twenty-four books of music published in New England before 1800. Oscar Sonneck's *Early Concert Life in America* and *Bibliography of American Secular Music* and Otto Albrecht's writings on Hopkinson, and *Early Music in the University of Pennsylvania* list titles of music found in this country. Lowens's and Britton's *Bibliography of American Tune Books,* to be published by the American Antiquarian Society, will doubtless add much to our knowledge about private collections. This was a period in which private collectors such as Alexander Wheelock Thayer, Lowell Mason, and Allen A. Brown were becoming active and H. F. Albrecht and Dr. R. La Roche were assembling material.

Lowell Mason was the first individual to purchase a European collection intact. Miss Eva J. O'Meara, writing from New Haven on January 10, 1961, says: "You will find Lowell Mason's own account of it [the library of Dr. Rinck of Darmstadt which he bought in 1852 and which came to Yale with Lowell Mason's library in 1872] in his *Musical Letters from Abroad*, p. 149; there he says that it contains, besides an extensive collection of organ works, 'the most approved treatises, and popular works on the literature of music, that are to be found in the German language; with books of music, and especially church music, in the greatest variety, from the sixteenth century down to the present day.' (The church music was for the most part Protestant, with many volumes of Choral books.)"

In the meantime James Warrington had been collecting psalm books, and Irving Lowens describes this collection in the *Bulletin of the Hartford Seminary Foundation* for January 1952. Although a check list was not published until 1898, Warrington must have begun his collection considerably earlier. It is one of the earliest to be devoted to a special field—psalmody. The next worker in this particular field was Frank J. Metcalf, whose collection I once saw in his home in Washington. It has since been absorbed by the American Antiquarian Society of Worcester and hence will be included in Lowens's and Britton's Bibliography.

An example of an early printed catalogue of a collection in the United States is that of the Harvard Musical Association in 1851. But the first public library containing music as a part of its general collection was the Boston Public Library, which opened its doors in 1853. Among its early contributors was Alexander Wheelock Thayer. This man's early education has been described by Christopher Hatch in *The Musical Quarterly* for July 1956. Eventually writing the great biography of Beethoven, Thayer had an ambition, so Hatch wrote, to compile a volume of specimens of New England psalmody. How he would have relished *The Printed Note* (1957), a catalogue of a loan exhibition published by the Toledo Museum of Art and including items from the

Museum's own collection and from the Newberry Library of Chicago, Hartford, Cincinnati, University of Michigan, Cooper Union Museum, the Historical Societies of Massachusetts and Pennsylvania, Harvard, the Library of Congress, the Pierpont Morgan Library, the Sibley Musical Library of Rochester, and others. He would have appreciated the examples from "The Bay Psalm Book"; Tufts's *An Introduction to the Singing of Psalm-Tunes* and Walter's *The Grounds and Rules of Music Explained.*

Thayer is often credited with having catalogued the Mason Collection, but there is no document extant to prove this. A catalogue of his own collection of music, miscellaneous books, and other property is noted in George L. McKay's *American Book Auction Catalogs*, New York Public Library, 1937, p. 240, as being sold February 8, 1898. A series of musical scores of Beethoven and Schubert was sold by Sotheby, Wilkinson and Hodge, London, February 18, 1899. Was it from the proceeds of these sales that Thayer made a bequest to Harvard of some $30,000?

It was through Thayer's interest that the first public library in the United States was to acquire the first research collection of theoretical writings—the Koudelka Collection in 1859. This collection, formed by the famous Austrian general who fought against Napoleon, was to make the Boston Public Library the first in America to have a music reference collection. It was housed in the Fine Arts Department in the building on Boylston Street until the Library was moved to the handsome building in Copley Square where, together with the great Allen A. Brown Collection, it has been housed on the third floor since 1894. Colonel Henry Ware, writing in the first edition of *Grove's Dictionary of Music and Musicians*, London, 1890 (Vol. II), under the heading *Musical Libraries, United States*, says, "The Boston Public Library (the largest in the United States) has about 2,000 volumes in its alcove devoted to music, but very little attention is given to increasing this department." This deficiency was speedily corrected when Allen A. Brown gave his personal collection in 1894.

The story of the development of the music library in America can be seen most aptly in successive editions of *Grove*. The present Reference Librarian of the Music Department of the Boston Public Library, Mr. Robert P. Giddings, has compiled the following information from *Grove:*

First edition (1879-89) mentions 7 libraries including cities and universities, signed by H[enry] W[are] and W. Barclay Squire. One column.

Second edition (1904-08) mentions libraries in 9 cities and 2 universities, signed by H. E. Krehbiel; 5¼ columns.

Third edition (1927-28) mentions libraries in 15 cities, 7 universities, and includes 3 libraries for the blind; 11 columns, signed by Carl Engel. Previous to the third edition there had been an *American Supplement* to *Grove* in which the editors, Pratt and Boyd, had referred to the great expansion of the number of music sections.

Fifth edition (1954) mentions libraries in 36 cities. University libraries are placed under the names of towns. Approximately 27 columns are devoted to music libraries; the article is signed by C. L. Cudworth.

Without recalling the details mentioned in *Grove* emphasis should be given to the *Catalogue of Music* in the Huntington Library at San Marino, California; the Leichtentritt Collection at the University of Utah, at Salt Lake City; the Riemenschneider Memorial Bach Collection at Berea, Ohio, the catalogue of which has just been published; the Joseffy Collection at the University of Illinois at Urbana; the George Stewart Collection in Luck's Catalogue at Detroit; the Clark and Stransky Collections at Los Angeles; the Reeves Band Collection at Providence, Rhode Island.

Otto Albrecht's *Catalogue of Manuscripts of European Composers in American Libraries* should be ranked as one of the most significant contributions to American librarianship. Florida State University can be proud of the Olin Downes Collection. The Stellfield Collection at the University of Michigan, the Shapiro Collection of American Sheet Music at the New York Public Library, the George Pullen Jackson Collection at the University of California at Los Angeles, the Guido Adler Collection at the University of Georgia, the Richard Aldrich Collection at Harvard, 1955, a large collection of American sheet music at Brown University, and the Slonimsky Scrapbooks at the Boston Public Library represent some of the recent acquisitions that should be mentioned. The latest addition to this notable list is the Lowens Musical Americana Collection given to the Moravian Music Foundation, at Winston-Salem, North Carolina.

The first to explore systematically the resources of music in several American libraries was Oscar Sonneck, first Chief of the

Music Division of the Library of Congress and Vice-President of G. Schirmer. The result of his study was the *Bibliography of American Secular Music*. His terminal date of 1800 will be brought forward to 1825 in a revision of this work currently being compiled by Richard Wolfe. H. Earle Johnson has followed in Sonneck's footsteps in *Notes on Sources of Musical Americana* (in *Notes*, March 1948), and *Need for Research in the History of American Music* (in *Journal of Research in Music Education*, 1958).

Added to the collections from time to time were items suggested by dealers' and publishers' catalogues. The author recalls distinctly a very attractive flyer issued fifty years ago by G. Schirmer advertising not only its own publications but very interesting foreign importations. Additions were based on requests of patrons, on items listed on programs of performing artists and organizations, and on reviews in periodicals. A few farsighted librarians subscribed to the important monumental series published in Europe. In 1937 Anna Heyer was able to publish a check-list of 113 libraries in the United States having complete or partial numbers of these series.

Reasons for the growth of music libraries in the United States are multiple. Where at first trained musicians and scholars were the prime users of music libraries, now a vast number of enthusiastic but unprofessional music fans and students are taxing the facilities of even the best-equipped libraries. Much of this can be attributed to interest in jazz and popular music, the influence of radio, and later, of television, and of the record industry. The popular use of libraries is perhaps exemplified by the fact that of the more than 7,000 public libraries in the United States, some 1,684 now maintain record collections. This does not include college, university, and other educational institutions.

The story of the music library in America includes not only its origin and its growth through three and a half centuries, but the facilities of the United States Information Service agencies overseas. Although the Voice of America is not heard in the United States, it maintains libraries and records for broadcasting abroad. The USIS supplies books, music, and records for the libraries, in addition to preparing films and making recorded radio and television programs for use abroad. The extent of this undertaking is illustrated by the fact that programs have been heard by 30 million people in 80 countries. The American Library in London is reported to have a mail order facility that can deliver American music, books, and records within 48 hours to all corners of the British Isles.

The Edwin A. Fleisher Music Collection in the Free Library of Philadelphia is unsurpassed. Through its facilities, says its present Librarian, Theodore A. Seder, orchestral scores and instrumental parts are lent free of charge to any musical organization in the world, after due consideration of copyright owners and their agents. Tapes are also available on a limited basis. The Drinker Library of Choral Music, now also housed in the Philadelphia Free Library although still owned by the Association of American Choruses, makes available to members of the Association multiple vocal scores and, in some cases, orchestral parts of titles in its collection.

The publications of the American music libraries are manifold. They began with small lists of their holdings. One of the earliest public libraries to publish such a list (including the Jenks Collection) was that in Fitchburg, Massachusetts. Catalogues of foreign collections reaching these shores included the Koudelka and the Drexel Collections. The Brown Catalogue (4 vols., 1910-1916) of the Boston Public Library remains one of the most important catalogues published by an American library, and with sets distributed in various centers here and abroad, it became a sort of universal catalogue of music published all over the world. Using it, a London editor located an important copy of Bach's *Aria with Variations,* which had once been a part of the Moscheles Collection. By comparing microfilms of this with other copies, he was able to establish several important questions relating to the original form of this work, the results of which appeared later in the London *Musical Times.*

The more recent library publications vary. Titles published in 1959 and 1960 include the New York Public Library's *Music Subject Headings,* and the revision made by the Music Library of Vassar College of *A Directory of American Publishers and American Agents for Foreign Publishers of Classical Music.* Two bibliographies, traditionally appropriate library publications, also deal with contemporary matters: The *Literature of Jazz,* compiled by Robert G. Reisner; and two volumes of *Some Twentieth Century American Composers,* compiled by John Edmunds and Gordon Boelzner. Both publications were issued by the New York Public Library.

A survey of American music libraries was made by Oscar Sonneck in the *Zeitschrift* of the International Music Society in 1904. He had been instrumental in founding the Music Division of the Library of Congress in 1897 and in starting the glorious series of publications described so well in *Grove's Dictionary* by Harold Spivacke, the present Chief, and in *Library Trends* (April 1960).

Several library periodicals have devoted special issues to problems of the music library. The latest of them is the above-mentioned issue of *Library Trends*, edited by Dr. Vincent Duckles. This issue contains valuable articles on personnel, content and services, and administration. Although directed primarily to British libraries, Eric T. Bryant's book, *Music Librarianship*, covers some of the same subjects. He concerns himself more with the public than with the research library, which is emphasized in *Library Trends*.

Without question the most important event in the American music library field was the formation of a Music Library Association in 1931 and the establishment of its quarterly publication, *Notes*, a magazine primarily devoted to musical bibliography and reviews of books, records, and music. The first article in a recent number is devoted to national bibliographies. Its authors, Donald W. Krummel and James B. Coover, "survey the world's musical output in national bibliographies . . . in hopes of publicizing some of the excellent but less-known tools." The Western Hemisphere, Western Europe, Eastern Europe, Africa, Asia, and Oceania are scoured. The authors conclude humorously, "Because there is little or no music published on the island of Mauritius, music publishers would do well to locate there because of the bibliographical advantages."

Once the Music Library Association was formed, it took on the task of indexing musical periodicals. A summary of this undertaking, the Newberry Project, was published in the *Notes* Supplement, No. 14 (March 1951). The index itself is now housed at De Paul University in Chicago. Supplement 15 (June 1951) contained a list of cumulative indexes from 1566 to 1950. (Note should be made that the *Musical Quarterly Cumulative Index* now runs through 1959.) Other publications of the Music Library Association are *Thematic Indexes* and a *Code for Cataloguing Music and Phono-*

records, prepared in cooperation with and published by the American Library Association. The climax of all the efforts towards periodical indexing was the *Music Index,* a private venture, which began to appear in 1949, and which is now in its eleventh volume. As is stated in the advertisement, it is "the only continuing subject guide to over 130 musical periodicals" available on a monthly or annual basis.

In 1955 the Reverend Redmond A. Burke, C.S.V., Director of Libraries at De Paul University, Chicago, made *A Survey of Music Periodical Indexing* (18 pp.). The bibliographical publications of the American Council of Learned Societies contained abstracts of the articles indexed (1940, 1942) and a record of graduate theses accepted. One difficulty about the *Music Index,* as is pointed out in the Burke survey, is that there are sources other than periodical literature for information on musical subjects. And there are articles in periodicals not indexed in the *Music Index.* The list of index cards on microfilm at the De Paul University Library includes 23 rolls in English, 8 rolls in German, 7 in Italian, with a total of 363,264 cards microfilmed.

Libraries have been immeasurably enriched by microfilm and microcards supplying out-of-print or unpublished material. These can be reproduced relatively inexpensively in microfilm, on microcards, and by xerography. Microfilms, especially, are made available through inter-library loans. The University of Rochester Press specializes in the microcard process. The University Microfilms, in Ann Arbor, Michigan, specializes in microfilms and xerography.

Beyond the geographical boundaries of the United States, mention should be made of the Canadian Music Library Association, which recently held joint meetings with the Music Library Association. It has published a pamphlet, *Standards for Music Collection in Medium-Sized Public Libraries. The Canadian Music Journal,* published by the Canadian Music Council, Sackville, New Brunswick, began publication in 1956, and the *Inter-American Music Bulletin,* published by the Pan American Union, Washington, D.C., features the music of Latin America.

Of all the efforts and activities in a music library, nothing national or international is more important than knowing one's own community: knowing the resources of musical individuals, their music libraries, their record collections, and concert proclivities; keeping a scrap-book of the obituaries of local musicians, even the most humble; keeping an employment file—for groups likely to need amateur performers—one, for instance, such as the New York Public Library Music Division's "Opportunity Book." The Philadelphia Library puts on exhibitions in store windows. The Washington Public Library, as noted in Mr. Bryant's book, expects the music librarian to participate in all sorts of activities. Between Dr. Kinkeldey's linguistic and professional requirements and those outlined at Philadelphia and Washington, the library and the librarian should be paragons unexcelled.

All these facilities are available to the general public in varying degrees. Universities, colleges, and conservatories also provide for their own students. Measures should be taken in public schools to direct assignments to their own libraries, rather than to material that should be reserved in the public libraries for adults. Miss Bernice B. Larrabee, head of the Music Department, Free Library of Philadelphia, in her excellent article in *Library Trends* (April 1960, p. 575), says that "student use of the library has increased to a point where it encroaches seriously upon the amount of time that can be given to research workers and general readers seeking help."

Now, what of the future? Is it too much to expect that libraries will have their own broadcasting facilities to answer questions by this medium, and conduct listening periods? Should libraries have a mail order system to circulate some of their material to the sick, or the aged who for reasons of safety should not be exposed to traffic hazards? Should libraries show the same enterprise as Sears Roebuck or Montgomery Ward by providing mail order service? Should they provide reading instruments for microfilms, microcards?

Among the projects of the future are the American Recordings Project and the International Inventory of Music Sources. The second of these has already made considerable progress.

The first of these projects has issued a progress report in the March 1960 number of *Notes*, giving an outline of the problem that is practically a history of American music in sound. The Committee contemplates a comprehensive set of recordings from the earliest

[254]

music in America down to the present. From 1620 to 1960 there is being prepared a "package deal," described in detail; no music librarian can afford to be ignorant of this vast project. To go with a history of American song, *A Pictorial History of American Music*, consisting of a set of one hundred 2" x 2" slides, has already been brought out by Musicamera of Chicago.

Many libraries now maintain circulating record collections. With these series of disc anthologies as an impetus, the concept of a "reference" collection may be further expanded to include the possibilities for both scholarly work and practical study inherent in an archival collection; i.e. the comprehensive acquisition of contemporary recordings to be preserved for future use. There are already national archives of sound recordings in France and Italy. There are a few such large-scale collections in American institutions, notably the Library of Congress, the New York Public Library, and the Stanford Archive of Recorded Sound, whose archivist, Edward E. Colby, discusses the future possibilities of such efforts with urgency and conviction in the April 1960 issue of *Library Trends*.

With the advent of Ussachevsky, Stockhausen, and others, whose compositions in electronically produced sound have raised knotty questions of performance and "notation" and consequently of preservation both in recorded and "notated" forms, librarians will still have to solve certain mechanical problems, as well as those of cataloguing and classification; e.g., just how do you keep a "score" in the Music Department that contains not musical notes, but acoustical graphs such as the Science and Technology Department is wont to call its own? In an article in the *Christian Science Monitor*, July 2, 1960, Vladimir Ussachevsky pointed out that electronic music "is attracting the increasing attention of young composers everywhere in the world." If this is so, then it behooves music librarians to be prepared for the results of their creative activities.

As music joins the scientific discipline on the creative level, and on the institutional plane of knowledge, efforts are being made to group music and the visual arts. Interestingly enough, of two experiments for the future whose plans remain to be completed, one is a national consolidation of the arts contemplated in a National Cultural Center in Washington, D.C. The other will be the Library

Museum of the Lincoln Center in New York. The reference and circulating collections of the Music Division of the New York Public Library will eventually move there to be housed with the other cultural offerings of the Center. Both these experiments are examples of long-range planning for the future, which will be watched with interest by musicians and librarians alike.

Music, Government, and the Law

Government and the Arts

By REPRESENTATIVE FRANK THOMPSON, Jr.

Government aid for the arts and official recognition for living artists and musicians have a low priority in the Federal government today, but state, county, and municipal governments have in some notable instances assumed their proper role in support of the fine arts. Federal priorities for the arts are, however, even lower than the priority for any meaningful program to provide Federal aid for education, which comes at the very tail-end of the Presidential "must" list if, indeed, it has been on any Presidential "must" list at all.

If the arts have not yet succeeded in making the Federal subsidy lists in a way that is noticeable to the naked eye, it is due in greater measure to the abysmal failure of America's educational and cultural leaders effectively to demand subsidy for the arts than to any doubt on the part of the President or his administration, or the Congress, that subsidy is a useful, indeed a vital, tool of the Federal government. For subsidy is the oldest economic principle written into the laws of the United States. When the Congress convened for the first time in 1789 its first act was to devise a system for administering oaths. The next business, according to a study of subsidy made by the Committee on Agriculture of the House of Representatives,

was the enactment of a tariff bill. Significantly, this legislation set up the subsidy principle to encourage the development of an American merchant fleet. It stipulated that goods imported into the United States on American vessels should have a 10 per cent reduction in customs duties, and a tonnage tax also was imposed in favor of American shipping.

The House Agriculture Committee study of subsidy goes on to point out that between 1827 and 1866 the Federal government granted 6,340,339 acres of public lands to private interests to encourage canal building and river improvement, and 183,000,000 acres of Federal and state lands were granted to private interests to encourage the expansion of railroads between 1850 and 1871.

In any discussion of subsidies one of the most commonly quoted and most authoritative sources is the Bureau of the Budget, which in recent years has put into the annual Federal Budget Message a statement on "Current Expenses for Aids and Special Services" for agriculture, business, veterans, and general aids. Federal subsidies in the fiscal years 1949 to 1955, inclusive, totaled $3,773 million for agriculture, $5,873 million for business, $32,687 million for veterans, and $9,880 million in general aids.

The people of this nation have as significant a heritage of cultural values as any people in the world. This heritage and our cultural traditions must be brought into clearer focus by the development of a national policy on the arts which has as its central feature a program of subsidy as significant as that given the sciences, agriculture, business, veterans, etc. We will, I predict, have such a national arts policy before much more time has elapsed and when we do it will be accepted as being as basic to the American tradition as any other Federal program.

Just think what a Federal-state grant-in-aid program could mean to the arts in our country, even if it were to be launched with a minimum Federal contribution of $5 million to $10 million a year. It has been estimated that $1 of Federal aid generates as much as $5 of state, local, and private support, so that a $5-to-$10 million Federal program could succeed in putting as much as $60 million more into American art each year than is being spent at the present time.

A nation that spends each year $2,681 million for cosmetics, $9,600 million for liquor, and $7,034 million for tobacco should find it comparatively easy to spend $60 million for the fine arts and to prime the pump with a cupful of Federal funds.

The British and Canadian Arts Councils are but two examples of national patronage of the arts by democratic governments which ought to inspire us in our own search for ways to establish a national arts policy including art subsidies.

The Soviet Union, it must be recognized, while far from being the "cradle of culture" its paid propagandists claim it to be, is far ahead of the United States in its financial support of the fine arts by government agencies. In view of the emphasis on the arts by the U.S.S.R. it behooves the citizens of our country in all walks of life to see to the health and vitality of our spiritual and cultural resources so that these do not become pitifully inferior to our strength and well-being in the sciences and other areas. Walter Lippmann recently called for an "American renascence" to restore the intellectual greatness of the West.

The absolute military power based on atomic weapons that is possessed by both the Soviet Union and the United States is so horribly dangerous that it cannot be used as an instrument of foreign policy as military power has been used in the past. The U.S.S.R. has, therefore, turned to the arts and other intellectual and cultural pursuits. In the January 1958 issue of *Foreign Affairs* a distinguished adviser on science to President Eisenhower, Dr. Lloyd V. Berkner, tells us that

There are intellectual fields in addition to science where the Russians have a brilliant tradition; and the Soviets have begun to show a desire to capitalize on the advantages that this tradition can provide. The Bolshoi Theater testifies as the once-brilliant Moscow Art Theater did before, to the Russian talent in the theatrical arts. In music, not even the heavy hand of political doctrine could permanently suppress the genius of Prokofiev and Shostakovich. And certainly a people that produced Pushkin, Turgenev, Tolstoy, Dostoievsky, Chekhov and Gorky have inherited great intellectual potentials.

A "cultural plank" to provide Federal subsidies and other means "to succor our failing arts" was urged upon the Democratic and Republican Platform Committees by Herman Kenin, president of the American Federation of Musicians in July 1960. Don Jacoby,

[261]

special assistant to Mr. Kenin, presented the case for America's musicians to the Democratic Platform Committee in Los Angeles with the observation that no one had ever seen a sign in a foreign land that read "Satchmo, Go Home," thus underscoring the universal appeal of the arts.

Mr. Kenin's statement to both platform committees declared:

In furthering our nation's primary objective of an honorable and lasting peace, our government has given scant recognition to a means that has demonstrated its effectiveness abroad among diverse peoples and ideologies, namely, music in particular and the living arts in general.

It is not trite to remind you and your colleagues of the Platform Committee that music is indeed the only universal language that provides ready exchanges and understandings between all peoples. Indeed, music could be called with complete justification, our national secret weapon were it not for the fact that it has long since been unveiled to the applause of millions living in foreign lands...

May I specifically recommend to you and your Committee the adoption of such language in the forthcoming Platform as will pledge governmental support for the living arts. Whether this support shall take the form of material aid such as is given the arts by most other nations, or whether it shall be through the establishment of cabinet-rank direction for arts and cultural affairs, or by what other means we are to succor our failing arts is for your Committee and the Convention to decide through the direction and force of your Platform declaration.

But, in the name of our national cultural heritage and in the name of an honorable peace, let us now declare boldy and affirmatively for the survival of music and the arts as a sacred obligation of government.

The 600,000-member National Federation of Music Clubs through its national chairman of legislation, Marie A. Hurley, in addition to the American Federation of Musicians and other cultural groups, called on both the Democratic and Republican Parties to include a "cultural plank" in their platforms which members of Congress and the candidates for President and Vice President could run on.

Our cultural leaders agree on many things but find themselves divided on the question of subsidy, and if the arts have not been subsidized in the United States as they are abroad it is due primarily to this division of opinion. The Congress can legislate only when there is a general area of agreement as to what needs to be done with regard to a particular problem, and this holds true for subsidy, which is a very thorny problem. Businessmen and farmers have strong nation-wide organizations demanding government assistance of all kinds, including financial assistance and subsidy. Recognizing this, Howard Taubman, former music critic of the New York Times, called for a national organization made up of leaders in the arts from all over the country. He pointed out that "the musical and theatrical unions are set up on a countrywide basis, and possibly they could lead the way. There are associations of concert managers and orchestra managers that could be represented. There are groups in the theater and the other arts to be drawn on. There are boards of directors for our variegated cultural institutions, and on these boards sit leaders of many phases of community activity."

Mr. Taubman added that

> Somebody must take the initiative to call a national conference of cultural leaders. If such a gathering could forge a unified policy in favor of Government support of the arts, it could, of course, be a powerful agent for the adoption of such a program. Even if unanimity on a policy could not be arrived at, the very discussion of the alternatives that face the Nation in the arts would be stimulating and useful.

Mr. Taubman wrote this in 1953, and the national conference of cultural leaders he called for at that time has not yet convened. Some heartening steps have been taken, but much more remains to be done. The National Music Council was given a Federal charter by the Congress in 1956, and it speaks with one voice for music in the United States, but it is afraid to speak above a whisper. It has signally failed to mobilize its vast potential strength for art subsidies in the United States, as it could well do by creating a special subcommittee to work for subsidies. Such powerful constituent groups of the Council as the American Federation of Musicians, the American Society of Composers, Authors and Publishers, the American Symphony Orchestra League, the Music Educators National Conference, the National Association of Schools of Music, and the National Federation of Music Clubs should be active on behalf of subsidies, for subsidies won't "just happen."

The National Council on the Arts and Government, headed by the distinguished dramatist Howard Lindsay, has taken a step along the road outlined by Howard Taubman. It is a group of cultural leaders drawn from all the fields of the arts. Among its members are Howard Hanson, Edwin Hughes, and Mrs. C. Arthur Bullock of the National Music Council. While it has been successful in hammering out a common cultural policy, it has failed to mobilize any grass-roots support to help push its program through the Congress. As the British theater director Tyrone Guthrie once observed in writing of one activity this National Council undertook:

over three hundred men and women eminent in the arts and public life in the United States subscribed their names to an appeal to Congress to enact forthwith legislation to set up a Federal Advisory Commission on the Arts. The names of the signatories were all nationally, many of them internationally, celebrated; the document was brief and moderate. Perhaps the very moderation of its demands and the mildness of its tone went a little against it. However that may be, it bombarded the ears of the populace with the stridency of a feather falling on velvet. There was very little press coverage and no political impact whatsoever.

A new National Council of Arts in Education has been formed which promises to take its place beside such powerful groups as the American Council of Learned Societies for the humanities, and the National Research Council for the natural sciences. President of this new council is Eldon Winkler, vice president of Lake Erie College. Others active in its establishment are Robert A. Choate of Boston University, Lynn White of Mills College, and Joseph C. Sloane of the University of North Carolina. Guiding genius of the group is Jack Morrison, former president of the American Educational Theater Association, and vice chairman of the theater arts department at the University of California at Los Angeles. The sponsors of this Council fondly hope the day soon will arrive when the country's cultural leaders will be able to develop national policies on the many problems affecting all of the arts and use the National Council of Arts in Education for this purpose.

The opponents of government subsidies for the arts are strong and capable men whose arguments must be met and answered by the proponents of subsidy before the Federal government embarks on any program of subsidy no matter how small. Let us, therefore, turn to a consideration of a few of the major theses of the cultural leaders who oppose Federal subsidies for the fine arts. I have chosen Willard Swire of the American National Theater and Academy, and Charles B. Fahs, who has charge of the purse strings as to grants of the Rockefeller Foundation, to present the case for the opponents of subsidy.

Willard Swire, long an influential leader in Actors' Equity Association, and executive director of ANTA, told the members of the powerful Ways and Means Committee of the House of Representatives that

it is my sincere desire that this Committee and this Congress encourage the continued and expanded undertakings of the cultural arts including theater and concerts and lectures, by removing the excise tax. In no other country in the world are the cultural arts subject to taxation, but to the contrary, those countries which are most notably recognized as cultural leaders actually subsidize the arts. Knowing and understanding the motivations and principles of American artists, I can state unequivocally that they are not seeking government subsidization but only desire the removal of this federal burden so that they may freely compete with commercially sponsored entertainment.

There would seem to be at least some division within the House of Rockefeller on the question of government aid for the arts. Governor Nelson Rockefeller recently signed a bill he had strongly backed to establish a New York State Arts Council. As Under Secretary of the Department of Health, Education, and Welfare he developed the plan for a Federal Advisory Council on the Arts, which President Eisenhower later supported. Recently, John D. Rockefeller, 3rd called for government aid to the arts. The Director of the Humanities for the Rockefeller Foundation, Charles B. Fahs, however, argues convincingly against Federal subsidies for the arts along these lines:

Nevertheless, I have some questions and reservations. These relate to the desirability at this time of Federal subsidies for state or local art activities and to the desirability of a centralized administrative authority for the arts within the Federal Government.

The arts need freedom and variety even more than do most other activities of the human mind. The United States is less experienced and less expert than is Great Britain in combining government aid with freedom from government interference. I fear it is unsafe to assume that a University Grants Committee or an Arts Council allocating national funds would work as well in this country as the originals do in Great Britain and I am not convinced that even there the system is without hazards. The difference in size of the two countries would alone be enough to make me wary of analogies.

I am convinced that there is a major and unprecedented development under way in the arts in the United States, but it is one which is missed by a large proportion of our foreign visitors because it is least in evidence in the few

[265]

major cities most frequently seen. It can be observed in the increase of music in our schools and of music, drama, art and creative writing in our universities, in the rapid spread of amateur painting, in the rural arts programs in such states as Wisconsin, Montana, and Washington, in the hundreds of symphony orchestras throughout the country, in Karamu House in Cleveland and Margo Jones' theatre in the round in Dallas, and in many other places. Our artistic future lies in pioneering an artistic life such as Europe has never known based on the large-scale participation suitable to a democratic society with mass education, high standards of living, and adequate leisure time. We are not a society trying to catch up with the culture of Europe but a society building its own culture on a new and broader base.

If this is so, is it wise to accept without very careful scrutiny European practices in national aid to the arts? If our strength is at the grass roots should we not hesitate before deciding on centralized leadership and support?

I do not mean that there should be no public aid for the arts—fortunately there is already such aid in a number of far-sighted communities. But decentralized or local aid seems safer than centralized national aid. Moreover, subsidy is not the only method open to the Federal Government and may not be the most effective one. There are many situations of significance for the arts in which the Federal Government has direct responsibilities and also some in which the Federal responsibility is comparable to that of local jurisdictions. In these cases it seems to me that the Federal Government should set an example of intelligent and generous interest in the arts. If it would do so it would thereby make a very substantial contribution to the arts in the United States without raising the problems inherent in a program of subsidy for state and local activities.

The first major Federal responsibility is the impact on the arts of general Federal legislation. An example is the good effect on many organizations throughout the country when they were exempted . . . from the Federal excise tax on admissions. Do the present income tax regulations give equitable consideration to the peculiar problems of the artist with his long training, sporadic creativity, erratic market, and in some cases early disqualification through age? Are there changes in the social security regulations which without favoritism would nevertheless help the artist towards greater security against unemployment, infirmity, and old age? Are there revisions of our copyright laws which would facilitate greater artistic development? These are the areas of legislation one thinks of first but presumably there are others in which revisions would assist artistic development in the United States without inequity to other interests.

The second major Federal responsibility is the use of the arts in Federal operations. The Federal Government has the constitutional responsibility for foreign relations, including surely artistic relations if these play . . . a significant role in the maintenance of American prestige abroad. The District of Columbia is peculiarly a responsibility of the Federal Government and a model program there for cultural development is clearly in order . . . I wonder, however, whether in thinking of developments in the District it would not be wise to think of it as another American community, a model community we hope, but nonetheless one in which the development of the performing arts must be based on the audience and the levels of artistic judgment which the community provides. In other words, if too much emphasis is placed on what the District should have for national prestige or what it can pay for only through access to the national treasury is there not some danger that the resulting program will neither have a sound local foundation nor serve as a practicable model for other American communities?

In addition to an auditorium the District needs a model program of art education in its schools. The other schools for which the Federal Government is responsible should also be leaders in this field: Howard University, the University of Alaska, the schools in the Indian reservations, the schools on Guam, Samoa, and Okinawa, etc. While some of the National Parks and the Department of the Interior have made a modest beginning in encouraging local arts much more could probably be done. The use of art in connection with new Federal buildings could be greatly improved. Almost nothing has been done to achieve good use of contemporary art in our existing public buildings and offices at home . . .

The use of art in return for fair remuneration to the artist is the best way to aid the arts and the Federal Government is potentially the nation's most important art consumer. Would it not be wise for the Federal Government to exhaust the possibilities of aiding the arts in America by example and within the scope of its own direct responsibilities before the decision is made that a program of broader subsidy and guidance is needed?

Raging now is a debate as to whether the citizenry of the United States is spending too much on private necessities and enjoyments such as tailfins, superhighways, advertising, tobacco, alcohol, cosmetics, and so on. We have a Gross National Product of $500 billion, and we spend $10 billion for advertising, $43 billion for leisure time activities, $45 billion for superhighways, etc.

Senator Eugene McCarthy of Minnesota recently asked whether the Federal road program was not hastening the day when we will "be able to drive eighty miles an hour along superhighways from one polluted stream to another, from one urban slum to another, from one rundown college campus to another."

As a people we must decide upon our national goals without further delay. There is nothing more important, in my opinion, than to decide where we are going, how we are going to get there, and how fast. For this reason I welcomed the establishment of the

National Goals Commission by President Eisenhower.

Even more important, from the point of view of our nation's cultural and artistic life, is the immediate establishment of a Federal Advisory Council on the Arts. Such a Federal agency could assemble and disseminate facts regarding the arts in the United States, and launch and complete comprehensive studies of all the professions dealing with the arts.

In testifying on my bill to establish a Federal Advisory Council on the Arts, Henry Kaiser, general counsel, American Federation of Musicians, on July 3, 1957, strongly supported my view that while the legislation to establish this Federal agency does not call for subsidy, it does not preclude subsidy. He said:

when this Council is created and completes its scholarly inquiry into the problems confronting the musician and other artistic folk, it will be compelled out of the realities and necessities to recommend subsidy.

I have been reminded of an editorial appearing, I think, on January 25, 1957 in the *New York Times* referring to the expenditures being made by Uncle Sam under the Humphrey-Thompson Act, the Fulbright Act, and the Smith-Mundt Act. These are all acts designed to lubricate and improve our relations abroad by cultural exchanges, and they are currently costing $30 million per annum. I think the $30 million more than well spent. But contrast that to the great big zero being expended by Uncle Sam on saving for our posterity the precious creative talents we have already demonstrated.

Mr. Kaiser, who undoubtedly reflects the majority view of those concerned with music in the United States today, then declared:

It has been observed that we are, after all, the cultural descendants of western European civilization. It is a fact that most of our cultural heritage is the product of subsidy, both private and public. It is a fact that in this country for many generations great private wealth has subsidized the arts. It is also a fact that because of our income-tax laws private wealth is no longer capable of maintaining that necessary burden. It is, finally, a fact that some of our State and city governments, even one as unsocialistic as the State of Vermont, have for years been subsidizing great musical combinations. It is not the word subsidy that is important; it is the control of subsidy. It is the democratic control of how government spends its money rather than a mere word that determines the freedom aspect of all our activities.

Despite the failure to establish a subsidy program for the arts, the interest of the Federal government in the arts was expressed simultaneously with the birth of our nation.

George Washington declared that "the arts and sciences essential to the prosperity of the State and to the ornament and happiness of human life have a primary claim to the encouragement of every lover of his country and mankind." In his First Annual Address to Congress on January 8, 1790, President Washington said:

You will agree ... that there is nothing which can better deserve our patronage than the promotion of Science and Literature. Whether this desirable object will be the best promoted by affording aids to seminaries of learning already established, by the institution of a national university, or by any other expedients, will be worthy of a place in the deliberations of the Legislature.

In Europe national governments consider the arts to be a basic part of the educational process, and offices or ministries of fine arts are usually to be found in the Departments of Education.

George Washington, Thomas Jefferson, and the other Founding Fathers were molded in the great European cultural tradition and were worthy exemplars of that tradition. They were living proof of the supreme ability of the classical tradition and a classical education to form outstanding leaders. A basic tenet of the classical tradition of Europe is that the arts are essential to the education of the whole, universal man. So Washington and Jefferson and the other great men of America's beginning years believed that an educational program that included the fine arts was essential to enable young Americans to develop a true understanding of our form of government and "the true and genuine liberties of mankind" in the democratic society they were instrumental in establishing.

It followed naturally, then, that the role of the Federal government has been part and parcel of this classical tradition. Thus we find President Truman's Commission on Higher Education stating in 1947 that

One of the tasks of American democracy is to heighten and diffuse esthetic sensibility and good taste, to make our people sensitive to beauty in all its varied forms: in the commodities and services of everyday life, in private and public buildings, in community and regional planning.

The study of the arts in general education should not be directed toward the development of creative artists of exceptional gifts, though it may in some instances lead to this. It should aim at appreciation of the arts as forms of human expression, at awakening or intensifying the student's sensitivity to beauty and his desire to create beauty in his everyday surroundings, at developing bases for discrimination and interpretation, at inducing sympathy with arts and artists and active concern for their welfare. Support of the arts can no longer be left to the patronage of wealth; active encouragement of artistic expression in its various forms must become the responsibility of all citizens.

After much groping, American educators and cultural leaders are finding their way back to the classical tradition which the Virginia aristocracy, in the persons of Washington, Jefferson, Madison, George Mason, and others, fostered in our country's formative years. To their evident surprise they find that Europe and the U.S.S.R., which have great national art programs with art subsidy as a central feature, have remained close to the classical tradition all the time.

A recent convert to the classical view of the central importance of the arts in our national life is Jacques Barzun, Dean of Faculties and Provost of Columbia University. In a recent article in the *Journal of the American Institute of Architects* (July 1960) Dean Barzun wrote:

What the country needs at this stage of its artistic fervor is an audience other than the haphazardly self-taught, and this implies leaders who combine an understanding of art in general with a professional capacity to perform or teach or direct in one of the arts in particular.

The place to do this teaching of audience and leaders is obviously the colleges and universities, where so many students already show their zest for the fine arts. The first step, therefore, should be to enlarge the conception of the liberal arts to include — the arts. It should be possible for an undergraduate to elect one or more of the fine arts as he now does the social sciences or the humanities. Why not round out the present offering of theory with studio work? The pattern is furnished by the sciences, which not only permit but require laboratory work. These would then be pre-fine-arts freshmen on a par with pre-engineers: there would be fine-arts majors as devoted to their practical work as chemistry majors.

In his 1955 Message on the State of the Union President Eisenhower proposed the establishment of a Federal Advisory Council on the Arts in the Department of Health, Education, and Welfare where, appropriately enough, it would work closely with the U. S. Office of Education and be represented in the President's Cabinet.

[270]

Unfortunately, President Eisenhower did not choose to push hard for the enactment of this splendid proposal.

A national program in the arts, including a significant subsidy program that would stimulate and supplement state, county, municipal, and private support for the arts, would fully utilize U. S. colleges and universities, their faculties and facilities, and indeed the educational system at all levels. It would seek, as a matter of primary importance, the development of an educated citizenry which would buy art and support artists as it buys all the other products and supports all the other segments of our affluent society. It would also seek to persuade the churches of all denominations to return to the traditional role of the church with regard to the arts and to assume again the great function of munificent patronage.

A new "center of higher learning" for the Protestant Episcopal Church in the United States is currently in process of formation at the University of Chicago. The idea was conceived four years ago by a small group of church leaders who were convinced that only through such a center could the church's cultural leadership and educational effectiveness be strengthened. The center will be in the nature of a religious counterpart of the English collegiate system and the Institute for Advanced Studies at Princeton, New Jersey. The leading Episcopalian backers of the new center have announced that the center will provide a much-needed focal point "for independent creative projects of all kinds, such as in the arts."

The National Council of Churches about four years ago established a Department of Worship and the Arts in the belief that "the church should have a vanguard of men and women qualified to interpret the significance of contemporary art for the believer in terms of Christian criteria." The Church, it was said at the time the new Department was established, must "reassume its ancient and proper responsibility and productivity with reference to all the arts."

Pope Pius XII in his Encyclical Letter on the subject of sacred music, *Musicae Sacrae Disciplina,* declares:

Music is among the many and great gifts of nature with which God, in Whom is the harmony of the most perfect concord and the most perfect order, has enriched men, whom He has created in His image and likeness (cf. Gen. 1, 26). Together with the other liberal arts, music contributes to spiritual joy

[271]

and the delight of the soul. On this subject St. Augustine has accurately written: "Music, that is the science of the sense of proper modulation, is likewise given by God's generosity to mortals having rational souls in order to lead them to higher things."

Cultural leaders and educators hold to the same ideals regarding the fine arts and they are in many cases, if not most cases, the same people. They recognize the importance of the arts in our national life. They recognize, too, the importance of the arts in the education of an informed citizenry capable of dealing with the problems of today's world both on a national level and in our relations with other nations of the world. Typical of this understanding approach to the arts is the following eloquent statement by Mason W. Gross, who recently called for a New Jersey State Educational and Cultural Commission:

It is obvious that education and culture are closely intertwined. Where the cultural commitment is low, the educational performance will be low also. Where educational dependence is permitted, cultural dependence will be justified and tolerated. Where activity of thought is held in low regard all the other educational and cultural values will suffer. In fact, a community with low cultural achievements simply can not know what good education is.

Present-day official recognition of the classical approach to the arts was voiced by Arthur S. Flemming, Secretary of the Department of Health, Education, and Welfare, in testifying in support of my bill for a Federal Advisory Council on the Arts. In a statement that cheered all those concerned with the development of a sound and significant national program to advance the fine arts in the United States Dr. Flemming declared:

Personally, growing out of my own experience in the field of education, I think we should put added emphasis on education in the arts. I think of it not only from the standpoint of the contribution which educational programs will make to the arts, but I emphasize it because I feel when people have the opportunity of participating in educational programs in the arts, it tends to stimulate the development of their creative abilities, and that those creative abilities will then show themselves and reflect themselvs not only in the arts but in everything they do.

In this kind of world we need more and more persons with creative abilities. So it seems to me that encouraging the strengthening of our educational programs along that line would be making a definite contribution to the strengthening of our activities in all lines of work.

[272]

The launching of the first sputnik by the Soviet Union shattered many of the popular conceptions about that country held by Americans. Overnight, we were shocked into a realization that the U.S.S.R. was training three times as many engineers and scientists each year as the United States is and that from now on education would be one of the most vital areas if not indeed the major area of the cold war conflict. To many well-meaning Americans this meant but one thing: more emphasis on the sciences and less on the humanities and the arts.

Looking back at that period, the education editor of the New York Herald Tribune, Terry Ferrer, wrote:

The rise of Sputnik I on Oct. 4, 1957, put American education under the greatest barrage of criticism it has ever undergone. A bitter and disappointed public accused its schools of being "soft," laced with "frills" and incapable of educating an intellectually productive citizenry. Public pressures on the schools to improve everything at once — but preferably without spending too much money to do it — reached hysterical proportions.

While the purblind advocates of cutting everything but science out of U. S. education were pressing their case on every occasion and from every rostrum the U.S.S.R. was stepping up tremendously its export of the most distinguished artists and cultural groups to all the major areas of the world as well as its support of the fine arts at home including support of the fine arts in education. All competent observers of the U.S.S.R. have reported on the major role that the arts have in that nation's educational programs.

James Bryant Conant, former president of Harvard University, a scientist and one of America's most distinguished educators, supports the arts in education. In his book, *The Child, the Parent, and the State,* published by the Harvard University Press, Dr. Conant says (p. 71) that "with a seven-or-eight-period day, there is room for art and music" in any minimum program for the academically talented (the top fifteen percent on a national basis) and, he adds (pp. 75-76), "Artistic and musical talents likewise are readily discernible. For this reason, and because of the long-term benefits to the individual that come from the development of musical and artistic skills, much time and money have been devoted to instruction in these fields in our public schools."

In his book, *The American High School Today,* published by

McGraw-Hill the same year (1959), Dr. Conant flatly declares that "All students should be urged to include art and music in their elective programs."

The American Association of School Administrators devoted their entire 1959 convention to the subject of the creative arts in education. School officials support the arts in education but they are pressured by school boards and others for more emphasis on the sciences because of the many newspaper and magazine articles demanding such emphasis.

In the 1919 Report of the Adult Education Committee of Great Britain there appears a statement that may prove enlightening and helpful to us as we consider the question of government subsidies for the arts:

> A people which reserves its religion for Sundays is not religious, and it is not educated if, while it multiplies schools, it takes pleasure in filling its evenings with bad plays, its houses with shoddy furniture . . . a conception of education which limits it to the training of intellect without seeking to humanize all social activities will lay no spell upon ordinary men, and will ultimately find that the very schools on which it relies as its strongholds are invaded by materialism . . . The natural bridge between the discipline of the mind and practical activities is to be found in the arts, which unite thought with emotion and action. An education which is merely one additional specialism is not education at all, and if the centuries which created English folk songs and ballad poetry had fewer schools and less information, it may be doubted whether, nevertheless, they were not, in some essential respects, better educated. If there is ever to be the reality of popular culture in England, it will not be achieved by reproducing the academic traditions of ancient institutions, however excellent. It must spring, like Welsh music, from the soil, and draw its inspiration from popular life. The natural vehicle is to be found in some form of art.

Much more, obviously, needs to be done by the public schools, by colleges and universities, by the churches, by state and local governments to advance the arts in America. Surely a great cultural breakthrough could be achieved if the Federal government were to provide the leadership in this area of human endeavor. I shall turn now to a partial survey of what the Federal government is presently doing for and with the arts, in the hope that an understanding of what the government is doing, as well as what it is not doing, will help us to come to grips with the issues involved in government subsidies for the arts at the Federal, state, county, and municipal levels.

The Federal government appropriates approximately $2,000,000 annually for the maintenance of the National Gallery of Art, which is largely devoted to European art of the past five or six centuries. The Federal government has yet to establish a great national gallery of American art and the National Collection of Fine Arts established by Act of Congress over a century ago has not yet been suitably housed. The 75th Congress, which accepted the gift of the National Gallery and a world-famous art collection from Andrew Mellon, authorized the establishment of such a gallery of contemporary art and this may soon be realized in the historic Patent Office Building in the nation's capital as the result of legislation that Senators Hubert H. Humphrey and Clinton P. Anderson sponsored in the Senate and I sponsored in the House of Representatives. Contemporary-art galleries, such as the Tate Gallery in London and the Luxembourg and Orangerie galleries in Paris, are common in Europe, just as state-supported opera houses are. When the Congress adopted the National Cultural Center Act it provided the land for the Center just as it previously had provided the land for the National Gallery of Art. Few of the detractors of Congress are aware that the Congress as of this writing has provided $31,417,526 for acquiring and clearing the land for the Lincoln Center of the Performing Arts in New York City. That this huge sum was in the form of an urban renewal grant rather than an outright art subsidy is the fact that is important in this context. It may well be that the forthright gift of the National Cultural Center site could usher in a franker approach to art subsidies on the part of the Congress and the Administration.

A franker approach to art subsidies is overdue because, among other things, the Federal government has forthrightly assisted several European countries to restore or obtain opera houses. A Federal agency, the District of Columbia Auditorium Commission, reported to President Eisenhower and the Congress in 1957 that its study showed that American tax dollars had helped restore a number of old European "opera houses and music halls" which had been damaged during World War II. This generous action was doubtless motivated as much by our desire to assist our allies to return to normalcy as it was by a concern for the preservation of cultural monuments. U. S. aid supplied under the Marshall Plan and the Mutual Security Program — totalling more than $78 billion to date — undoubtedly has had the effect of making it possible for nations receiving such aid to spend their own tax dollars on programs and projects, such as opera houses and music halls, that are close to their hearts.

The Act establishing the National Cultural Center is similar, though not identical in all details, to the Act establishing the National Gallery of Art. Both are bureaus of the Smithsonian Institution and both have members of the President's Cabinet as trustees, and both are national and international in scope. The National Cultural Center Act provides (Sec. 4 [3]), interestingly enough, authority for resident companies in the performing arts — a factor that so far seems to have escaped the attention of the Center's officials.

There is growing criticism of the architectural plans of the center, which call for a series of five auditoriums under one roof. In any order of priority a great hall for symphony concerts, opera, and ballet productions would come first, and could be established and endowed for $30 million. Since, as with Lincoln Center and the National Gallery of Art, funds must be raised from private sources to build the Center, such a sum is much more likely to be raised than the $75 million to $100 million figure being suggested by some of the Center's officials. I do not think the nation's capital should try to duplicate New York's Lincoln Center or attempt to compete with it. After all, New York City is the wealthiest city in the world, with a population in its metropolitan area of nearly 15,000,000, while Washington has only 2½ million in its metropolitan area. I would like to see rise in Washington a cultural center that other U. S. cities could think of as a prototype, one that would stimulate the development of cultural centers across our land. There is a cultural growth of unprecedented proportions taking place in our country today, and I would hope that the nation's capital would stimulate and contribute to this growth. To do this a new pattern must be developed, which will be an expression of the democracy that this country represents in the world.

The Library of Congress is, like the National Gallery of Art, one

[276]

of the cultural glories of the Western world. For those skeptics who fear Federal subsidy of the arts as a step, and a long one, towards Federal domination and control, a year spent at the Library of Congress studying its vast number of art activities and programs should be enough to convince them of the groundlessness of their fears.

In the nation's capital, which the Federal government largely controls since the President appoints the members of the Board of Commissioners of the District of Columbia and the Congress acts as City Council, the Congress appropriates the piddling sum of $16,000 annually for the Watergate concerts and other art programs. This is only $3,500 more than the little town of Hagerstown, Maryland, contributes to the arts. Let us note some other embarrassing comparisons. San Francisco contributes $449,314 to the arts each year. Yet, Washington has over 100,000 more people within its boundaries than San Francisco and is much wealthier per capita. Baltimore contributes $448,000 to the arts, Philadelphia $824,000, and New York City $4,718,824. These figures were determined in a recent survey of municipal support for the arts which the Library of Congress prepared for Representative Harris B. McDowell, Jr., Democrat of Delaware.

Legislation has been introduced in the Congress to provide financial support for the National Symphony Orchestra, the Washington Opera Society, the Washington Ballet Guild, the Washington Civic Opera Association, and other non-profit art endeavors in the nation's capital similar to the financial support given the arts by other U. S. cities. Sponsors include Senators Humphrey and Wayne Morse, Representative McDowell and myself. The title of these legislative measures is instructive: "to provide for the establishment of a municipal arts council representative of local non-profit organizations and institutions, including educational organizations and institutions, in the District of Columbia with active programs in the arts, to set aside for such local cultural activities one mill out of each $1 of tax revenue of the government of the District of Columbia and for other purposes." What other U.S. cities do by simple resolution of their city councils must be done in the nation's capital by act of Congress or not at all. About $175,000 would be provided from local tax funds for the worthy cultural endeavors I have listed above, and this sum — under the provisions of the several bills — would be matched by the one major industry in the nation's capital: the Federal government.

If we are to be enabled to display in our international relations a culturally strong United States both deserving and capable of the highest form of world leadership, the Congress, as Washington's "city council," and the President, who appoints the District of Columbia Commissioners, must take action to end forever the provincial status of the nation's capital and to bring it abreast of other capital cities of the world in cultural matters.

The French Minister of Culture, André Malraux, was recently forced to give his Parliament an explanation of how the French art masterpiece *The Fortune Teller* was taken out of France. The acquisition of this 17th-century painting by the Metropolitan Museum of Art in New York City, for a sum reportedly of nearly $800,000, produced an angry reaction among Frenchmen, who insisted that the canvas, part of the national patrimony, never should have been permitted to leave the country permanently.

Keeping up with the Joneses, a familiar part of American family life, has no counterpart at the national level in a determined effort to do as much for U. S. art and artists as other nations do to encourage their art and artists. While little is done for art at home, there is a rapidly growing appreciation and understanding of the propaganda value of art. Perhaps it was this developing sense of art's value as a tool in international relations that led the Federal government to support a new amendment to the Mutual Security Act to help save the millenia-old architectural and art treasures of Egypt which otherwise would soon be covered by the waters to be impounded by the Aswan Dam. This amendment to the U. S. annual $4 billion Foreign Aid Program will permit our Government to contribute up to one-third of the expense of the historic preservation program in Egypt, which is expected to cost about $90 million. Sponsored by UNESCO, this gigantic rescue operation represents the common interest of many nations in preserving mankind's heritage in one of the cradles of civilization.

Hundreds of thousands of Americans tour Europe each year and spend over $2 billion to steep themselves in the art festivals, the art galleries and museums, attend opera and ballet productions, and visit the ancient cities. Yet, as the *Architectural Forum* noted editorially in April 1957,

The very things that Americans adore abroad they destroy systematically at home. Old buildings are broken up in the US as fast as used packing boxes to make way for new ones. We have no cultural custodians to sort out the values . . . [such cultural custodians as we do have] judge old structures by their sentimental associations rather than by their intrinsic, esthetic significance, or their contributions to beauty, as if it were magic just to stand where Mark Twain stood or to sleep where Washington lay awake. If we had a Sainte Chapelle in New York and it stood in the way of speculative office building, we would pull it down at once without further question. The Pyramids, having already stood through five thousand years, have a better chance of rounding out another cinco-millenium than any five-year-old American masterpiece has of rounding out the decade.

In the field of our nation's foreign policy a new and significant program was launched in the fall of 1954, known as the President's Special International Program for Cultural Exchange. This was continued on a temporary basis for two years and was made permanent in 1956 by the Congressional adoption of the International Cultural Exchange and Trade Fair Participation Act of 1956 — legislation that was co-sponsored by Senator Hubert H. Humphrey and myself.

Unfortunately, the President's Program has been primarily concerned with sending American cultural programs overseas and does not provide for a true, reciprocal cultural and artistic exchange with other nations. In his letter to the Congress under date of July 27, 1954, President Eisenhower explained the purposes he had in mind in the following terms: "In the cultural and artistic fields as well we need greater resources to assist and encourage private musical, dramatic, and other cultural groups to go forth and demonstrate that America too can lay claim to high cultural and artistic accomplishments."

The Humphrey-Thompson Act assured continuing Congressional support for this program, including the appropriation of the necessary funds. Between $2,150,000 and $2,500,000 is appropriated each year, and a recent report showed that 3,500 performers have gone abroad in 132 attractions since the program's inception. The cost of the undertaking to date has been $12.6 million, with about 95 per cent of this amount going for travel expenses. Attractions are screened by committees on music, dance, and drama.

Unlike the Fulbright and Smith-Mundt Acts, which are truly reciprocal and under the authority of which more than 35,000 students, teachers, and leaders — about 10 per cent of them from the arts — have been exchanged during the past ten years with many nations of the world, the lack of a provision for reciprocity in the Humphrey-Thompson Act (Public Law 860, 84th Congress) has seriously hampered our relations with other countries. As a result of this defect in the President's Program (which State Department bureaucrats hastily renamed the "President's Special International Program for Cultural Presentations" without changing or amending the law) the box office and the gate receipts are the final arbiters of the foreign cultural attractions that are seen in the United States.

A factor in the overwhelming reliance on commercial talent by the President's Program to date is the exclusive concentration on commercial talent by the Soviet Union, which stems from its well-known reluctance to let its young people travel abroad where they would come in contact with young people and new ideas in the democratic West. Imitation is the sincerest form of flattery, and the American policy-makers of the last Administration paid the Kremlin's propagandists the highest form of compliment possible in casting the President's Program so largely in the Soviet mold. Despite the widely acknowledged success of the Fulbright and Smith-Mundt educational exchange programs involving young people, which are also under the auspices of the State Department, the President's Program continues to be largely one of commercial artists. Howard Hanson, director of the Eastman School of Music, and president and chairman of the board of the National Music Council, assures us that educational talent "will contribute even more importantly to the cultural exchange program than the exchange of 'commercial' professional groups."

This program will undoubtedly grow in stature and Federal financial support, and will utilize a much larger number of educational talent groups in the future when, it is hoped, abler and maturer Federal officials will direct it without delegating their key responsibilities under the Humphrey-Thompson Act to others because of the peculiar view of present State Department officials that "the government doesn't know anything about art."

Economic progress alone is not an accurate measure of the

interests, values, and achievements of a great and free people. By enriching the lives of individual citizens, we envision that they will in turn contribute to the flourishing of arts and culture in the nation. Robert Frost told the members of a Senate subcommittee: "I've always said it would be sad if a great nation like this got so great and prosperous and famous without the help of the arts at all—like Carthage. My respect is always for nations that have had art and literature, language of their own."

The United States surely can find ways to provide at least as much support for the fine arts, which make civilization endure and flourish, as many less affluent nations do in our era. The philosopher Hobbes once described man's life without culture as "solitary, poor, nasty, brutish, and short," and so it is. The degree of culture that any community achieves can be measured in terms of its commitment to activity of thought, and receptiveness to beauty and humane feeling.

If we are to accomplish our purpose of furthering cultural activities throughout the United States and displaying our accomplishments throughout the world, we must supplement private support of the arts in this country with a significant subsidy program on the part of Federal, state, county, and municipal governments.

We must, in addition, place much more emphasis on the arts as an integral part of the education process at all levels and with all age groups, and this must include pre-school as well as adult education programs. We must encourage the churches to do more than they have done for a great many decades. In short, we must see to it that all of our citizens are educated to understand and appreciate and support the fine arts. For, as Woodrow Wilson, who deeply loved music and the arts of the theater, once wrote,

the educated man is to be discovered by his point of view, by the temper of his mind, by his attitude toward life and his fair way of thinking. He can see; he can discriminate; he can combine ideas and see where they lead; he has insight and comprehension. His mind is a practiced instrument of appreciation. He has the knowledge of the world which no one can have who knows only his own world or only his own task.

[281]

Copyright and the Creative Arts

By ROBERT J. BURTON

The first 60 years of the 20th century have witnessed more changes in man's way of life than any comparable period in the recorded history of mankind. In the field of communication of ideas, technological developments have resulted in the everyday use of media so revolutionary that a short century ago no reasonable man could have considered their description anything but pure fantasy. Yet certain basic legal principles affecting the protection of intellectual property have remained essentially constant and are today being applied to situations unforeseen at the time of their development or enactment. Nowhere can we find any more striking example of this historical paradox than is to be found in the development of copyright law in the United States as it relates to communication in the form of musical composition.

What may be described as the current lag in laws affecting musical compositions and composers is not without historical precedent. Music was one of the earliest means of communicating thoughts and ideas from one human being to another. Yet as men have developed vast legal systems to deal with almost every aspect of their communal life, the legal concepts which most directly affected transmission of thought by music have lagged behind even laws protecting other kinds of intellectual or creative property and these laws are themselves far behind branches of the law affecting other areas of man's activities.

I shall make no attempt here to deal in intricate legal analysis or even to attempt to summarize or generalize a vast and fairly complex body of law. My sole objective will be to sketch briefly the historical background of the development of the law protecting intellectual property and to focus some attention on the sad fact that in the sixth decade of the 20th century composers of music are still living under a system of law which, with but a few exceptions, is identical with that which existed almost 150 years ago and which has undergone almost no revision at all since 1909.

The origin of statutory copyright protection is attributed by some historians to the chartering of the Stationer's Company in England in 1556. I have always dissented from this point of view because the main objective of the chartering of the Stationer's Company by the Crown was the suppression in England of the religious ideas which were in conflict with those of the Church of England. The effect of the chartering of the Stationer's Company was to forbid the printing of any book unless it was registered by a member of the Company. Thus, in effect, the Stationer's Company was a device to effect censorship and control of the printing press and had no bearing whatever upon protection of intellectual property as such. In 1694 the Licensing Act under which the Stationer's Company operated expired, and from the expiration date until 1709 there was no copyright protection whatever in Great Britain. Finally in 1709 the Statute of Anne was passed and this is actually the beginning of our present copyright system. The Statute of Anne was restricted to printed materials, principally books. In 1735 the Statute was extended to cover engravers of historical and other prints. There is no indication that the Statute of Anne was applicable to music.

What is more significant, however, is that this earliest attempt at creating protection for intellectual property dealt solely with the right to reproduce intellectual property in printed form. Of course, one could hardly have expected the members of the British Parliament at the beginning of the 18th century to enact legislation which would have envisioned the development of radio, television, stereophonic reproduction or the like. Certainly at this point in the 18th century people were aware of the fact that musical compositions were performed by artists in public and that the public performance of the music intended for the enjoyment or edification of the listener was a basic use for this type of intellectual property. The Statute of Anne is silent, however, as to any such concept of musical usage. Thus, the birth of copyright law occurred solely in context of a legislative intention to protect the reproduction of intellectual property such as books and periodicals by prohibiting unauthorized printing or dissemination.

As further evidence of this one-dimensional thinking, one can examine copyright laws enacted by some twelve of the original thirteen American states between the period 1783-1786. Without exception these statutes refer to the printing and publishing of books and other writings. Some of the statutes included protection for maps and charts, but essentially they were limited to books, pamphlets and similar periodicals. In none of these statutes do we find any reference to music as such, nor, quite obviously, do we find any suggestions that the right of public performance of music should be protected.

As late as the adoption of the Constitution of the United States in 1787, copyright protection was limited to "writings" of authors of books, maps and charts. The first federal Copyright Act enacted on May 31, 1790, similarly contained no reference to any form of intellectual property other than the traditional forms heretofore mentioned.

It is abundantly clear from a review of all of the historical evidence that the first theory to present itself to the state legislators and to the Congress of the United States at the close of the 18th century was that the copyright clause in the Constitution of the United States was intended to protect literal "writings," having reference to such objects as books and periodicals—words written in a form comprehensible to all who could read. I do not mean to suggest that this early limitation was based on any theory of constitutional limitation as to the scope of copyright protection. I think this limitation resulted purely from the fact that commerce of the late 18th century, to the extent that it dealt with intellectual property at all, concerned itself with intellectual property only in its printed form.

Although musical compositions were protected prior to 1831 under the loose category of books or pamphlets, music did not warrant specific inclusion in a federal copyright act until 1831. Even at this late date, however, the protection was limited to printing and vending of musical compositions. Thus 120 years after the enactment of the Statute of Anne do we find music — one of man's oldest and best loved means of communication—achieving for the first time the dignity and importance of statutory recognition. Even here, however, the legislative intent was clear—to restrict the protection to what was then a comparatively unimportant potential source of revenue for composers of music.

Although, quite obviously, no valid historical information is available as to the sale of published music in the United States in the 1830s, one can very readily assume that the number of people in our infant nation who were capable of reading printed music and who possessed an instrument on which to perform printed music, constituted an insignificant proportion of our population. Music in the United States not only in the 1830s but well past the conclusion of the Civil War was essentially communicated by public performance and, as a matter of fact, indigenous American folk music, passed down from grandfather to father to son, had little, if any, recognition in printed form until well into the 20th century. Yet no attempt was made by the legislators to give the composer any right to derive revenue from the public performance of his music.

In 1856 our copyright law was amended and for the first time recognized the protection of performance rights in dramatic works. If there indeed be an ancient art form it would be the public performance of the spoken drama, and yet no protection was afforded this venerable art form until a little less than a century ago.

Music, as always, lagged well behind. It was not until 1897—a mere three years before the beginning of the 20th century—that our federal copyright law recognized that the composer should have a right to derive revenue from the performance of his music. Musical performance was not even recognized under our laws as being deserving of legal protection until such a late date. As a matter of fact, it was not until the enactment of our present Copyright Law in 1909 that we find an adequate spelling out of protection for composers against the unauthorized public performance for profit of their works.

In this very brief review of the development of our laws protecting musical property, I have very carefully avoided any mention of protection for the mechanical reproduction of musical compositions. Although it is historically fair to criticize the lack of understanding or appreciation by legislators prior to 1909 of the need for protecting public performances of music, one can not equally deplore their inability to foresee the onrushing technological developments of the phonograph record, sound motion pictures, radio, television and the like. As I shall hope to demonstrate, the present law, enacted in 1909, has afforded some measure of protection to composers in their relations with our new technology, but the Act remains at the present day outmoded, inadequate and unjust. Before discussing the specific areas of substantive copyright law and their individual developments, such as term of copyright, standards of copyrightability and the like, it might be enlightening to appraise briefly the economic and sociological atmosphere which formed the backdrop to the enactment of the law of 1909.

Fundamentally, legislation in a free society is the result of a compelling need of public welfare or economic growth, or for the strengthening and defense of our national system. The music industry, if one can even use so broad a term, had little existence in the United States until the beginning of the 20th century. Publishers of music existed during the latter part of the 19th century in many principal American cities. These establishments, however, played an insignificant role in our national economy. The manufacturer of musical instruments similarly was not a major factor in the dynamic American Industrial Revolution which followed the conclusion of the Civil War. Although minstrel shows and the variety stage, vaudeville and music halls did develop rapidly and successfully after the end of the Civil War, the spotlight was on the performer and little, if any, thought was given by the public or by the Congress to the plight of the composer whose works were being performed. The oft-told history of Stephen Collins Foster, certainly the most widely performed composer of his time, is more than sufficient evidence to illustrate the simple proposition that 19th-century America loved music, sang music, danced to music but saw little social reason for enacting legislation to compensate the composer for the enjoyment which the public was deriving from his works. It is equally significant to bear in mind that as a pioneer nation, the musical heritage of our educated countrymen was almost exclusively of European origin. We, as a young nation, were too busy building railroads and opening up vast new frontiers to occupy ourselves with the development of an American musical tradition. Thus both the economic and sociological forces necessary to bring about enactment of legislation in any area of human affairs were demonstrably lacking in the United States until the beginning of the 20th century.

It is for these reasons, among others, that the United States entered the 20th century in a climate which paid little heed to the rights of composers and showed no national desire to make a substantial contribution to their well-being as important members of our society.

Returning now to the enactment of what remains our present copyright law, namely the Act of 1909, we find a number of statutory changes which have enabled composers to achieve genuine progress during the past fifty years. From an economic standpoint, certainly the protection given against unauthorized public performances for profit of musical compositions has been proved by history to have been the most significant part of the law of 1909. From a modest beginning in 1914 when the American Society of Composers, Authors and Publishers (ASCAP) was organized, annual income to American composers from the public performance for profit of their music has risen from a modest sum of several thousand dollars to a position where payments for public performing rights in the United States are approaching $40,000,000 in 1961. Although more than 90% of these payments result from the public performance of music by radio and television broadcasting, a source of dissemination which developed after 1909, payments are predicated upon rights granted by the 1909 statute. This statute, incidentally, contains a provision which exempts from payment performance of music by means of coin-operated machines commonly referred to as juke boxes. Once this morally unjustified exemption in our law is removed, the amount of money available for distribution in the

United States as the result of public performances for profit will be very substantially in excess of its present high-water mark.

The second major innovation contained in the Act of 1909 is the much discussed and very complex right to record mechanically a musical composition. No single subject causes as much discussion, and even confusion, among so-called copyright authorities as does this right. While this area cannot be here explored except in its most general aspects, it may be useful to examine briefly its historical background in order to understand some of the present problems.

In 1908, the Supreme Court of the United States decided that the making of a player-piano roll was not an infringement of a copyright (*White-Smith Music Pub. Co. v. Apollo,* 209 U.S. 1). The Court said, in effect, that the player-piano roll, which was merely a device to reproduce sound when used in conjunction with a mechanical device, a player-piano, was not a *copy* of music and thus did not violate the Copyright Law.

In 1909, Congress took notice of this decision and when the present law was adopted in that year, it provided specifically for the protection of the copyright proprietor against the unlicensed recording of his music. However, Congress imposed certain fundamental restrictions upon this right. The first restriction was that once a copyright proprietor had licensed anybody to make a recording, then thereafter any person could make a recording without express permission from the copyright proprietor, upon the payment to the copyright proprietor of 2¢ for each recording manufactured.

This provision of the Copyright Act, 1(e), is generally referred to as the "compulsory licensing clause." In practice, this clause is not usually used because most copyright proprietors are willing to give manufacturers of recordings a somewhat better arrangement, namely, a license under which the manufacturer need only pay a royalty on records actually sold, rather than on records manufactured. However, the provision does exist and enables a manufacturer of recordings to proceed without permission of the copyright owner by complying with the terms of the Act. It also has, in effect, established a maximum royalty rate which a copyright owner can get from a record company notwithstanding the fact that the price of records has increased many times since 1909.

The second restriction imposed on a copyright owner under the provisions of Section 1(e) is a requirement that the copyright owner file in the Copyright Office a "notice of use" once he has licensed his first recording. This is an extremely important provision. In the event that a copyright owner fails to file a notice that he has granted permission for a first recording, then his mechanical rights, and perhaps even the copyright itself, may fall into the public domain.

The really interesting and complex questions, however, under Section 1(e) relate to the problem of "what is a mechanical recordation?" for the purposes of the Copyright Act. There is a minority of copyright lawyers who contend that the provisions of the act relate only to commercial phonograph records. There are others, (and these have the support of some of the cases) who contend that the provisions apply to *any* form of mechanical "recordation." In the present rapidly developing technological age, there is a wide variety of types of mechanical recordings. Tapes, wires, sound motion picture films, kinescope recordings on television, are but a few of the many devices that contain mechanically recorded music as an integral part. A number of cases have dealt with the problem of whether music recorded on a motion picture sound track does or does not fall within Section 1(e). It would now appear quite clearly that it does, and although trade practices have not, as yet, adopted all of the implications of this doctrine, there is some reason to believe that they may.

Up to the present time, motion picture producers have not treated motion picture sound tracks as coming within Section 1(e), at least for the purposes of negotiating recording licenses with copyright owners of musical compositions. However, with the advent of television film as a major form of communication, it is certain that this whole problem of the legal aspect of music recorded on a film sound track will be something to watch carefully in the very immediate future.

In the case of radio and television, where programs are frequently recorded either on tape or on kinescope film for delayed broadcasting, certain trade practices have evolved whereby such recording can be done either without fee, or for a very nominal fee. In other words, because of time-zone differences, program time availability, and other technical considerations, it sometimes becomes necessary to tape or kinescope a program; usually the making of these tapes or kinescopes is not regarded as an act requiring a separate license —providing such tapes or kinescopes are used within a very short period after they are made, and are used for a one-time performance only. In the case of motion picture film made expressly for television and which may be used and re-used over an extensive period of time, the question of recording licenses requires greater study.

The Act of 1909 contained a third significant departure from prior copyright history which directly affected the developing music publishing industry in the early part of the 20th century. Section 1(b) of the Act of 1909 gave the copyright proprietor the exclusive right to arrange or adapt his musical work. This was the first recognition by the Congress that copyright proprietors of musical compositions needed protection against the reproduction, whether by printing, recording or public performance, of their works in forms other than the original form of the work as actually copyrighted.

This new provision in the law gave to copyright proprietors of musical compositions the right to reproduce their own works in orchestral and vocal editions of all kinds and to meet any possible public demand. It was significant in that it gave to the copyright proprietor a right to prohibit a person from recording or performing a musical composition in any form except that in which the work was originally copyrighted unless permission was obtained from the copyright owner.

In practice, copyright proprietors, generally speaking, have not enforced this right against artists who record works on phonograph records or against performers who arrange works for various types of public performance for profit. There has grown up in the United States a sort of permission by implication which gives to performers a right to arrange musical compositions to suit the particular needs of their individual renditions. Nevertheless, the right to prohibit this type of practice does exist and is asserted from time to time at least in the field of concert or "serious" music.

The true commercial value of the right to arrange and adapt is found largely in the printing field. A music publisher fortunate enough to publish a composition which receives wide popular acceptance and which ultimately becomes what is commonly known as a "standard" (that is, a musical work having a more or less permanent place in our current musical literature) exercises his right to reproduce such a standard work in literally dozens of orchestral and vocal editions to meet varying public demand.

Another significant departure in the Act of 1909 is found in Section 7 thereof which provides that compilations, abridgments, adaptations, arrangements, dramatizations, translations or other versions of works in the public domain when re-published with new matter shall be regarded as new works subject to copyright protection. This provision of the law has had a substantial effect on the music publishing industry, not only for United States publishers but also in the case of foreign publishers who, during the 20th century, have been able to secure protection for their works in the United States. It has become a world-wide common practice for music publishers to reproduce their "own" editions of public domain classics and to place them on the market as copyrighted musical compositions under the authority of Section 7 of the present Copyright Law. Unfortunately for legal and other scholars, the courts have not had much opportunity to adequately define what constitutes "new matter."

The Copyright Office itself has indicated in its rules that mere transposition of a musical work, altered harmonization of a musical work, or editing, fingering and phrasing of a musical work do not constitute "new matter" for the purpose of achieving copyrightability within the meaning of Section 7. The courts have indicated that a public domain work, in order to be moved over into the field of a new work, must contain "original" musical creativity. By the same token, the courts have indicated that lack of artistic merit would not necessarily defeat a claim to protection for an arrangement of a work in the public domain.

I believe it to be impossible to define a precise boundary line at which point the contribution of new matter is sufficient to create protection. It is a field in which musical experts can and do differ very substantially. The fact remains that almost any substantive change in public domain musical literature including perhaps mere rhythmic alterations *may* be sufficient to achieve protection as a new arrangement of a public domain work.

Perhaps the most practical answer to this much under-litigated section of the Copyright Law is to be found in the fact that if a music publisher brings out a commercially successful series of public domain arrangements which bears the name of a well-known contemporary musical figure (an editor, educator, performer, etc.) as arranger or adapter, no other publisher is likely to challenge the copyrightability of such a series. In the first place, much of the sales appeal of such a series is undoubtedly due to the prominence of the name of the arranger, editor or adapter, and the name of such an individual clearly could not be used by any other publisher without appropriate contractual arrangements with the individual. In the second place, it must be borne in mind that in view of the sparsity of substantive case law bearing upon this issue of copyrightability, a publisher seeking to "pirate" what is claimed to be a copyrighted arrangement of a public domain work would never know whether the claimed arrangement would hold up or not until the case was actually tried on its merits. Under these circumstances, commercial practice has dictated that publishers content themselves with their own "new versions" of public domain works rather than to copy other publishers' "new versions" at the risk of incurring severe penalties.

With some minor exceptions having little or no bearing on the field of music, copyright development in the United States came to an end with the enactment of the Statute in 1909. The development of new problems in the field has been less static. Even concepts which have been embodied in copyright law for longer than recording or public performances desperately need re-evaluation. The first and most fundamental of these concepts is that of publication itself. The essence of statutory protection was to permit an author to publish a work for general distribution and to secure copyright protection of such published work during a limited period of years. I need hardly remind my readers that were it not for legislation which permits publication with protection, the common law which is still in effect destroys the author's rights in a work upon its publication. To this very day if a work is published without compliance with the requirements of our statutory copyright system, all rights in the work are lost immediately upon publication and the work falls into the public domain.

Up until a few years ago it was generally assumed in the United States that "publication" meant the dissemination of music in printed form carrying an appropriate copyright notice as provided for in the Copyright Law and in the various rules and regulations promulgated by the Register of Copyrights. It was assumed that a work might be freely performed publicly and for profit without being considered "published," and it was equally freely assumed that a work might be recorded and disseminated widely on phonograph records without being considered "published."

A few recent decisions in the United States have thrown doubt upon the proposition that the dissemination of a phonograph record does not constitute publication of a musical work. As a matter of fact, at least one or two cases have rather expressly indicated that dissemination of a musical work by means of a recording *must* be considered as a publication.

If a recording is to be considered as publication, several new problems must follow, one of which is how one may comply with the statutory requirement of depositing copies of the publication. Until very recently the Copyright Office has consistently refused to accept a recording for registration purposes. Within the past year, however, the Copyright Office has accepted for registration magnetic videotape containing a performance of Gian Carlo Menotti's opera *The Consul*. This radical administrative departure by the Copyright Office early in 1961 is still without any judicial sanction. However, one may, at least as of this writing, suggest the possibility that if the Copyright Office is willing to register videotape it may also now be prepared to accept for registration phonograph records or other mechanical devices used in the reproduction of musical compositions.

In the light of the recent judicial indications that a recording constitutes publication, it is interesting to note the definition of publication as contained in Article 6 of the Universal Copyright Convention. This definition represents the most recent attempt by copyright authorities from all over the world to define this troublesome concept. The article states, "Publication as used in this convention means the reproduction in tangible form and the general distribution to the public of copies of a work from which it can be read or otherwise visibly perceived."

Another concept which badly needs review is the fundamental issue of the length of term of copyright protection. The Constitution of the United States merely grants to Congress the power to secure protection for "limited times." I submit that the power of Congress, therefore, to determine what is an appropriate time within the framework of the Constitution is virtually unlimited. The question is whether the "limited time" presently embodied in the statute represents the best possible balance between the rights of the composer and the public.

The Statute of Anne provided for a term of 14 years with a right of renewal for an additional 14 years under certain conditions. The first United States Copyright Law of 1790 adopted the original theory of the Statute of Anne by providing for two 14-year terms.

In 1831 Congress granted an additional period of 14 years by increasing the original term to 28 years, and retaining a renewal term of 14 years.

Finally, in 1909, Congress took a further step and provided for two terms of 28 years' duration each. Thus, since 1909, maximum copyright protection in the United States remains at 56 years from date of publication.

It is, however, a fallacy to speak in terms of our having a system of protection for 56 years. The fact is that under our present Copyright Act, obtaining protection for the second 28 years is enormously complicated and the statutory provisions applicable to securing protection for the second 28-year term represent a series of pitfalls for even the most experienced lawyer. As a matter of fact, during the past twenty years, there has been more copyright litigation involving technical questions relating to the renewal copyright provision of our law than to any other section of the Copyright Act.

It is most important for those interested in intellectual property to bear in mind that 56 years of protection is the *maximum* in the United States and is dependent upon successful passage around the legal pitfalls which surround the obtaining of a valid renewal copyright for the second term. While we in the United States have remained static, virtually every nation in the world having a copyright system has adopted another basis for term of copyright, namely the life of the author plus 50 years after the author's death. Obviously, such a system gives, almost inevitably, a longer term of protection unless we assume that an author writes a work and dies almost immediately thereafter. I do not think, however, that the mere granting of a longer term under this almost universally used system constitutes the sole significance of this method.

One of the great advantages of the life-plus-a-stated-term-of-years system (some nations have terms shorter and some have terms longer than fifty years) is that all of the works of an author enter the public domain at the same time. Under our present American system, if an author has the good fortune to live to a ripe old age, he will witness the spectacle of many of his works written during his earlier years passing into the public domain while he is still alive and then after his death the fruits of a life of labor drop into the public domain at odd intervals.

I find neither social nor economic basis for our obsolete system of two terms of copyright. I do not suggest that the only available system would be life of the author plus a stated term of years. It would be possible to grant an author a single term of copyright for a period in excess of 56 years and perhaps accomplish something of the same purpose achieved in the many nations that use the life-plus-a-term-of-years-after-death system.

The historical argument in the United States for two separate terms of copyright was that the author might, in his early years, dispose of a work on improvident terms, having no basis at the time of disposition to believe that the work would achieve enormous commercial value and that, therefore, the second term of copyright would enable the author to make a new bargain in the light of the work's successful history. However, the courts in the United States have thoroughly disposed of this theory by upholding contracts in which authors have granted both terms of copyright at the time of original publication. In practice the author who is alive at the time of renewal is likely to be bound by his assignment of both copyright terms; if he is deceased at renewal time his heirs may reap the benefit of being free to negotiate anew for the renewal term.

In all of the countries using the life-plus-a-term-of-years system, no provision is made to give an author (or his heirs) such a second opportunity.

To the extent that copyright law revision in the United States may involve an argument between "long-termers" on the one hand and "short-termers" on the other hand, it would seem to me that the long-termers have all the best of the argument in the field of music — and specifically in the field of popular music — since only a very small handful of works retain great popular appeal for more than a few short years. To the extent that protection for these works which live a short but merry life is granted, no public interest is harmed if the works are protected by copyright for a longer period; such transitory works are just as dead even though copyrighted as they would be were they to fall into the public domain. However, with respect to that part of our musical literature which does have continuing appeal, and particularly with respect to contemporary works of a serious nature, it is mandatory that longevity be recognized and adequate protection granted.

For the few popular works that become successful "standards" and live on for many decades, there is every moral reason to continue protection for a longer term and no moral reason to force these works into the public domain. In the case of contemporary serious composers, the history of this field of creativity indicates that many composers are likely to achieve true recognition many years after the initial introduction of the work and, in many cases, not until after death. Clearly, the public interest dictates an appropriate length of copyright to suit the needs of people who do not write solely for today's hit and tomorrow's oblivion.

The third part of our present law which has long passed into antiquity, although still the law of the land, is that which relates to the ever-changing field involving the mechanical reproduction of music. The compulsory licensing clause, the statutory royalties of 2¢ per record manufactured, the ambiguity in the present Act as it relates to such recent developments as tape and other electronic forms of recording, all of these subjects are in desperate need of modernization.

During the last 30 years, the development of sound motion pictures, radio and television broadcasting, the long-playing phonograph record and other similar devices have made music an indispensable partner, as well as a permanent ingredient, of industries involving billions of dollars.

The musical printing press, although naturally still with us, is in the sixth decade of the 20th century economically overwhelmed by the importance of the mechanical usage of music. Although the sale of musical instruments in the United States continues to show growth, and although musical education in our primary and secondary schools continues to expand, the total sales of printed music in all forms in the United States constitute an insignificant sum of dollars when compared to the monies involved in the motion picture, broadcasting and recording industries, all of which are, to varying degrees, dependent upon the use of music.

Within the past several years a series of studies was prepared under the auspices of the Copyright Office of the Library of Congress, with a view to considering a general revision of the Copyright Law. One aspect of these extensive studies concerned itself with what one might characterize as the economics of individual copyright industries. As an indication of the relative insignificance of the sales of all forms of printed music in the United States in the past ten years these studies are of considerable help. They point out, for example, that in 1954 the gross receipts from the sale of sheet music aggregated a maximum of $12,000,000 and this figure, it is conceded, is a somewhat high estimate. During the same period the total gross receipts of book publishers aggregated $665,000,000. Gross sales of phonograph records totalled almost $85,000,000. Radio and television broadcasting and motion picture production are, of course, billion dollar industries respectively, although the amount of the contribution of music to these grosses is a complex and controversial question. In reviewing, however, the relative unimportance of total printed music sales I would, referring again to the same report, call attention to the fact that greeting cards grossed approximately $75,000,000 in 1954 as against the outside estimate of $12,000,000 from the sale of sheet music.

It would seem that these figures indicate very clearly that Copyright Law revision must of necessity pay the most careful heed to the new economics of the so-called copyright industries.

The only point on which it may be assumed that all interested parties must agree is that a statute placed on the books prior to the invention of sound motion picture, radio or television broadcasting and actually prior to any commercially significant emergence of the then infant recording industry is obsolete and inadequate.

I have deliberately refrained up to this point from any attempt at either describing or evaluating the international copyright relations of the United States. Perhaps my reluctance to approach this subject is due to the fact that I view with dismay our posture in 1961 as the great leader of the free world on the one hand, and on the other our traditionally isolationist and insular attitudes toward international copyright.

Historically, the facts are as brief as they are distressing. Until 1891, foreign authors enjoyed no copyright protection in the United States. We were until then, in effect, an outlaw nation practicing a type of international intellectual piracy. In 1891, our Copyright Law was amended in order to provide for a system of bilateral treaty copyright protection. In its most elementary form, this system functioned on the hypothesis that we would grant copyright protection to works written by nationals of a foreign state if, in turn, such foreign state would agree to grant protection under their domestic law to United States nationals. No attempt was made, under these treaties, to equate differences in local substantive copyright protection. In some cases, nationals of countries entering into these bilateral treaty arrangements received less protection in the United States than our nationals received abroad. The reverse occurred in a number of cases.

This concept of protection by reciprocity was continued in the 1909 Copyright Act and is still the law. At the present time, by treaty and/or presidential proclamation, copyright protection is afforded in the United States to authors who are citizens of approximately forty countries, and United States nationals, in turn, receive copyright protection in these same countries. Under the Act of 1909, a foreign author domiciled in the United States may obtain copyright protection even though he be a citizen of a foreign state with whom we do not have reciprocal copyright relations.

While the United States was busily engaged in building its international copyright relations based upon this hodgepodge of treaties and presidential proclamations, other nations of the world were attempting to approach international copyright relations in a more orderly fashion. With rare exception all of the important nations of Europe, as well as of Latin America and elsewhere, brought into being the Berne International Copyright Convention in 1886. This Convention has been revised several times: in 1908 at Berlin, in 1928 at Rome, and most recently in 1948 at Brussels. The Berne Convention provides that any signatory to the Convention receives copyright protection automatically within the borders of all other signatory powers. The Berne Convention also provides for certain minimum standards and requirements for domestic copyright legislation within the borders of each signatory power.

As an example, United States copyright law until very recently denied any copyright protection to books in the English language not printed within the borders of the United States. This provision of our domestic law was in violation of the basic minimum standard established by the Berne Convention, and this (among other reasons) made it impossible for the United States to adhere to the Berne Convention. Putting it another way, the Berne Convention attempted to establish certain minimum international standards with respect to the protection of intellectual property. The United States took the position that as an isolated power we chose to set our own domestic standards and did not wish to conform domestically to any standards and requirements that might be imposed upon us by adherence to an international treaty.

In 1954, as a result of many years of efforts by UNESCO, the United States ratified the Universal Copyright Convention, commonly referred to as UCC. UCC, with minor exceptions, represents an international compromise in order to bring the United States into some form of international copyright agreement. In principle, UCC permits each signatory power to establish its own domestic copyright rules. There were a number of minor changes which the United States agreed to, such as a shortening of the copyright notice by permitting the use of © instead of spelling out the word "Copyright." The United States also agreed to some minor changes in its requirement that books in the English language must be printed in the United States in order to secure copyright.

Despite the very modest beginning represented by UCC, the United States still remains outside of the international copyright structure and even UCC, as a practical matter, represents but a pious hope for better international copyright relations in the future.

Historically, therefore, in the field of copyright, the United States still evidences an attitude comparable to its attitude toward the League of Nations after the end of World War I. This is but another example of how far behind the time our concepts are with respect to intellectual property and its protection.

No discussion of the history of United States copyright developments would be complete without a brief mention of our concept of copyright notice, registration and deposit.

From the first Federal Copyright Law down through the present Act, we have had, with varying technical requirements, a system which, in effect, has made the obtaining of a valid copyright dependent upon (a) the publication of a copyright notice in a stated position on each published work, and (b) the registration and deposit of copies of each such published work in the Copyright Office.

There is little doubt that this system grew up in a pioneer society where title to real property, the greatest single item of personal ownership in the 18th and 19th centuries, was dependent upon a form of deed registration. Of course, the theory of copyright notice went beyond the theory of deed registration in that it had as its basic *raison d'être* putting any member of the public on notice that a particular work was subject to copyright protection because of the printed notice. The only change that we have made in our history in this regard has been the change referred to in connection with our ratification of UCC, namely that we now permit the substitution of © for the word "Copyright"—but this is more a matter of shadow than substance.

Nations adhering to the Berne Convention do not require a copyright notice. Whether future copyright law revision will continue the requirement of notice, deposit and registration is a subject of debate which rages quite as furiously as some of the other topics I have discussed earlier in this article.

I do not believe that copyright notice in and of itself has significant bearing on the future development of our substantive law to protect intellectual property. I do not see that the requirement of notice imposes any great burden on those seeking copyright protection nor, by the same token, do I feel that the lack of notice necessarily entraps an unwary user. I refer to the problem with a slight feeling that we should continue our system of copyright notice, registration and deposit, but with the suggestion that the usefulness of the procedure be subjected to the most careful legislative scrutiny.

It is my everlasting conviction that laws protecting intellectual property are among the most important which men in a free society can consider and ultimately enact. It is clear that in our society we have woefully failed to meet our responsibilities with respect to legislation in this area of our community. To the extent that intense economic conflict has now entered the arena, the problem becomes even more pressing.

In the Preamble to the New Jersey State Copyright Statute enacted in 1783, we find the following language, "Whereas learning tends to the embellishment of human nature, the honour of the nation and the general good of mankind; and as it is perfectly agreeable to the principles of equity, that men of learning who devote their time and talents to the preparing of treatises for publication, should have the profits that may arise from the sale of their works; therefore . . . . ."

Historically, the New Jersey Preamble is as significant and as true today as it was almost 200 years ago. Our challenge is to supply the substantive material following that ancient legal word "therefore."

Epilogue

Epilogue

By HANS W. HEINSHEIMER

Anyone who, like this writer, spent the better part of his youth in the business of serious music in Europe and has now, for more than twenty years, occupied a similar front seat in the amphitheater where the vast spectacle "Music in America" is being enacted, is both immensely impressed and deeply puzzled by what he observes. The newcomer — more, perhaps, than the native, who is prone to take too much for granted and grumblingly to underestimate the scope of American musical achievement — is impressed by the magnitude and the breadth, if not always the depth, of the musical activity shown by the America of the mid-century. But he is also puzzled that under the unique conditions prevailing in the United States it could ever grow to its present dimensions, and he is sometimes a little worried about its future.

Reared in a world of Stadttheaters, Staatsopernhouses, Landes-symphony orchestras, and Staatlichen Musikhochschulen — in a world where music in all its facets is the concern of states, cities, or government-operated radio stations — he looks with startled admiration at the completely different foundations on which American musical facilities are built, at the different economic machinery of music-making here, and at the very philosophy that has created it all and keeps it going and growing. He soon realizes that the undisputed, accepted premises on which the musical activity of most of Europe is and always was built, do not exist here, are looked upon with suspicion, and are not likely to be adopted in our lifetime.

For one active in music in America today, such trends of thought cannot stop in study and analysis. They have to be translated from recognition of the unalterable facts into positive conclusions. If an American publisher of serious music takes a position of responsibility and creative action, he has to accept the basic conditions, the philosophy that underlies American musical life, and make it the basis for his own decisions, for his policy, and for his creative contacts with writers and composers.

The European composer writes for more than a hundred publicly supported opera houses. If one, ten, fifty of them were bombed out, they were rebuilt before new factories, houses, or schools were completed. If he wants 135 men in the orchestra pit, he has 135 men in the pit when his *Elektra* or his *Wozzeck* is performed. If he needs 50 orchestra rehearsals for his *Moses and Aaron* he gets them. If one of the 26 full-time radio symphony orchestras of Western Europe performs his symphony, which it does without any consideration for rehearsal time, degree of difficulty, or audience appeal, he has a good chance that many of the remaining 25 will repeat the performance from tapes.

The publisher shares in these bonanzas. He works under conditions entirely unknown to his American colleague. While he is not directly subsidized, he participates handsomely in the subsidies given to opera houses, orchestras, and radio stations. A considerable share seeps down to him in the pleasant disguises of large rental fees, enormous extra bonuses for world or local premières, performing fees, theater royalties, payments for the playing of tapes or recordings of serious music on radio and television stations, and many similar lovely entries in black ink which are unknown to the books of American publishers.

Under these rather extreme circumstances the means by which composers, writers, music publishers, and some others in America substitute a positive, creative attitude for resigned envy, regret, or despair are among the most fascinating aspects of musical life in America today. Perhaps one can best explain the successful, positive interplay between typical American conditions and the creative mind of a composer and writer through the case of Gian Carlo Menotti.

From the very beginning of his career this Italian graduate of an American music school — already a contemporary *unicum* in itself and a significant reversal of the accepted position that Americans study music in Europe, not Europeans in America — from the beginning of his career Menotti has written his operas not for the traditional facilities of the European opera houses — for their unlimited forces on and off stage, for their lavish monetary resources, for the professional brilliance of their artists — but for the operatic facilities of a country where the subsidized opera house does not exist and where large-scale professional operatic performances are limited to a handful of opera houses in a few large cities and to short seasons—two or three operas in a year, repeated twice or perhaps three times — in another handful of cities throughout the land.

His first opera, *Amelia Goes to the Ball*, was first produced at the Academy of Music in Philadelphia, mainly by a cast from the Curtis Institute of Music, Menotti's musical alma mater. *The Old Maid and the Thief*, which followed, was a commission from an American radio station, where it had its first performance. Menotti is now writing in English, an important step in a country where opera in English (this is 1939) is still looked at suspiciously. A brief excursion to the traditional professional stage, a production at the Metropolitan Opera (*The Island God*), meets, to quote the tactful author of *Baker's Dictionary*, "with indifferent success." Menotti's reaction to the setback is immediate and radical. It is a new departure, a creative solution of the problem of opera in America, unthinkable anywhere else: he writes an opera for a college theater, for the opera workshop at Columbia University in New York — for a type of theater, then, and for producing conditions that do not exist anywhere else. *The Medium* was scored for an orchestra of thirteen men because the tiny Brander Matthews Theater at Columbia couldn't seat many more. The opera has no chorus because there was none. It has a single, simple set, a small cast and is written for voice ranges and tessituras that can be managed by accomplished amateurs while at the same time providing a rewarding challenge for professional singers.

The event took place in 1946. What happened afterwards is, again, a "first" in the long history of opera. From the university workshop the opera, now preceded by a curtain-raiser — the celebrated *Telephone* — moves to the small Heckscher Theater for a series of performances, sponsored by the New York Ballet Society (with a single American Ludwig of Bavaria in the background). The success grows. Encouraged by the reaction, three young people form a producing unit — all three brand new in the game of Broadway producing — and bring the two works to a professional theater, this time with a professional cast, selected by the composer-librettist who is also the stage director of the highly imaginative production and who with this first display of his flair for the discovery of unknown talent adds still another facet to his kaleidoscopic talent.

The operas run for almost a year. Nobody gets rich but nobody loses money and a new dimension has been added to the Broadway scene. From here, from a workshop beginning, there begins a worldwide professional career for the two operas, there begins — most important and to be discussed presently — the dissemination of the works to innumerable very recently created workshops in America. It is difficult, indeed, to say which came first, the egg of *The Telephone* and *The Medium* or the hen of the many workshops that produced them avidly. A film, produced in Italy and directed by the insatiable Menotti, propels *The Medium* into still another sphere.

The story of *The Consul*, the next Menotti venture (1950), is perhaps even more remote from the traditional operatic launchings in Dresden, Bergamo, or Paris. Here an opera — and the *Tarnhelm* "musical drama" didn't fool anybody — was written for a Broadway production. The producing unit that had presented *The Telephone* and *The Medium*, the C. Z. & L. company, had amicably parted ways. The Z, Mr. Efrem Zimbalist Jr., had gone to Hollywood and eventual TV fame; the L, Miss Edith Lutyens, had become a successful costume designer, and the C, Mr. Chandler Cowles, a man endowed with unsuppressible charm, a strong, very stubborn belief in Menotti's talent, and a gentle but never failing way of persuading the most hard-boiled angel to part with some money for unorthodox Broadway ventures, presented *The Consul,* first for a few try-out dates in Philadelphia (where we all were sure that we were facing disaster, except Menotti) and then, a few weeks later, in a brilliant opening on Broadway (where we all were happily surprised when we knew we had a hit, except Menotti, who had known it all the time).

From Broadway, from a performance by American singers (among them Pat Neway, yet another Menotti discovery) with an American conductor, Lehman Engel, in the pit, who soon was to be replaced by one Thomas Schippers from Kalamazoo, Mich., *The Consul* went all over the world, reversing, as its author had done once before, the established tradition that music traveled westbound as an import to, not an export from, the United States, and probably setting a record among contemporary operas by being translated into 19 languages (including Turkish, Polish, Serbo-Croatian, Flemish, Dutch, Finnish, and Hebrew) and being, so far, performed in 27 different countries.

Lately, *The Consul* has been selected for yet another unbay-reuthian, American pilot project: it has been made into a film to be the first opera to be used on Paid Television. So far, the opera has been offered only to the 5,800 subscribers the International Telemeter Company has lined up for its test project in Etobicoke, a suburb of Toronto. However, since a subscriber has to put $1.50 in the handsome box on top of his closed-circuit TV set in order to get *The Consul* on his screen, and since it is expected that Pay TV will reach New York and other large American cities soon, some rather startling new possibilities loom in the operatic future for American composers and publishers. "Suppose only a million viewers tuned in on *The Consul* at $1.50," daydreamed a New York newspaper after the Etobicoke experiment. "That would mean a box office take of $1,500,000 for one night."

Well . . .

And where are the shades of Bergamo, the memories of Vienna, the echoes of Bayreuth in the story of the birth of *Amahl and the Night Visitors?* The history of this gentle Christmas opera begins in a skyscraper in Manhattan, with a letter written on the somber

[309]

letterhead of the National Broadcasting Company, Inc. The letter, dated March 25, 1949, begins: "Dear Mr. Menotti: This will confirm our understanding and agreement as follows: (1) You will select the subject for, write and compose an original one-act opera expressly designed for television broadcasting purposes and within a period of twelve months from the date hereof will deliver to us one complete copy of the score. The opera shall comply in all respects with the NBC program policies and in particular shall contain no obscene or off-color themes, jokes, songs, sacrilegious expressions or any other language of doubtful propriety. We shall pay you the sum of . . ."

Half of the sum was paid to the composer upon signature. Twelve months went by. March 25, 1950, slipped into limbo and yet another year passed. Once in a while, a timid call came from NBC, and as time marched on, the calls became a little less timid and a little more urgent. Menotti, occupied with other chores, was unable to think of any subject, either on or off-color. Finally, he instructed us to return the advance to NBC and to ask them to please forget the whole thing. But luckily NBC didn't want their money back. They were quite willing to wait. Their calls became again less urgent and much more timid.

And then, one day out of a blue October sky in 1951 Menotti called and asked us to tell NBC he would have a Christmas opera for them! He had gone to an exhibition of paintings, all dealing with the Christmas story and arranged by the Metropolitan Museum of Art at the Cloisters, the lovely ghost-gone-west castle overlooking the Hudson and the George Washington Bridge, which looks particularly impressive when seen from the ramparts of a medieval *Kreuzgang*. Here, in this superbly unique combination of European beauty and American grandeur he had seen the painting *The Adoration of the Magi* by Hieronymus Bosch. It had, suddenly, fired his imagination. Within a day or two, the story had become so alive in his mind that he was certain he could bring the opera off in time for a Christmas production.

When we called NBC they were overjoyed. "Where is the score?" they asked. When we told them "In Menotti's head" they used language of doubtful propriety.

And so October drifted away, and November — only 54 writing, casting, rehearsing days till Christmas — entered threateningly. By now word had seeped down that the lead part of the opera was to be taken by a boy soprano: Menotti had found one — the great discoverer of hidden talent was at it again — at the Columbus Boys Choir School in Princeton. One of our copyists would take the morning train to Mt. Kisco, where the cook, driving down from Menotti's house, would meet him with a few pencil-sketched pages. The southbound train left a minute or two later. The copyist would snatch the pages from the cook, cross the tracks, and jump on the train to New York. By nightfall the pages had been copied and a messenger would board another train for Princeton to deliver them for next morning's rehearsal. The piano score was completed early in December. There was no time left for Menotti to write out the complete orchestral score: he had to dictate many of its pages to several composer-friends who came to Mt. Kisco for long nightly sessions to help him get the score on paper.

We heard *Amahl* — the title, too, was a last-minute stroke of inspiration — for the first time about two weeks before the performance, which took place as scheduled on Christmas Day, 1951. Toscanini was among the small number of people who had been asked to attend. Olin Downes was there, a few musicians, a few friends, at least one Italian countess.

They sat on broken-down chairs, among empty Coca Cola bottles, paper cups, cigaret butts, in the dingiest, dustiest, motheatenest ballroom, in an Eighth Avenue hotel. An old upright piano. No props. A few hints at costumes. Amahl's crutch and, for the first time, the unforgettable voice of Chet Allen.

Tears. Happy smiles. The certain knowledge of having been present at an important event.

*   *

*

Here, then, are some of the birthplaces of American opera: the university workshop, Broadway, the billion-dollar Radio Corporation of America with a preview in a walk-up ballroom on Eighth Avenue.

From here *The Consul* went to the Vienna State Opera, the *Medium* to Piccadilly, and *Amahl*, repeated year after year not only on television but in hundreds of American churches, colleges, and workshops, became also *Amahl und die nächtlichen Besucher* and *Amahl e gli ospiti della notte.*

It has been our good fortune to be godfathers to still another very special child in the growing family of American opera, and the story of Kurt Weill's *Down in the Valley* must keep us here for a brief moment.

When I joined Schirmer's in 1947, the first repercussions of the new Menotti boom had just begun to rock the startled firm and when I inquired — keen, as may be forgiven, to begin my new association with a bang — what I could possibly bring as a welcome *Morgengabe,* a new opera of interest to and within the technical and musical reach of amateurs from the high school level up was pointed out as a desirable but difficult-to-find venture. As luck would have it, I had — many years back, in Vienna — staged and therefore become intimately acquainted with one of the few operas written for amateurs by a professional European composer, Kurt Weill's school opera *Der Jasager.* The connection of the half-forgotten past with the scarcely hoped-for present was immediate. I went to see Kurt Weill.

Our meeting in New City, in Weill's lovely home by the brook, remains unforgotten. He listened carefully. Then he went to a chest and took out the score of an opera. It was called *Down in the Valley,* written, at the suggestion of Olin Downes, for a radio series that never came off. The composer had put it away after the sponsors had decided that this type of opera wasn't soapy enough.

It was a little short for what we had in mind. Weill called in Arnold Sundgaard, who had written the libretto. The two expanded the material to about 45 minutes' duration. Within a few months the new work was ready. It was exactly what we had hoped for. "It can be performed wherever a chorus, a few singers, and a few actors are available," Weill explained when he delivered the score. "The physical production can be as simple as a dramatic concert performance. Scenery and lighting can be just as elaborate as equipment allows. The leading parts should provide a good training for the specific type of singing actor who has become such an important asset to the musical theater in America."

No attempts were made to launch *Down in the Valley* through a professional operatic setup. That came later. Instead, the première of the opera (it is perhaps significant that the printed score does not title the work an opera, or, in fact, anything else: it is just "Kurt Weill's Down in the Valley") took place at Indiana University in Bloomington in the summer of 1948. Since then, the work, another product of the intriguing interplay between American performing facilities and the creative response of writers and composers, has been performed in more than 2000 different productions in this country: in high schools, in colleges, in summer camps, in huge open-air presentations, in prisons, off Broadway in a church basement on 13th Street, on records, radio, and television and, lately, in professional theaters in Europe.

*   *

*

Up to the arrival of *Down in the Valley* and the two Menotti works there had been little, with the exception, perhaps, of Copland's *Second Hurricane*, Moore's *The Devil and Daniel Webster*, and a few similar pieces, to cater to the rapidly growing demand for new workshop material and to take over where Gilbert and Sullivan — brilliantly but for too long a time — had reigned supreme. Now many writers began to get interested. Arnold Sundgaard, after the death of Kurt Weill (in April of 1950) found in Alec Wilder a congenial musician who understood the specific requirements of the new style; with him Sundgaard proceeded to write a series of works for the ever-increasing workshop and school opera circuits. Douglas Moore wrote music to another Sundgaard sketch. Leonard Bernstein and Lukas Foss, writing their own librettos, supplied colorful works, and many others contributed to what, in fact, amounted to a new chapter in American music. To the short, easy-to-stage and easy-to-produce works were added more extended operas, designed both for professional performances (which, soon, with new facilities springing up in Santa Fe, in Houston, in Dallas, in Central City, in Washington, Boston, and in some of the large-sized university theaters such as Bloomington or Los Angeles, became of greater interest to composers) and for the more ambitious workshops. There has been created, within the short period of ten or twelve years, a whole new repertory for a new field of operatic production which soon, as we will see presently, began to attract the interest and support of new and powerful allies. As more works became available, more workshops and other operatic facilities were created. As more facilities promised performances and the liberation of the American opera from the oblivion of desk drawers, more operas were written and many were published.

In response to the growing demand there has also been created in this last exciting decade a new repertory of standard operas in singable, contemporary translations. It is interesting to observe how little attention earlier American editions of standard operas gave to English words. The large catalogue of such operas, published some sixty years ago, contains translations mostly written in an operatese that could never have been meant to be sung in actual performance but was obviously added only so that the public would be able to follow the story while the opera was performed in the original language.

Today, hundreds of opera workshops and professional companies in America give English performances of *Carmen, Traviata, Così fan tutte,* and *The Marriage of Figaro,* dozens are doing *Falstaff, Aida,* or *Tosca,* and a few are even trying their skill on *Parsifal, Don Carlo,* and *Pelleas and Melisande.* For all these producers and many more the question whether opera should be performed in the original language or in English is no longer a subject for debate. The decision has been made, the point of no return has been passed. A whole new world of opera is being offered to American audiences by American singers in the language the audience can understand and the singers can pronounce. While there was some confusion at the beginning, with too many translations offered and every stage director and conductor adding his own, there is now emerging a series of generally accepted standard translations of the great operatic masterpieces, translations that begin to become part of the repertory of American singers and are used everywhere, just as the German, the French, the Italian translations of the standard repertory are used, identically, in every opera house in each of those countries.

*   *

*

While these forces were at work to create new musical dimensions in America, a very different but likewise new and unexpected force began to make itself felt on the musical scene in mid-century America. That music — in the absence of "official" help — would have to be assisted by somebody and could not be left alone, drifting in a free enterprise pool where, for the obvious lack of profits, it was bound to sink and drown, had always been recognized. The American symphony orchestra is one brilliant result of such recognition and of the practical application of the thought that man does not live by bread alone. As everywhere else in the world, the average American orchestra earns only about half of its expenses through ticket sales, royalties from recordings, radio fees, or similar income. The rest, since it doesn't come from the *Stadt,* has to come from the citizens who want it. And it has always been one of the most impressive sights on the American cultural scene to see how out of endowments made in last wills and testaments, out of tea parties, balls, and bingo games, out of telephone drives, young ladies and old ladies committees, out of a few large donations and out of thousands and thousands of small ones has grown a tradition of symphony orchestras in America that has weathered every storm of recession or war and is still growing both in scope and in quality. Mr. Severance built his hall in Cleveland. Mr. Higginson founded and royally maintained the Boston Symphony for many years. The splendor of the New York Philharmonic playing in Moscow and Tokyo has outglamored queens and princely ambassadors, and in hundreds of less glamorous but just as important American towns the symphony orchestra has become the beloved and ardently supported center of cultural and social life.

For a long time, however, these efforts paid little if any attention to the basic source of all musical activity, to the composer. For the first time — or, at least, for the first time on a large scale — a new approach was made when, in 1930, Serge Koussevitzky suggested to the trustees of the Boston Symphony Orchestra that they celebrate the fiftieth anniversary of the orchestra by commissioning new works and by performing them during the anniversary season. Not only were commissions given to international celebrities such as Igor Stravinsky (*Symphonie des Psaumes,* dedicated appropriately to the glory of God and the Boston Symphony Orchestra), Paul Hindemith (*Musik für Streicher und Bläser*), Serge Prokofiev (Fourth Symphony), Arthur Honegger (First Symphony), and Jan Sibelius (Eighth Symphony — never completed), but American composers such as Aaron Copland and Howard Hanson were asked to write new works and were given performances by one of the leading orchestras of the country.

This, of course, was only the beginning of what later grew into the famous Koussevitzky Music Foundation, established in 1942 after the death of the conductor's first wife in her memory and continued, after Dr. Koussevitzky's death in 1951, in connection with the Library of Congress in Washington under a permanent endowment and under the tireless guidance of that quiet but energetic champion of contemporary music, Mrs. Olga Koussevitzky. The catalogue of works commissioned by the Foundation contains today more than 80 compositions by 70 different composers and it is still being augmented. The practice of 'commissioning new works has since been taken over by many orchestras in America, large and small. The Boston Symphony reaped a rich harvest at the occasion of its seventy-fifth anniversary (1955) and other orchestras have followed suit.

All these efforts centered around the initiative and personality of conductors, artists, or an occasional individual Maecenas. Something importantly new, however, made its entry onto the scene of American musical life with the famous, now historical, Louisville experiment. For the first time one of the great foundations took an active interest in music and centered it around the composer. Everything in the experiment was new, refreshing, different.

Here was a small American city with an orchestra of modest size and adequate but provincial status, quite different, of course, from the splendor and international fame of the Boston Symphony and its leader. The town had, however, a mayor, Charles Farnsley, who, among other cultural obsessions that he managed to impose on the citizens of Louisville, had a violent dislike for the music of the 19th century and a burning love for the composers of the 18th and 20th centuries. He started modestly but daringly enough by giving commissions to contemporary composers, taking the money from some city department that had never heard of Virgil Thomson, Norman Dello Joio, or Paul Hindemith and that now suddenly found out it was not only supporting these strangers by paying them handsome commissions but the boss also expected its members to attend — en famille — the performances of these works. There were no limitations imposed on the composers — I remember with delight the première of William Schuman's Judith with Martha

Graham as the dance soloist before an appreciative audience in Louisville — the only exception being that the Louisville orchestra was limited to about fifty players. Whether the mayor kept it to pre-Berlioz size because he didn't like Romantic music or whether he didn't play Romantic music because he didn't have the orchestral forces nobody knows.

This went on for several years. But no matter how successfully he channelled funds from the Municipal Slaughterhouse towards the creation of twelve-tone music, the mayor found himself limited in the pursuit of his Hoffmannesque hobby. He came to New York to find money on a larger scale. Farnsley is a wonderful fellow, a smiling, outgoing politician charming everybody, even people like myself who would never have an occasion to vote for him. From him I learned one of the basic approaches one should always take in a big country. "If I ask a foundation for $100,000 they'll laugh at me," he told me before he went to see the Rockefeller Foundation. "If I ask for a million they'll take me seriously."

He came home with a grant for $400,000, by far the largest sum of money ever invested in the commissioning, performing, and recording of new music. Yet, the money itself, lavish as it was, was not the most important part of the story. The fact that one of the big American foundations would become interested in music — in any facet of musical life — was a new departure in the economics and in the philosophy of musical life in America.

The Rockefeller investment in contemporary music, concentrated as it was on a single community with limited resources and a limited possibility to absorb it all, was, perhaps, more handicapped than helped by its bigness, which imposed an obligation on the people of Louisville to commission so large a number of orchestral works and operas that they couldn't possibly find enough material on a high level and thus had to spread their magnificence sometimes pretty thin. However, the Louisville experiment, if perhaps not the most successful, was at any rate the first such undertaking in America and, whether by accident, because the time was ripe, or by setting an example that stimulated others, the beginning of many more.

The Ford Foundation and its programs in the field of music (which are only a small section of its enormous endeavors in the humanities and the arts) are of such creative imagination and of such stimulating variety that they have already made a great impact on the contemporary musical scene. The program was only established in 1957 — the newness of all these ideas and efforts, the changing of the American musical climate now, today, in these decisive, formative years cannot be stressed enough.

Here are some of the fields of music where the Ford Foundation has stepped in — and, again, it should be observed how important if not decisive the composer looms in most of these projects:

In 1958, the Foundation selected ten artists "whose abilities had been widely recognized on the concert stage but who had not yet achieved the peak of their careers." Each artist was asked to pick an American composer who would write a work for him to perform with orchestra. The Foundation not only commissioned the new composition, it also offered help to the orchestra for rehearsals of the new scores and paid a grant-in-aid to the artists. The orchestras of Atlanta, Denver, Detroit, Houston, Indianapolis, Los Angeles, New York, Pittsburgh, San Antonio, and Seattle participated in the first realization of the plan. The works are not only given a première performance (which is always easy to get) but will be repeated by many if not all of the participating orchestras. Already some very successful works performed by outstanding artists have made their appearance under this highly original program.

A grant of a very different nature — recognizing the importance of "amateur" music-making in this country which, with its 25,000 high school bands, its opera workshops, its countless choral societies and community orchestras, has more of it than any European country — was the one devoted to "The Young Composer and High School Music." "The young composer," the Foundation stated, "today has little opportunity to practice his craft upon conclusion of his training. With no outlet for his compositions, he is generally forced to find a teaching position. Writing in his spare time with no assurance of performance, the young composer thus tends to compose in a more and more technically complicated fashion."

The Foundation gave $200,000 to help twelve young composers spend a year each in a secondary-school system, not to teach but to compose for school orchestras, choruses, and bands. The program has since been repeated and has been extended for at least four more years.

There ·were other musical stimuli — the latest, a $400,000 grant to the Peabody Conservatory of Music in Baltimore, establishes a program to give promising American conductors practical training in the fields of orchestra and opera — but probably none is as important as the carefully planned and spectacularly executed assistance given to opera in America. In the spring of 1958, with the assistance of a grant of $105,000 from the Ford Foundation, the New York City Opera Company presented, for the first time in history, a five-week season of opera by ten contemporary American composers. The results were so stimulating that the experiment was repeated the following year (with three operas carried over from the previous season and seven new ones added) and a national tour was organized, subsidized by the Foundation and presenting some of the most successful works that had emerged from the New York seasons to audiences in Boston, Cleveland, Detroit, Chicago, Pittsburgh, Washington, and Philadelphia and to some college and university communities along the way. In addition, thirty American composers were invited to attend the rehearsals of these operas at the City Center and to observe how they were prepared for production.

From here it was only one step to the Foundation's most ambitious program so far, the $950,000 grant to find eighteen new operas by American composers and to have them produced during the next eight years. "The American operas produced with Foundation assistance by the New York City Opera during the past two years," the Foundation said when it announced the program in 1960, "have established that an American operatic repertoire exists and that there is a growing public interest in it."

The money will be available to composers and librettists for commissions, and to the Metropolitan Opera and City Opera in New York, the San Francisco Opera and the Chicago Lyric Theatre for productions of the new works. The New York City Opera will introduce six new works at the rate of one or more a year and will also probably be the first one to present one of these new operas: *The Wings of the Dove* with music by Douglas Moore.

Before we leave this remarkable subject it is important to point out that none of these projects are designed as permanent subsidies. They are carried out, frequently in repeated grants over a number of years but always with the idea that there is a time limit to them. They are experiments to test an idea, to test the climate of the country, to stimulate, to show the way, and then to be terminated in the expectation that others may take over. The Rockefeller bonanza in Louisville has come to an end. The Ford projects are deliberately designed as pilot projects, and they are very important while they last. However, unless they lead to something of a more permanent nature, they might leave a dangerous vacuum if and when they expire.

*   *
*

The Ford Foundation, as we have seen, seems sometimes a little worried that "the composer tends to compose in a more and more technically complicated fashion." Nothing can be complicated and advanced enough to suit the taste and solicit the support of the foundation established in 1952 by Mr. Paul Fromm, who feels that "the composer of today occupies an anomalous position" and thinks that, while "his creativeness is the source of musical culture, his status in the musical world is uncertain." In order to make it a little more certain, Mr. Fromm, by profession a successful wine merchant, converted a considerable segment of his business profits into a foundation which, as he put it, "wishes to bring the living flow of musical creation closer to the public and to return the initiative to the composer, thus strengthening the most vital source of a healthy musical culture: composition."

The Fromm Foundation gives cash awards for new, unpublished works, sponsors public performances in various parts of the country, helps with the publication of award-winning compositions, sees to it that they are recorded, and occasionally, branches out into other ambitious and stimulating endeavors, such as the Festival of Contemporary Arts, given by the University of Illinois with the help of the Foundation. Recently, Mr. Fromm was host to the Princeton Seminar in Advanced Musical Studies. Under the sponsorship of the foundation, twenty-five musicians from all over the country, most of them from isolated places where they have little if any contact with fellow composers or with people close to the sources of the new trends in music, were invited to a three-week seminar in Princeton under an outstanding faculty headed by Roger

Sessions and treated to lectures by such composers as Aaron Copland, Edgard Varèse, Ernst Krenek, and Elliott Carter. In addition, three programs of contemporary chamber music were presented.

Mr. Fromm has sponsored other high-caliber concerts of contemporary works at Tanglewood, in Aspen, and in other places. New York is obligated to him for some of its most stimulating concerts, highly experimental and different in their programs, always performed on the highest professional level and given with such audience appeal that they are usually played twice on a Sunday, in the afternoon and at night, to an SRO assembly of fascinated and fascinating eggheads.

The efforts of Rockefeller, Ford, and Fromm only expand some of the assistance that the composer had been accustomed to find. The Guggenheim will help for a little while. The MacDowell or Huntington Hartford colony will give him a place where he can compose for a few months without having to worry about his next meal, which is left, discreetly, on his doorstep in order not to disturb the ministrations of Euterpe. And there is always the Prix de Rome with its not always quite successful transplantation of young Americans from the rigors of Minnesota or the dust storms of the great plains to the oh, so tempting sidewalk cafés and osterias of the Eternal City and to a leisurely way of life which, if one looks at it without glasses blurred by Tiber water, while it may be an enviable relief from the hardships of life at home, has not added too many immortal pages to the annals of music in America . . .

*   *
*

This, then, is the scene as Schirmer's enters its second century, hopeful, excited, grateful to be permitted to participate in this great musical adventure. It is a scene of many colors, of lights and shadows, of bright hopes and of dark spots, of progress and frustration.

Here is the America teeming with hundreds of symphony orchestras, with thousands of glee clubs and choral societies, with composers in residence and string quartets on campus — yet an America that enters this period of the 20th century without a single radio symphony orchestra and with a TV opera theater that becomes more anemic from year to year, for lack of a sponsor.

Here is the America with 500 or more FM Good Music Stations that play nothing but recordings from Gesualdo to Stockhausen — yet when asked to pay $25 for the broadcasting of a full-length contemporary opera hurriedly take it off the air.

Here is the America with the most up-to-date, the most expensive, the most futuristic electronic musical machine, the RCA synthesizer at Columbia University — yet with a copyright law whose basic thoughts were codified under the reign of Queen Anne in 1790, retaining provisions, clumsily applied to LP's, stereophonic tapes, television, juke boxes, written into the law in 1909 before any of these and many other modern devices were even thought of, and never changed.

Here is the America with hundreds of opera workshops but with 350 of its excellent native singers gainfully employed in the professional opera houses of Europe.

And here is the America that, through a public outcry of heart-warming intensity, shocked even a state legislature and a city council into action and stopped the bulldozers at the very threshold of Carnegie Hall, the America that, at this moment, is erecting in the Lincoln Center for the Performing Arts the largest and most ambitious combination of cultural edifices in modern times.

A symbol, we take it, of a bright future and of great and wonderful things to come.